Topics in Mathematics

for the 9th Grade

Topics in Mathematics

for the 9th Grade

Based on teaching practices in Waldorf schools

Peter Baum, Arnold Bernhard, Sidurd Bindel, Karl-Fr. Georg Uwe Hansen, Friedrich Hartmann, Markus Hünig Klaus Labudde, Rolf Rosbigalle.

Editor: Robert Neumann

This book is available as e-book (pdf) at www.lehrerseminar-forschung.de/shop/

Printed copies of this book are available at www.awsna.org

Published by the Lesson Plan Initiative of the Pedagogical Research Center in Kassel in cooperation with the AWSNA and the Research Institute for Waldorf Education. Printed with the support of the Waldorf Curriculum Fund.

Impressum

All portions of this book are protected by copyright. All rights reserved, in particular the rights to translate the material, and the rights to any form of reproduction or even partial reproduction in any way. The translation has not been revised by the authors.

© Bildungswerk Beruf und Umwelt

1. Edition (Version 1.0)

ISBN: 978-3-939374-30-5

Typesetting: Robert Neumann, Freiburg

Contents

Remarks on methods of mathematics instruction in the high school
    (UWE HANSEN) 9

On the Treatment of the Conic Sections in the 9th Grade
    (UWE HANSEN) 15

The conic sections as symmetry figures and their construction using thread
    (MARKUS HÜNIG) 18

Plane geometry as a way into high school mathematics
    (ROLF ROSBIGALLE) 24

A remark on geometric locus
    (UWE HANSEN) 81

A contribution concerning the metamorphosis of curve forms
    (SIGURD BINDEL UND KLAUS LABUDDE) 85

The Irrational in Arithmetic and Geometry
    (PETER BAUM) 103

On Arithmetic and Algebra for the 9th Grade
    (F.J. HARTMANN) 128

Division by 9 and Casting Out Nines
    (ARNHOLD BERNHARD) 139

Division by 11 and 11-check
    (ARNOLD BERNHARD) 151

Theory of equations
    (KLAUS LABUDDE) 158

Theory of equations
    (UWE HANSEN) 174

Combinatorics Main Lesson 9th Grade
    (KARL-FRIEDRICH GEORG) 177

A contribution regarding the combinatorics main lesson in the ninth grade
    (KLAUS LABUDDE) 198

Calculating probabilities and combinatorics
    (UWE HANSEN) 216

Additional sources 223

Index 224

Preface to the English Edition

It might seem surprising that the translation of the book for grade 9 – the lowest high-school grade – is the last one to be published. This is just due to the fact that the translation process for our math book series started when grade 10 was the featured grade at the first international refresher course week in Kassel in 2009.

This year, the preparations for the 10th anniversary of the refresher course are already underway., and we hope to have the 9th grade printed book available by course begin this Easter.

With this book for the 9th grade published, all grades for the Waldorf high school are now completed, although there is still a second volume for grade 12 to come, on geometry.

This book series has been a source of inspiration for many years. Because there is not just "one" way of teaching math,In this spirit, the books try to offer multiple articles on one theme. So the reader can sample different perspectives on the topic and choose the approach that seems most fitting.

The articles mention many additional sources. We kept the German ones and added information identifying translations or additional English sources available.

The book is dedicated especially to the many teachers around the world who are new to the Waldorf school. May it be a source of ideas and inspiration to them as they seek their own way to successful classroom instruction.

Special thanks goes to Charles Gunn for the translation.

Kassel, January 2018

Robert Neumann

Preface

The ninth grade of the Waldorf school poses new challenges for students as well as teachers: The students are released from the era of the class teacher, a freeing they generally experience as healthy, and they look expectantly, oscillating between optimism and uneasiness, towards the time of high school. High school teachers chosen to teach a ninth grade class have the responsibility to stand the test of these expectations, and not to disappoint them. To this task belong courage, inventiveness, and humor – along with the necessary measures of strictness and leadership. It's quite normal that even experienced colleagues approach the task of teaching a ninth grade with a measure of respect. Particularly in mathematics, where, in the eyes of the students, it's time for "genuine mathematics" to be taught by an real "expert", it's possible to exert a long-lasting influence on the relationship of the student to this subject. Here lies a great opportunity, one connected with an equally great danger.

So it seems like a good idea to re-publish this book on mathematics for the ninth grade – for many years out-of-print – in a slightly revised form and with a new look, in order to be able to meet the challenges posed by today's pedagogical reality. The colleagues of the Mathematics Curriculum Group, responsible for this volume, continue to meet about four times a year, in the framework of the Research Institute in Kassel, with a slightly-changed membership (with respect to the original publication). They have critically reviewed the articles in the original book with respect to their quality and their relevance for today. The unanimous verdict was to give a green light to the re-publication, especially since no further german publications on the theme of mathematics for the ninth grade in the Waldorf school have appeared in the interim. Also the articles by Arnold Bernhard (2007) regarding the 9- and 11-division checks, which are also appropriate for the eighth grade, are again included, as they show in commendable fashion how to fashion a path into the web of numbers in a methodologically careful way, and how this can lead to deep insights.

In the not-too-distant future, we plan to publish a further volume for this grade on themes which in the current volume are either not handled at all, or not adequately handled. This should be viewed against the background situation, that fewer and fewer of the new teachers on the Waldorf school have completed a Waldorf training, and hence they bring a pressing need for literature about, and suggestions for, concrete instructional themes. In this context, it's worth mentioning the further volumes devoted to the tenth and eleventh grades, also produced by the Curriculum Group. Additionally, there are plans to publish two volumes in 2010 and 2011 for the twelfth grade, to be supplemented by a main lesson book featuring a detailed commentary, to serve as introduction to calculus.

Finally I would like to particularly thank Peter Schwab, who carried out the laborious task of integrating the corrections, produced the layout, and worked over all the figures.

Kassel, February, 2009

Stephan Sigler

Preface 1999

The current collection contains 15 articles devoted to the mathematics instruction in the 9th grade of the Waldorf school. Five of these articles appeared in a previous version of this collection and appear in a slightly revised form here. All the articles are based on practical experience. The authors are mathematics teachers in Waldorf schools, and meet about four times a year to discuss questions of the curriculum. These articles were also included in these discussions. They are not however intended as revelations of the divine word, but rather as stimulation for the practicing teacher, to find his own way in the landscape of mathematics. For the beginning teacher, they may serve as an aid in preparing his lessons both in regard to content and method. They of course do not replace a standard training in mathematics.

The variety of approaches can be seen in the presence of several articles devoted to the same theme. Sometimes the discussions led to the emergence of controversial topics, for example, the significance of combinatorics as an instructional topic. We include such discussions at the end of this volume. (This discussion has been dropped in the current version.) It is, we hope, self-evident that all the articles reflect the personal opinions of the respective authors and not the intentions of the group, even though they have all been approved unanimously for inclusion.

The mathematics instruction on the Waldorf school, as every other subject taught there, has essentially two aspects, that according to the age group of the children, carry different weights: on the one hand, it should put into the students' hands a tool which will serve them practically in later life; on the other, is serves the spiritual-psychological and physical development of the child. For example, algorithms for extracting square roots are not intended as an aid to actually calculate roots – after all, there are pocket calculators for that – but rather as an exercise in thinking. The student should have the experience of understanding and then carrying out a mathematical process.

May the reader think along these lines, as he reflects on the sense and purpose of some of the included details. Naturally, the authors are grateful for all constructive criticism.

The tedious task of bringing the manuscript to a publishable form has been carried by Peter Schwab, who also prepared the figures, and detected numerous errors that had crept in. Heartfelt thanks to him!

Kassel, March 8, 1999

For the authors:
Peter Baum und Manfred v. Mackensen

Methodology – Remarks on methods of mathematics instruction in the high school

Uwe Hansen

The following description of the significance of thinking (given by Rudolf Steiner in the 1st part of his "Theosophy", GA 9), can provide orientation for the choice and treatment of themes for the 9th grade – and, to a large degree, also for the subsequent grades:

> "Thinking leads the human being beyond his own life. He acquires something that extends beyond his own soul. For him, it is a self-evident conviction, that the laws of thought are in agreement with the organization of the world. He therefore observes himself as a native inhabitant of the world, based on this agreement. This agreement is one of the important facts, through which the human being gets to know his own being. The human being seeks in his soul for the truth, and through this truth speaks not only his soul, but the things of the world also. What through thinking is recognized as true, has an independent significance, in regard to the things of the world, not merely to the own soul."

The whole instruction should be permeated by this mood: my thoughts are not tied to myself in the same way that my feelings and sensations are. When I construct thoughts, when I recognize the laws of thinking, then I release myself from the tight bonds of my separate life and discover thereby anew a being-together, that had disappeared in the previous years as a result of my own development. Going through puberty is indeed like a fall from the paradise of being protected and held, into isolation, vulnerability, and the solitude of the own soul.

These very painful experiences bring forth a yearning for inner stability and a new being-together. This yearning will be satisfied, when the young person penetrates the world with his own thoughts, when he experiences the creative power of his own thinking, when he realizes, how through these new capacities he can find truths that are significant for the whole world and for other people.

In this age (14-15 years), one has to arouse in the student the feeling, that he himself has discovered the laws, that he has recognized the truth from within himself through the creative power of his own thinking. This joy in discovery has to permeate the whole learning experience; one has to dive whole-heartedly into the adventure of thinking.

The completely new qualities of thinking have to be experienced by ninth-graders: for example, that it's not necessary to carry out an action, in order to arrive at the result; it's sufficient to carry it out in thinking. The number of seating arrangements in a classroom, for example, is arrived at not by actually trying them all out, but by thinking about it. For this reason, the thoughts arising out of combinatorics and probability theory satisfy the students of this age-group.

The inner imagination is also schooled through thinking: if one cuts a cylinder with a plane neither parallel nor perpendicular to the axis, then one obtains an elliptical cross-section. This fact may lead one to the conclusion, that this cross-section will no longer be an ellipse if the cylinder is deformed into a cone. Through a series of thoughts one can come to the insight, that this conclusion is false, so that thinking can correct and refine the inner imagination.

Through working with geometric loci, one practices the observation and mobility of one's own thinking. One turns away from the concrete, isolated situation and turns toward the all-inclusive law; just as all of mathematics is characterized by this embedding of the single case in in a larger connection, and thereby is a release from the immediately given. This activity is a metamorphosis of the human activity of standing up. This can be more generally phrased: everything mathematical has its origin in movement processes, in processes whereby the human being works actively into space. This inner "standing up" and release from the immediately-given helps to understand the following discussion by Rudolf Steiner, that appears in the writing "Mathematics and Occultism" (GA 35):

"When I think mathematically, I think about the sense-perceptible, but at the same time I do not think *in* the sense-perceptible... That is the essential thing about the mathematical approach, that a single sense-perceptible element leads beyond itself, that it can serve as an analogy for me, for a encompassing spiritual fact. The mathematical object can be the means, whereby I get to know, in a sense-perceptible way, super-sensible facts."

Experience reveals that mathematical concepts lie on the border between the sense-perceptible world and a purely spiritual world. This proximity with the super-sensible has as consequence, that in mathematical activity, the young person submerges himself in a domain of sublime harmony, absolute purity, beauty, and clarity.

This submersion has a cleansing effect on the not-yet strongly formed, indeed, often chaotic soul of the young person. This healing effect of the mathematical, this freeing from personal moods, which is a deep yearning of the growing young person, is addressed in a beautiful way in a lecture from Rudolf Steiner:

> "Let's assume that we have the thought of a triangle. We have to inwardly give ourselves up to it, without this Mr. Thought worrying about whether I have a headache or a stomach-ache. It's really a matter of indifference to him, what my personal disposition is. He doesn't care a whit, if I'm feeling this way or that way, sad or happy, whether something hurts or feels good – the thought of the triangle rules with a particular unrivaled nonchalance in my consciousness and doesn't concern himself with my subjective mood." (GA 212, 4th lecture)

Steiner repeatedly made the point, that doing mathematics is simultaneously an inner construction activity and an observation of this activity (GA 324, 3rd lecture). The mathematical concepts arise out of the will nature of the human being. These activities of the will are then raised into the light of mental pictures, so that mathematical concepts acquire a pictorial quality. This mutual interpenetration and fertilization of will and imagination is a necessity of all mathematical activity. When the side of the will is too weak, then the mathematics freezes into formalism; when the imaginative side is too weak, then it lacks the necessary clarity.

Steiner's recommendation to derive numbers and operations more strongly out of division, rather than putting addition in the foreground, reveals an emphasis on the side of the will. One-sided reliance on mental pictures is to be avoided. In the same vein, he often brings attention to a false confidence in pictorial representations:

"When a person is exposed only to instruction based on pictures, then in his soul he becomes completely dried out, then the inner driving forces of the soul slowly die away." (GA 296, 4th lecture) In contrast, Steiner presents the following thought:

> "We have to remain conscious of the creative force of our soul and should not awake in the child the impression, that before he has recognized the triangle *within* himself, he can grasp the essential nature of the triangle in the outer world." (GA 301, 13th lecture) Steiner then points out, that one should characterize, not define, that one "should communicate not dead, but living, concepts, living sensations. And so one should try, for example, to teach geometry as lively as possible.. The geometric can be so experienced – by those who have a certain experience with geometry – that it can gradually be transformed from something static into something living... So it's quite good, to draw forth from the child the mental picture of the triangle, that is in inner motion, so that one doesn't actually get the imagination of a static triangle, but rather that of a mobile triangle..."

It's also valid in the domain of numbers to aim for this inner liveliness, in the introduction of negative numbers, of powers, of logarithms, etc.

These hints are actually valid in all domains. Weaker students, for example, have difficulties setting up equations, They don't understand where the two sides should come from; after all, there is only one situation being described. This experience shows that these students don't manage to bring their own willing activity into the picture. Their own experience and the equation go their separate ways.

We can illustrate this on a simple example: What number do you have to start with, so that after you after added 5 to three times this number, then divided this result in half, you get 13?

In order to get the students involved, you can write the separate steps one after the other like this:

the sought-for number	x
times 3	$3x$
5 more than 3 times the number	$3x + 5$
half of this	$\frac{3x+5}{2}$

It makes sense, first to go through the path to the solution first without equations, purely conceptually: If $\frac{3x+5}{2}$ is equal to 13, then $3x+5$ has to be twice 13, that is, 26. The increase by 5 is likewise reversed, so that $3x$ has to be the same as 21. The desired number then has to be 7.

From this, one notices that the student has to be able to undo a sequence of different actions. He has to be able to observe his actions, in order to undo them. To multiply both sides of an equation by 2, or to add 5 to both sides, is a strange thought at first for the students. The immediate experience is that one doubles one thing, not two. One thinks about the same thing differently at different times, and consequently symbolizes it also it different ways. Bringing this all together, one can write out the process as follows:

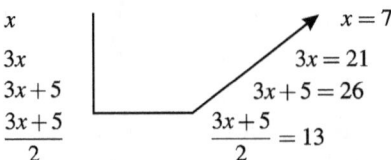

In this way one emphasizes the symmetry to be seen in setting up the equation and solving it.

It's sufficient to carry out this exhaustive treatment on just a few examples. Later, the students are then happy, if they then can solve the exercises in the usual way. This example should show, how one brings the underlying activity stronger into consciousness, when one emphasizes the temporal element and doesn't set up the standard pictures to begin with.

The recommendations of Steiner for the lower school can also be applied to themes in the high school. In this way one can carry over the suggestion, to go from the whole to its parts, to the three-dimensional geometry in the high school:

How can one cut a cube with one slice into two parts of the same volume?

One can align the cutting plane to go through the center point, parallel to two opposite faces, or as diagonal plane through two opposite edges, or in such a way, that it cuts a space diagonal of the cube at right angles. One sees: every plane going through the center of the cube divides the cube into two congruent solids. In general they are mirror images of each other. The cutting surface can be a square, a rectangle, a rhombus, a parallelogram, or a hexagon. The number of sides can't be larger than 6, since there are only 6 cube faces. Due to the symmetry of the cubes, the number of sides has to be an even number.

If one additionally takes a second cutting plane, one can arrange it so that both parts are divided again in half, which yields four bodies with the same volume. Is it possible to divide the cube also into 3 equal parts? If you connect the vertices of one face of the cube with one of the vertices of the opposite face, one obtains a skew pyramid. You can then easily verify that the cube can be decomposed into three such pyramids.

If you connect the center of the cube with the four vertices of one face, you get a right pyramid[1], that encompasses one sixth of the cube's volume. From this it's not far to the thought, that a right

---

[1] One whose apex lies directly over the center of its base.

pyramid, whose tip is the middle point of a face, and whose base the opposite face of the cube is, has the volume of one third of the cube. The volume of the pyramid is, after all, unchanged if you move its tip in the plane parallel to the base (that is called a "shearing" movement in space).

Taking this as the point of departure, one can divide the cube in very distinctive ways. Here are some examples:

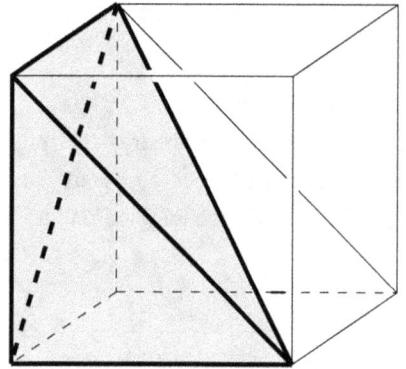

Dividing into two prisms.

$$1 = \frac{1}{2} + \frac{1}{2}$$

Then one of the prisms is divided into one pyramid and a tetrahedron.

$$1 = \frac{1}{2} + \frac{1}{3} + \frac{1}{6}$$

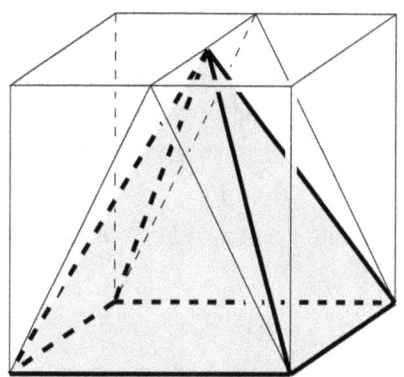

Dividing the cube into three prisms.

$$1 = \frac{1}{4} + \frac{1}{2} + \frac{1}{4}$$

The middle prism is divided into two tetrahedra and one pyramid.

$$1 = \frac{1}{4} + \frac{1}{12} + \frac{1}{3} + \frac{1}{12} + \frac{1}{4}$$

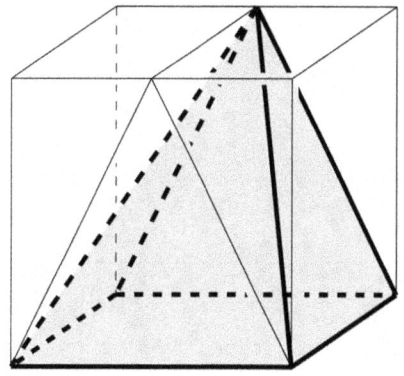

When the tip of the pyramid is moved to the side of the face, one of the tetrahedra disappears and the other becomes twice as big. One obtains:

$$1 = \frac{1}{4} + \frac{1}{3} + \frac{1}{6} + \frac{1}{4}$$

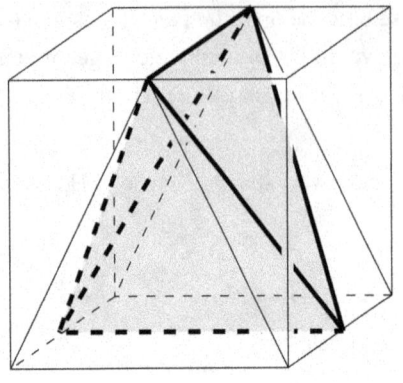

The middle prism can also be divided into a tetrahedron and two pyramids.

$$1 = \frac{1}{4} + \frac{1}{6} + \frac{1}{6} + \frac{1}{6} + \frac{1}{4}$$

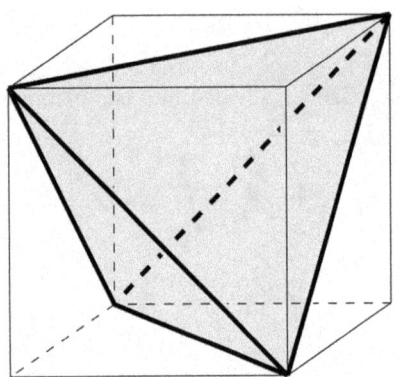

A cube can be divided into 6 tetrahedra – the three congruent skew pyramids introduced above are each split in half. Or, one can divide the tetrahedron into 5 tetrahedra:

$$1 = \frac{1}{6} + \frac{1}{6} + \frac{1}{3} + \frac{1}{6} + \frac{1}{6}$$

Here the middle tetrahedron is twice as big as the other four.

This example can serve to show how the division of a whole into parts opens up a field of creative activity. This approach can serve as a general principle, not only for a main lesson as a whole, but also for the individual instructional units. In the course of the high school, this principle will be further enriched by the principle of metamorphosis.

In the following articles, the points of view presented in this introduction will be presented in more differentiated form.

On the Treatment of the Conic Sections in the 9th Grade

UWE HANSEN

In the future it will become ever more necessary to strengthen intensively the imaginative powers of young people. For this reason, it is justified to practice the visualization of spatial configurations.

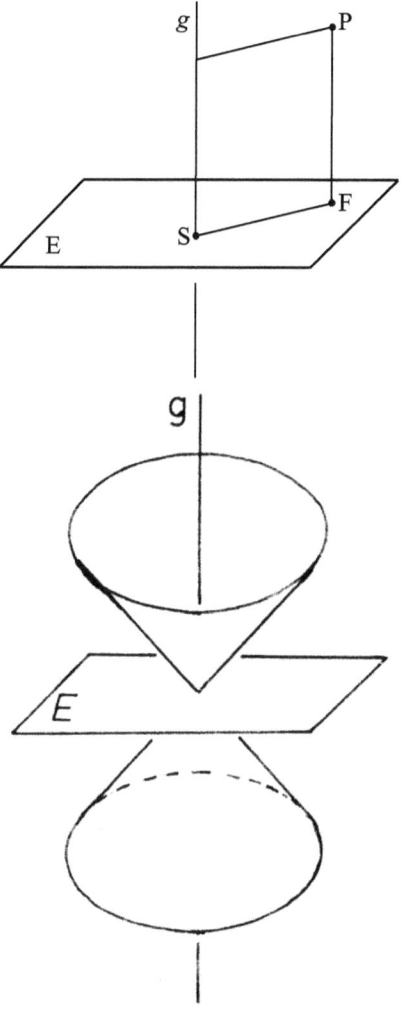

Example 1: Given a plane E and a line g, that intersect at right angles in the point S. We want to find all the points P that are exactly as far from g as they are from E. A point P with this property is so positioned, so that angle is $\sphericalangle\,\text{PSF} = 45°$. (F is the base of the perpendicular from P to E), since the line SP has to bisect the right angle at S. That means: All the points P lie on the surface of a double cone, whose lines form an angle of 45° with the cone axis.

One can also present this exercise in the following form: a horizontal plane E, moves with constant velocity upwards, or downwards. A line g that is perpendicular to E is the axis of a cylinder Z, whose radius grows at the same velocity as E moves, beginning with the radius 0. What surface is created by the intersection of E and Z? One obtains the same double cone as above: due to the identical velocities, the distances of a point on the cone is always the same to g and to E.

This double cone arises therefore, in that an constantly expanding circle moves up/down at a constant speed.

Both exercises lead to the same result. In the second one, however, the double cone actually comes into being, hence demands from the student a heightened activity.

Experience shows that 9th graders gain satisfaction from such visualization exercises; the required concentration brings an orderly atmosphere into the classroom. The movement of the students' own hands can be a decisive help, especially for weaker students.

When the plane and cylinder move with two different constant velocities, then a double cone arises with a different opening angle. To stimulate the reader, we give some further examples here:

Example 2: The radius r of a sphere increases with a constant velocity; the center stays fixed and lies at the start, when $r = 0$, in a horizontal plane E. E moves up (or down) with half the velocity (of the radius increase) parallel to itself, hence remains horizontal. What surface does the intersection curve of the sphere with the plane sweep out? In this case, one obtains also a double cone with the opening angle of $\alpha = 120°$.

Example 3: A and B are the centers of two spheres that grow with constant and equal velocity. At the beginning both have radius 0. The intersection of the two spheres is (in case it exists) a circle which, as the spheres grow, sweeps out a plane, the perpendicular bisector of the segment AB.

Example 4: As in Example 3, but one of the spheres should begin with a non-zero radius. The intersection curve sweeps out in this case not a plane but one "half" of a two-sheeted hyperboloid.

Example 5: As in Example 3, both spheres begin with radius 0, but now the one radius grows, for example, twice as fast as the other. The intersection curve now sweeps out a sphere – called a "division sphere", in analogy with the concept of "division circle".

Example 6: Again one has two spheres, but now the one shrinks at the same velocity that the other grows. The intersection curve now sweeps out an ellipsoid – if the parameters allow it, that is, if $r_1 + r_2$ is greater than the distance between the two centers A and B, which are then the two foci of the ellipsoid.

Example 7: As in Example 1, but now the center point M starts out above the plane E. The radius of the sphere grows at the same speed as the plane moves up parallel to itself. What is the surface swept out by the intersection curve of plane and sphere? Answer: a paraboloid.

All these exercises can be carried out successfully with ninth graders – of course a cautious and systematic approach is required, in order that the weaker students can also participate in the class. Meaningful repetition is very important here. We hope it is obvious, that the students are not expected to draw the results of the exercises! The following exercise can be solved only by particularly gifted students:

Example 8: Two cylinders, whose axes don't intersect, but whose directions are perpendicular to each other, increase their radii with equal velocity. What surface does the intersection curve of the two cylinders sweep out? Answer: a hyperbolic paraboloid. (See the sketch).

By varying the initial conditions one can also produce a one sheeted hyperboloid. g_1 and g_2 are the two cylinder axes.

I always used these exercises at the beginning of the main lesson – as a entryway into the lesson.

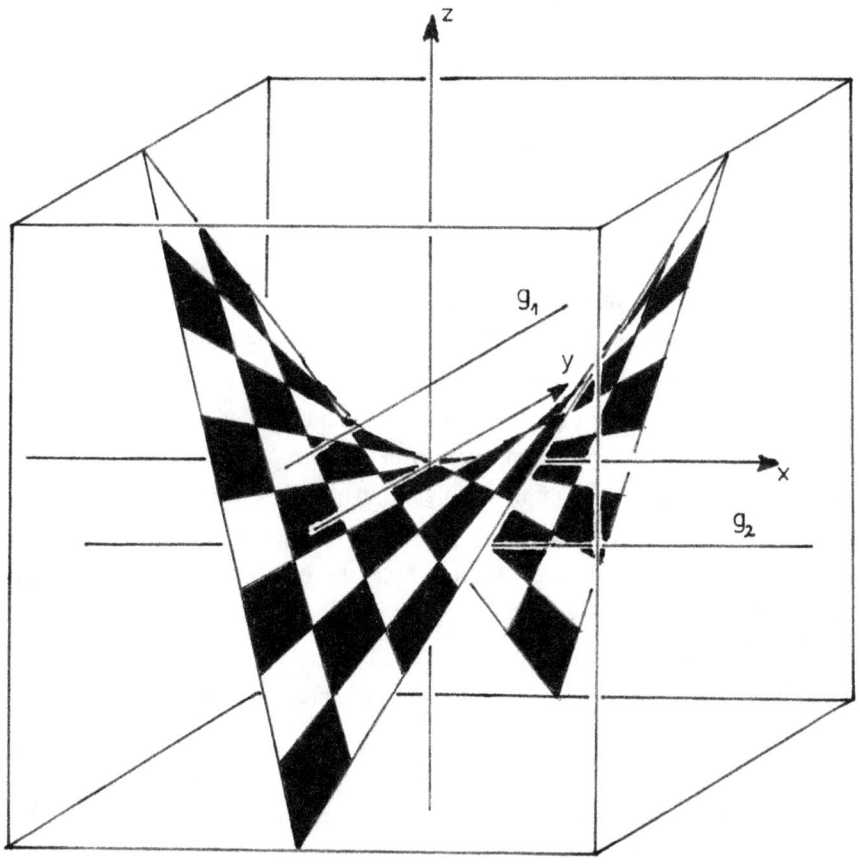

Figure 1: Example 8: $x^2 - y^2 = 4z$ $g_1 : z = 1, x = 0$ $g_2 : z = -1, y = 0$

The conic sections as symmetry figures and their construction using thread

Markus Hünig

1 Preliminary Remarks

Young people at the beginning of high school find themselves in a phase of necessary re-orientation (change from class teacher to high school collegium, crisis of puberty, etc.) Finding the right way to relate to different requirements counts as one of their most urgent tasks.

The treatment of the curves commonly known as "conic sections" in the ninth grade can help to meet this challenge, when these curves are introduced and handled as symmetry curves in the plane. Perhaps one should dispense completely with the term "conic sections" and refer to them as "curves of the second order" or simply as "ellipse, hyperbola, and parabola".

The term "symmetry curve" in this context serves to denote a geometric locus, that in some form is defined through an equal distance.[1] For example, the perpendicular bisector of two points satisfies this condition, as does the angle bisector of two intersecting lines.

A constant length can be represented by a thread of a certain length. Thread constructions for the circle and ellipse are well-known. Less well-known are thread constructions for the other conic sections; we want to derive these in what follows from the thread construction of the ellipse.

What follows, is not enough to fill a main lesson. The intention here is rather that the teacher of the corresponding main lesson receives a stimulation that can perhaps have a fruitful effect on the pedagogical quality of this domain.

2 The ellipse

One is given a circle ("Guide circle" k_l) as well as a point ("focal point" F) within this circle. The goal is to find the set of points, which lie the same distance from both focal point and guide circle. We will call this set of points the *symmetry curve* between focal point and guide circle.[2]

The symmetry curve obtained in this way is an ellipse. For each point of the ellipse, there are two segments d_f and d_l of equal length; we call d_f the *focal line* and d_l, the *guide line*. Call the segment from the center of the circle to a point on the ellipse d_m. Then $d_m + d_l = r_l$, where r_l is the radius of the guide circle, since by the above, d_l lies on a radius of the guide circle.

Since we are assuming that $d_f = d_l$, then $d_m + d_f = r_l$; this constant length can be represented by a thread of length r_l, whose ends can be attached to the points F and M_l, for example, by thumbtacks. When the thread is pulled taut by a pencil, then the tip of the pencil lies on a point of the ellipse.

---

[1] See also the article on geometric loci by Uwe Hansen in this volume, p. 81]
[2] The distance of a point P to a circle is defined to be the shortest distance from the point to any point of the circle. If one calls this closest point of the circle N, then it's geometrically obvious that line PN must be a radius line of the circle, and consequently, perpendicular to the tangent to the circle at N.

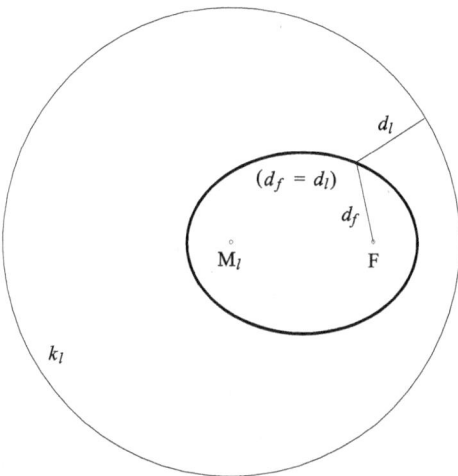

Thread construction of ellipse (Guide circle added for clarity)

Note that to obtain the traditional thread construction of the ellipse, we have made a transition from the equality of two segments to the constant sum of two segments, in that we subtracted the one segment from a third (constant) length. This is the basic idea which will help us find thread constructions for the parabola and the hyperbola.

3 The parabola

If one imagines that the radius of the guide circle grows ever larger, so that the curvature becomes more and more flat, then in the limit one obtains a guide line. Once more, we seek the symmetry curve:

Given a line ("guide line" l) as well as a point ("focal point" F) not lying on the line. We seek all points, which are the same distance from the focal point and the guide line. The resulting curve is a parabola.

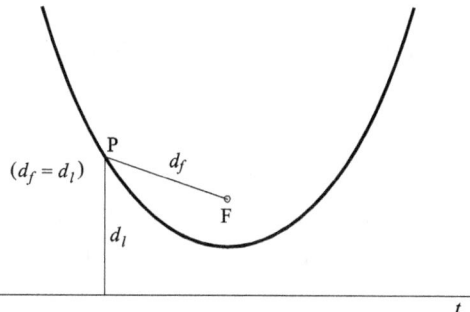

A string that is stretched between two points can only represent a constant length. Here we have as before $d_f = d_l$. Through rewriting we obtain:

$$d_f - d_l = 0 \Leftrightarrow d_f + c - d_l = c \Leftrightarrow d_f + (c - d_l) = c$$

In order to arrive at a thread construction for a parabola, we therefore begin with a thread of arbitrary length (c) and imagine one of the two segments as belonging to a segment of this total length (it's easier to take the guide line for this purpose). The guide line l is represented by a ruler, and a right triangle gliding along this ruler represents the perpendicular line d_l. One end of the thread is attached to the focal point F with, for example, a thumbtack, the other to the tip of the right triangle. The length of the thread c is exactly the length of the vertical side of the triangle. With the tip of the pencil, one stretches the thread as far as possible on the side of the triangle. The resulting position of the pencil tip is a point of the parabola, since it's easy to see that the distance from focal point to pencil is the same as the "missing" distance along the edge of the triangle (the line d_l) from the pencil to the ruler (guide line). Thus, as the triangle glides along the ruler, the tip of the pencil traces out the desired parabola.

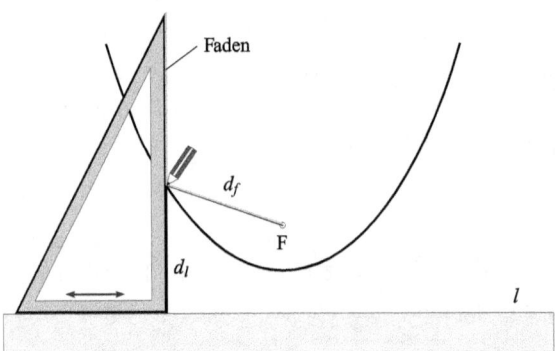

Thread construction of a parabola ("Faden" = Thread)

4 The hyperbola

When one continues the deformation of the guide circle which led to the guide line, we obtain a circle once more, which however is curved in the other direction to the original circle so that we have now to consider the focal point F outside the guide circle.

That is, we are given a circle (guide circle) and a point (focal point F) lying outside the circle, and we want to find all points which lie the same distance from the circle and from F, that is, the symmetry curve determined by the focal point and the guide circle. To begin with, one branch of a hyperbola appears.

One obtains the second branch of the hyperbola, if one uses the farthest point of the guide circle in the construction, instead of the closest one. It also meets the tangent line there at right angles. How can we devise a thread construction in this case?

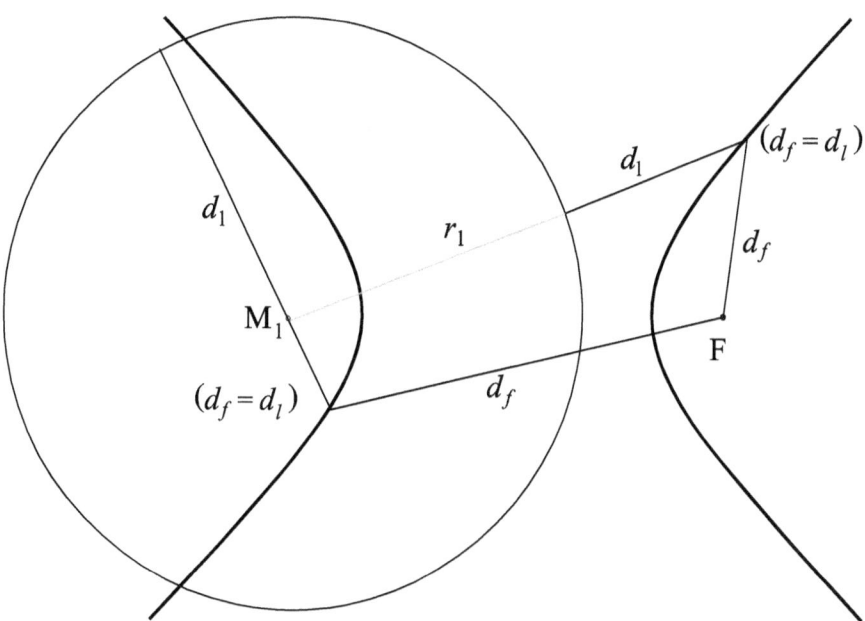

In order to obtain a reliable process, we need to make special tool, that fortunately is easy to produce. It is essentially a ruler that can be fixed to pivot around one of the points of its "line":

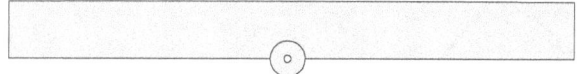

The pivot point is then fixed to the middle of the guide circle with a thumbtack. The thread is attached to one of the ends of the ruler, and its length is adjusted so that it reaches exactly to the guide circle (either the nearest point or the farthest point, depending on which branch one seeks to draw). The free end of the thread is attached to the focal point. When we now stretch the thread against the ruler, it's clear that the distance from the focal point to the pencil is the same as the distance of the pencil to the guide circle (although depending on the branch being drawn, the thread from pencil to the guide circle will either avoid the center of the circle or pass through this center).

It then becomes clear that the symmetry properties of the conic sections are closely connected to the possibility of making the thread construction. The distance, which remains constant, between the two different locations is, via the detour of a third segment of constant length, converted into something which can be represented by a thread of constant length (see the equation in the section on the parabola). Through this construction, some students will find their access to the geometry of conic sections made easier; for some it may make this access possible for the first time. In any case, the balance between competing reference objects (guide circle and focal point) can be here experienced as a continuous process that leaves behind a unified trace (the conic section as curve).

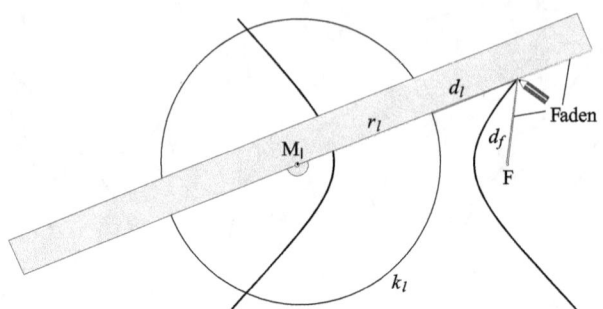

Figure 2: Thread construction of hyperbola (right branch, "Faden" = Thread)

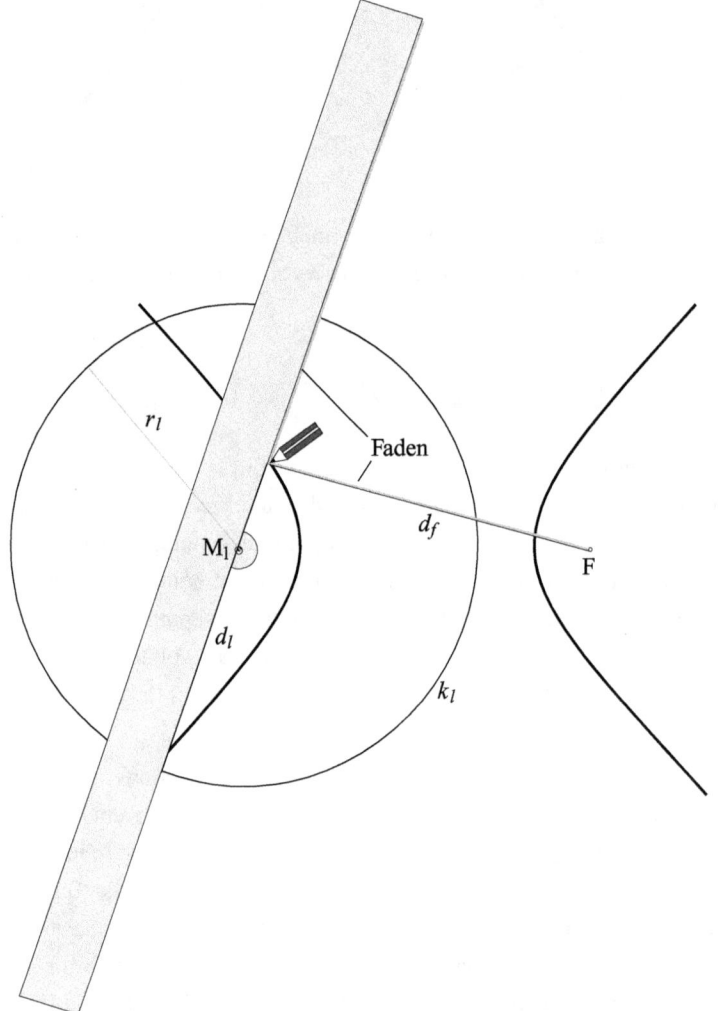

Figure 3: Thread construction of hyperbola (left branch, "Faden" = Thread)

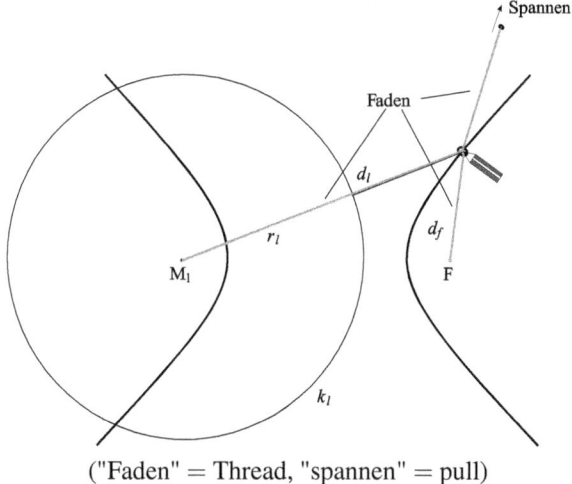

("Faden" = Thread, "spannen" = pull)

The ordinary constructions of single points of these curves with ruler and compass is not intended to be replaced by the thread construction; some aspects of these curves can be much better worked with, with their help.

In practice, experience shows that the thread can also be attached using pins or various clips (available from office supply stores). On the blackboard one can work well with suction cups (this is difficult however with painted boards).

Students can also construct the special ruler for the hyperbola from hard cardboard with a cardboard cutter (the part surrounding the rotation point doesn't have to be round!). One can use a flat wood panel; in the vicinity of the rotation point, make a hole and then screw in a screw-eye. This provides a stable rotation point.

There is a variation of the hyperbola construction that doesn't require the rotating ruler. One attaches one end of the thread to the middle of the guide circle, and stretches its other end in some direction; there one ties it to a second (shorter) thread, whose other end is attached to the focal point. Then a small ring is positioned around both of these threads, and the common, outer end of both threads is pulled tight. The pencil is then placed at the location of the ring. As the common end is moved (keeping both threads taut), the position of the ring/pencil traces out one branch of the hyperbola.

The construction is certainly easier to set up, but the drawing of the curve is hardly any easier, and the second hyperbola branch only appears by exchanging the role of the center of the circle and the focal point. It therefore seems to me that the first method, involving the rotating ruler, is superior to the use of the ring.

One stimulating aspect of these constructions is that the students have to work together to carry them out. While one holds the thread in place with a pin, for example, the other draws the curve with a pencil. This leads to a continuous switching between "serving" and "leading" rolls.

Plane geometry as a way into high school mathematics

Rolf Rosbigalle

1 Introduction

When you take over a ninth grade class as mathematics teacher, you do well to quickly find out, what the students can. For this purpose, it's good to find easy, but not uninteresting, approaches that:

- have no prerequisites,

- provide a solid foundation in a short time, without tiresome repetition, and which generate a feeling of confidence,

- can lead directly to more difficult and novel themes, and

- in the process, lead students to become to self-reliant problem-solvers.

The following examples describe the first main lesson blocks[1] of the first mathematics main lesson for the ninth grade (can also be treated as seeds for skills classes[2] or main lesson units). They are so arranged, that they represent a self-contained sequence of lessons. Some of the "theme clusters" can, however, be extracted and handled on their own. Often the unit begins with a *mental reckoning phase*, and one is shown – starting from there – how to arrive at new challenges (See *Path in the main part of the main lesson*), or, on other occasions, it's shown how one can pick up and deepen the content from the previous day's lesson. Care is taken to achieve this in a playful way, so that "math anxiety", which can be a relic of the class teacher time, doesn't have a chance to rear its head. I have described the *first four main lesson periods* in a particularly detailed way. I hope that will help the beginning teacher to practice careful preparation of the course of a lesson, as well as the precise planning of how to lead a classroom discussion, etc. An *alternative path* is provided as a supplement.

Everything presented here has been repeatedly tried out and has proven its validity, but it goes without saying that it must be always taken up anew and in different ways; there's always room for improvement! The content and the method presented here orient themselves on what I've *found* in beginning ninth grade classes, not necessarily on I might *wish* to have found. There's plenty here that belongs in the eighth grade, according to some authors (A. Bernhard, G. Ott); note that this material is not treated here as something new but rather given as a short, pregnant repetition for a class that is now one year older.

---

[1] By "block" we mean a single meeting of a class, typically for a main lesson one and a half or two hours
[2] "Skills classes" denotes regular mathematics instruction that lies outside the main lesson.

2 The course of the main lesson with commentary

2.1 Period 1 – simple Figures

Mental reckoning: calculating percents

How many € is $3\frac{1}{2}\%$ of 6000 €? Several such exercises follow. How did you calculate that? Divided by 100 and times $3\frac{1}{2}$. Or: drop 2 digits from 6000, multiply by 3 (that is, 3 times 60), then add on half of 60. Take several such exercises, with accompanying calculations, possibly including also the divisibility test of "casting out 9's"[3] Choose the difficulty level so that *all* students can be called on to participate verbally – and make sure that all have a chance to do so! Then you can increase the speed and raise the difficulty level. This mental reckoning phase doesn't have a direct connection with the content of the main lesson but has proved itself as a valuable path into the mathematical activity of a ninth grade class. That's why it's introduced here. It serves to establish an initial contact with the students and as a "wake up" call. Then, as a transition into the main lesson, one brings a visualization exercise. Or, you can leave the mental reckoning phase out and begin directly with the visualization.

Visualization exercise

We imagine a square lying in a vertical plane, whose base edge is horizontal. We inscribe a triangle in the square, whose vertices P, Q, and R, are positioned as follows: P lies on the upper edge, Q on the right edge, and R is the lower left vertex of the square.

- Where do P and Q lie, if the triangle is isosceles?
- Which special positions arise, as P and Q move along their respective edges?
- In these special cases, how big is the area of the triangle?

The blackboard is then flipped around (or opened) to reveal the following picture: [4]

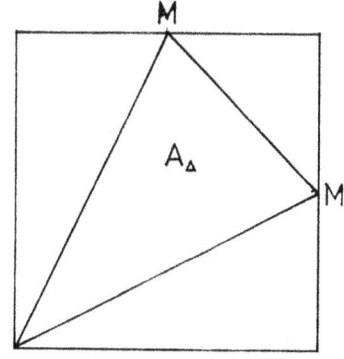

$A_\square$: Area of the square
M: Midpoint of the respective side

Figure 1: $A_\triangle : A_\square = ?$

---
[3] See the treatment of this theme in the article by A. Bernard in this volume S. 139.
[4] See P. Eigenmann: Geometrische Denkaufgaben, Klett Verlag, Stuttgart 1981, Aufgabe 10 aus Teil I

One collects suggested solutions, discusses them (perhaps letting students present them on the board), and preserves one or more suggested solutions on the board. The essential steps – each of which has to be consciously carried out – are

- the notation used for areas, possibly also for edge lengths
- the area of a (right-angled) triangle
- the desired area as a "remainder" (after removal of some areas)

One obtains in this way $\underline{\underline{A_\triangle : A_\square = 3 : 8}}$.

Possible direction for further work include:

1. What percent of the square's area is covered by the inner triangle? is covered by the other triangles? For this, I have to convert a fraction to a decimal number, then express it as parts of a hundred, to arrive at the percentage.

2. The question "What kinds of triangle do you find in this figure?" leads to the considerations

    - What do we know about isosceles triangles?
    - What do we know about right triangles?

    and to further observations about the angles on this or the other figure, or perhaps the Theorem of Pythagoras.

4. Proportion equations [5] can be easily found in the figures and used as practice material in mental reckoning. The pedagogical importance of such equations in really understanding the intercept theorem and the angle relationships in a right triangle are sometimes underestimated.

Any of the above connections which don't get handled in the main lesson can be handled profitably in the skills classes.

The direction 2. above makes it possible to discuss, just why the area of *any* triangle is given by "base times height divided by 2". Students might proceed from here in different directions:

---

[5] Of the form $\frac{a}{b} = \frac{c}{d}$ which arise, for example, from the similarity of two triangles

(1) Students might complete the triangle to a rectangle (Sketch 1), which encounters problems for triangles of the form △. In this case, one can complete the triangle to a parallelogram (Sketch 2) which can in turn be transformed into a rectangle by "cut and paste" (Sketch 3). Or, the students start immediately with a parallelogram for Sketch 1, and skip the rectangle completely.

Sketch 1

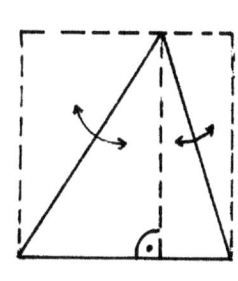

Sketch 2

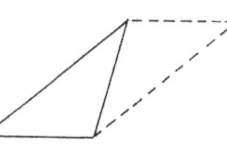

Sketch 3

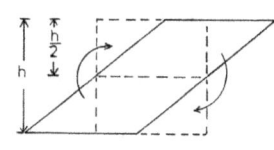

(2) Students might arrive immediately at the principle of shearing. Given a triangle as in Sketch 1, one brings in the idea shearing by a drawing as in Sketch 4. Given a triangle of the form △, one must first establish the invariance of the area, as done in direction (1).

Sketch 4

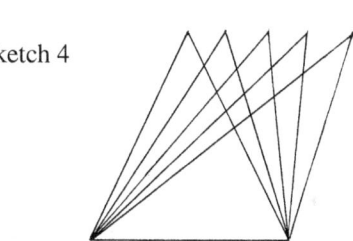

In "*Quiet work phase*", the students enter Figure 1 along with the solution, into their notes, and the above sketches (as drawn by the teacher on the board), and area formulae for triangle and parallelogram (rectangle and square as special cases).

> When choosing the exact form for the students' classroom activity, it's always good to keep in mind, whether the goal is for the students to work alone, or to work alone and help each other out as needed, or to work in self-chosen groups. It makes good sense, to develop skills in the latter form of working, as practice in social life. Decisive for this phase of the instruction, is that every student achieves some degree of self-reliance in doing exercises, testing ideas, drawing, etc. See also p. 52.

In the remaining time, students can already begin to work on the homework. For this purpose, the following figures are drawn on the board: [6]

---
[6] From P. Eigenmann: Geometrische Denkaufgaben
Exercise 1: Part I, 26; Exercise 2: Part I, 22; Exercise 3: Part I, 4

Exercise 1

Let the area of the square be: Q.

Let $A = \dfrac{Q}{7} \cdot x = ?$

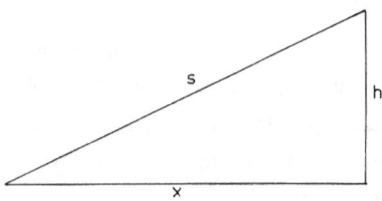

Exercise 2

$A = ?$

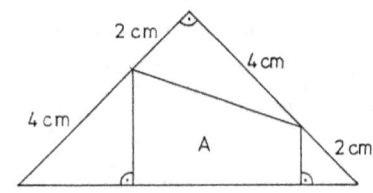

Exercise 3

Let M be the midpoint of the slanting side.

$A_1 = ?$
$A_2 = ?$
$A_3 = ?$

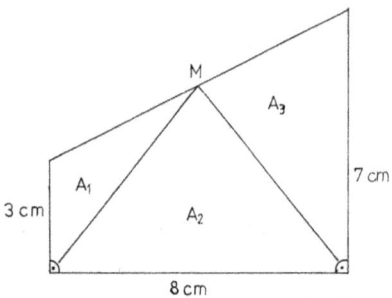

Here we would like to insert a *recommendation regarding the work ethic of the teacher*. Someone with a skill in elementary mathematics will always be finding more possibilities for solutions; occasionally these solutions are based on this or that result, that has not yet been handled in class. The teacher is therefore well-advised to think through, precisely and from different points of view, the possible paths to a solution, *before* he handles them in class. On the one hand, it can happen that in classroom discussions, when the suggestions for solutions arrive at a dead-end, the teacher's offer of help instead leads the students onto a confusing path, resulting in catastrophe. On the other hand, a well-prepared teacher, even when he allows the students to work on their own, creates the fruitful atmosphere necessary for successful problem solving. The teacher is further well-advised, to empty himself to a certain degree when he is teaching, in order to be open to everything the students say, even the most peculiar combinations of thoughts.

Solutions: Exercise 1: $x = 8\,9$cm; Exercise 2: $A = 9\,\text{cm}^2$; Exercise 3: $A_1 = 6\,9\text{cm}^2$, $A_2 = 20\,9\text{cm}^2$, $A_3 = 14\,9\text{cm}^2$

Supplement

In this context, the following problems are also appropriate:[7]

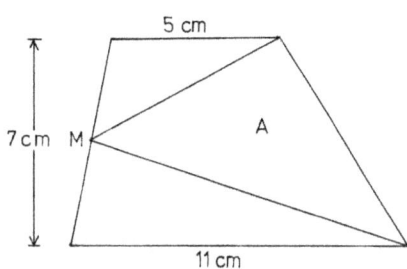

Exercise 4
$A = ?$

Exercise 5
Sei $A_1 = A_2$
$A = ?$

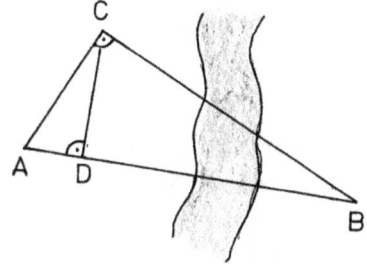

---

[7] From P. Eigenmann: Geometrische Denkaufgaben
Exercise 4: Part I, Exercise 18 (Solution: $A = 28\,\text{cm}^2$; Exercise 5: Aufgabe 20 (Solution: $A = 28\,\text{cm}^2$).

2.2 Period 2 – calculation of simple figures, area-transformations

Mental reckoning unit 1

$7 \cdot 13 = ?$ $3 \cdot 13 = ?$ $13 \cdot 13 = ?$

How did you figure that out?

$11 \cdot 13 = ?$ $9 \cdot 13 = ?$ $6 \cdot 13 = ?$
$5 \cdot 14 = ?$ $9 \cdot 14 = ?$ $4 \cdot 14 = ?$ $14 \cdot 14 = ?$

What was $13 \cdot 13$? And now $13 \cdot 14$? How can you calculate that? $10 \cdot 14$ and add $3 \cdot 14$, isn't it? $13 \cdot 13$ and add 13. Right? Or, $14 \cdot 14$ and then subtract 14.

One can then shift over to less-easy reckoning sequences, that lead towards the square numbers. Depending on the preparation of the students, one can go to 20^2 or 25^2. If nothing else suggests itself, it's possible to calculate $19 \cdot 19 = 10 \cdot 19 + 9 \cdot 19$, that is, one doesn't have to apply the binomial formula here (see below).

To conclude, review: What was $13 \cdot 13$? What was $14 \cdot 14$?, etc. In this way one progresses through all the square numbers up the chosen upper limit and enters them onto a **memory board**, that stands somewhat to the side:

$$1^2 = \ldots \qquad 11^2 = \ldots \ldots \qquad 41^2 = \ldots$$

$$\vdots \qquad \vdots \qquad \vdots$$

$$50^2 = \ldots$$

As you can see, the completed display table can go up to 50^2, or even further. One extends it beyond 25^2 in the course of time, something that can take place in the mental reckoning phase. In this regard, see particularly the Mental Reckoning Unit 5 (p. 62). This table should be left standing for some time.

The next phase of the mental reckoning moves over to calculation of areas, relying on the square numbers. The following kinds of exercises can be recommended:

- In a square piece of tin with side length 10 cm a square hole with side length 5 cm is cut out. How big is the remaining area?

- We take a rectangular piece of tin with side lengths 15 cm and 7,5 cm and cut out two square holes of side length 6 cm. Area of the remainder?

 (Fastest calculation of the rectangle area: $15 \cdot \frac{15}{2} = \frac{15^2}{2} = \ldots !$)

- We have three square wooden boards of side length 15 cm, 20 cm, 25 cm. Is the combined area of the first two bigger than the area of the third?

  How is it with the side lengths 14 cm, 19 cm, 24 cm? etc. Find the side lengths of 3 square wooden boards, so that the combined area of the first two equals the area of the third!

- Saw from the square board with side length 25 cm a square hole with side length 20 cm, and from this a square hole with side length 13 cm. Which of the "passepartouts" has the greater area?, etc.

- Saw out of the square piece of side length 13 cm (from the previous exercise) a square so that the area of what's left is approximately half the original area. How long should the side of the square hole be?

2.2.1 Remarks on mental reckoning:

When this phase leads over *thematically* into the main lesson, for example, when what's done in mental reckoning lends itself to some generalization, that then will be further investigated or applied, then it can be relatively long. When the mental reckoning is primarily for awakening the students and making them receptive for the themes of the main lesson, then it can be quite short. In any case:

- it should move along at a good clip

- it can be "amusing"

- by simple reckoning, keep the speed up; by difficult, *wait*

- it's forbidden to blurt out unsolicited answers

- employ the very good students for correcting wrong calculations, assuming no weaker students volunteer for the task

- those who don't volunteer answers are occasionally called on to answer a question of appropriate difficulty

- for every mental reckoning phase one should choose a broad range of exercises, with respect to level of difficulty.

All this applies as well to visualization exercises. By the Mental Reckoning Unit 1, the ability to make rapid, short-term observations is particularly in demand, in a way that intensifies step-by-step. Exactly this capacity is only weakly developed among young people in many industrialized countries these days, and can be improved in this way.

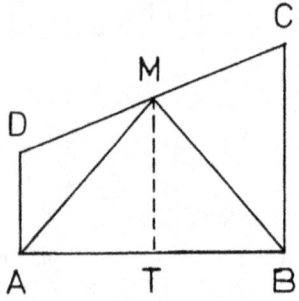

M is the midpoint of $\overline{DC}$, hence T is the midpoint of $\overline{AB}$.

The homework problems are still on the board and it's a good time to discuss them, preferably with closed books. Here the teacher asks the students for solutions to exercises 1 and 2. Students present their solutions one after the other on the board. Questions from students or the teacher during this phase serve to clear up any uncertainties.

One should invite presentation of alternative solutions. The main thing here is a general understanding of the path of the solution, rather than a precise formulation, which can come later (it is presented in Exercise 3).

After – or during – the discussion of Exercise 3, something like the following should be entered on the board:

- In $\triangle ABM$ we have $g = 8$ and $h = \frac{3+7}{2} = 5$, hence $A_2 = \frac{8 \cdot 5}{2} = 20$.
- In $\triangle AMD$ we have $g = 3$ and $h = \frac{8}{2} = 4$, hence $A_1 = \frac{3 \cdot 4}{2} = 6$.
- In $\triangle BCM$ we have $g = 7$ aund $h = \frac{8}{2} = 4$, hence $A_3 = \frac{7 \cdot 4}{2} = 14$.

In this way we obtain:

$\underline{\underline{A_2 = 20\,\text{cm}^2}}$ $\underline{\underline{A_1 = 6\,\text{cm}^2}}$ $\underline{\underline{A_3 = 14\,\text{cm}^2}}$

2.2.2 Remark on the specification of physical units

As a teacher, one is naturally aware that the numerical results calculated for h and A_2 (resp. A_1, A_3) are actually magnitudes, and, on top of that, different types: length and area. I allow the calculation to run its course with pure numbers – whereby one has already agreed previously on the units being used – and I bring the unit back in only when the result has been found. That sensitizes the student to the various qualities the makes possible a conscious, and not just mechanical, relationship to number, unit, magnitude, etc.

One now turns to the question: how can one find the total area without any detours through triangle areas, etc.? That leads, under favorable conditions, to the formulation of the area formula for a trapezoid. But perhaps someone makes a suggestion related to "cut and rejoin". One takes this suggestion on, applying the transformation of areas via shearing, introduced in the previous unit. One repeats briefly the shearing of a triangle and a parallelogram and presents the students with enough interesting shearing problems of various degrees of difficulty. Here, it's advantageous to have prepared exercise sheets for this theme, in order to avoid losing valuable "think and test" time for the drawing of figures; students with a particular temperament run the risk thereby of losing themselves in the drawing itself, which isn't really important at this point. We now present *some examples of shearing exercises*, that are to be "plowed up" by the students in the quiet work phase that now begins.

(1) Transformation of a given triangle while preserving the area

1. with changing base line:

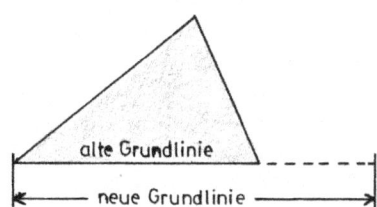

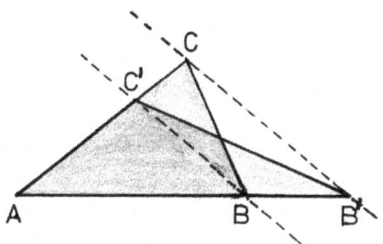

"alte Grundlinie" = old base line
"neue Grundlinie" = new base line
(works also with a smaller base line)

The parallel to $B'C$ [8] through B cuts AC in C' $\triangle AB'C'$ is the sought-after triangle
Justification:[9] $\triangle BCC'$ goes by a shear to $\triangle BB'C'$, the triangles have hence the same area. Furthermore, $\triangle ABC'$ belongs to both $\triangle ABC$ und $\triangle AB'C'$. Hence $\triangle ABC$ and $\triangle AB'C'$ have the same area.

2. With changing altitude

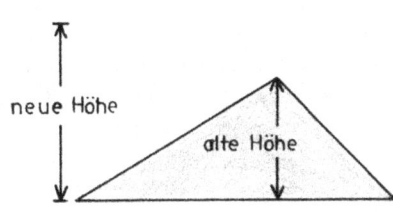

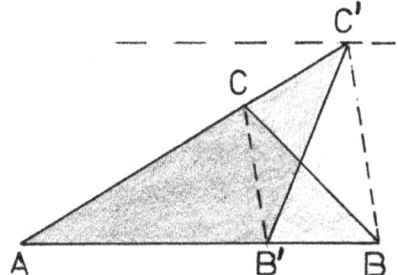

"alte Höhe" = old altitude
"neue Grundlinie" = new altitude
(works also with diminished altitudes)

AC cut the new altitude parallel in C' ; the parallel to BC' through C cuts AB in B'; $\triangle AB'C'$ is the sought-for triangle.
Justification: analogous to that in a).

(2) Transformation of a given polygon

1. Into a triangle of the same area:

---

[10] I denote the line through A and B as AB, and the segment from A to B as $\overline{AB}$.
[11] This figure plays the central role in *one* proof of the intercept theorem. If you want to treat this theorem in the current context, you can help easily help the students to the necessary insight in this way.

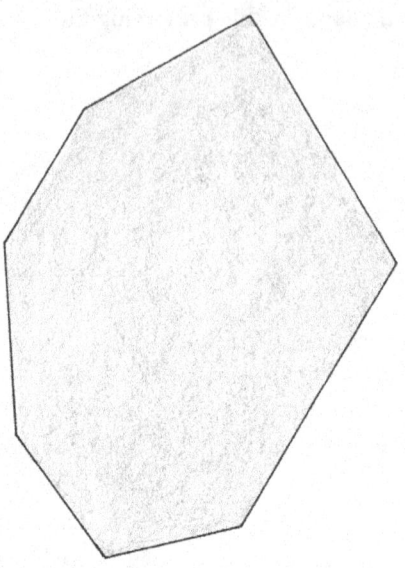

Example solutions

Transformation I

- △CAB becomes △CAB′
- △GEF becomes △GEF′
- △CGB′ becomes △CGB″
- △F′B″D becomes △F′B″D′

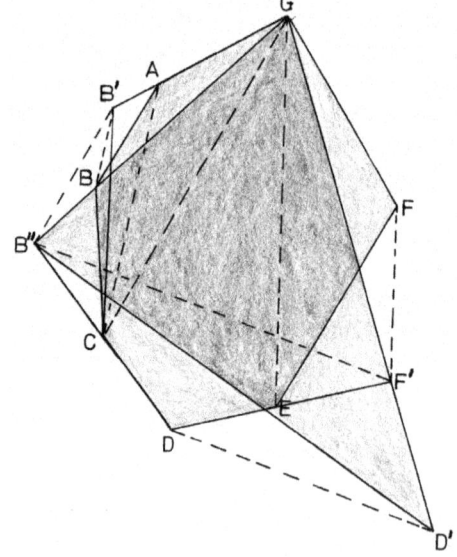

Transformation II

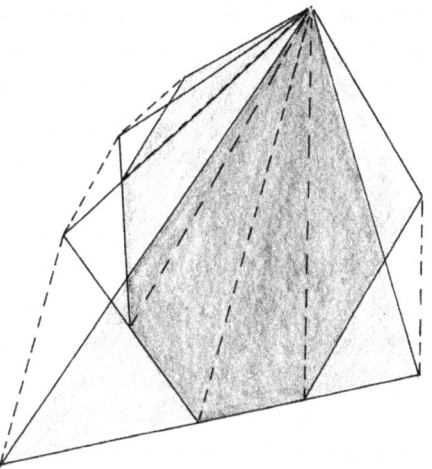

Hence, we obtain as solution triangle $\triangle GB''D'$. In similar fashion, one finds other solutions.

2. **Transformation of a given polygon into a square of the same area,** *with the goal of finding its area*

   Transform the given pentagon into a square of the same area, and determine in this way the area of the pentagon.
   (Result: $A = 196 \, \text{cm}^2$. This exercise is due to a suggestion from A. Bernhard, the numerical values are only introduced for the reader!).

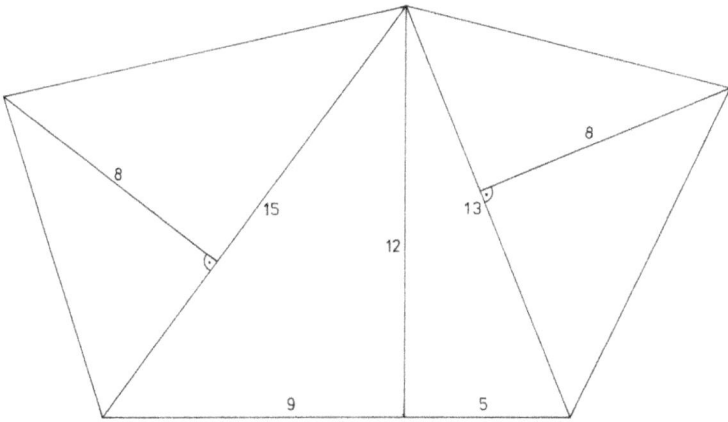

Concave polygons are also interesting, but they are not so simple to deal with. An extension of the concept "Polygon" to include concave figures appears to be desirable. That frees us from mental pictures that are too narrow. That will be particularly important in connection with projective geometry.

(3) Examples of transformations of rectangles:

1. Transformatiom of a given square into a rectangle with a given length:[12]

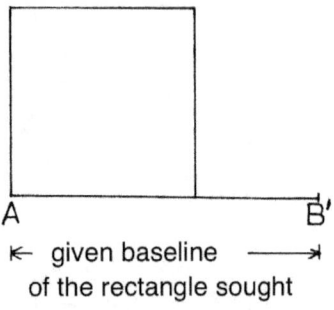

A   B'

← given baseline →
of the rectangle sought

Solution 1:

- ABCD becomes B'B'' CD
- B'B'' CD becomes B'C'D'D
- B'C'D'D becomes B'C'D''A

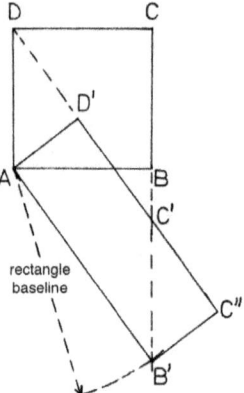

- Solution 2:
  ABCD becomes AB'C'D
- AB'C'D becomes AB'C''D'
  But take note of b)!

2. Transformation of a given rectangle into another rectangle with given length:
   Note that solution 2) of a) doesn't work, if $\overline{AB'} < \overline{AB}$ and $\overline{AB'} < \overline{BC}$. No such problems arise with the following solution:

---

[12] One can of course start with a rectangle instead of a square, see below. See also below, "Supplementary parallelogram", as well as what follows in Mental Reckoning Unit 4; there the Altitude Theorem and Euclid's Theorem are brought together with the shearing principle; what is presented above finds there another application, resp., solution.

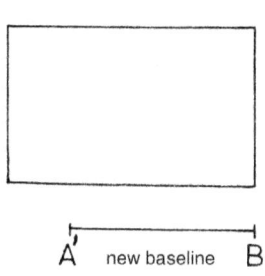 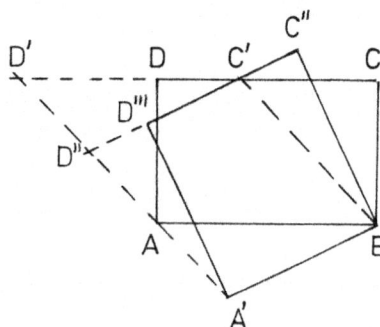

Solution:

- place the new base line $\overline{A'B}$ transverse to $\overline{AB}$
- $A'A$ cuts DC in D', the parallel to $A'A$ through B cuts DC in C'
- so ABCD becomes $ABC'D'$
- the parallel to $A'B$ through C' cuts AD' in D''
- so $ABC'D'$ becomes $A'BC'D''$
- $A'BC'D''$ becomes $A'BC''D'''$

(4) Examples of non-trivial parallelogram transformations

1. Transformation of a given parallelogram into one of the same area, with the same side a and a new altitude h'_b:

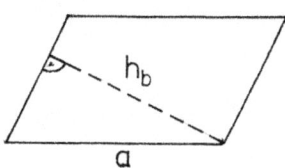 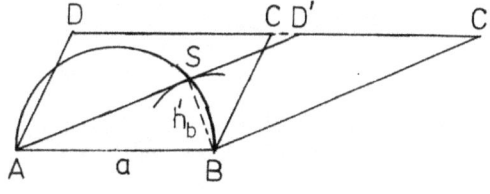

Assume: $h'_b < a$! New altitude h'_b ⊢——⊣
Solution:

- Circle centered at B with radius h'_b cuts the Thales circle constructed over diameter $\overline{AB}$ in S
- AS cuts DC in D', the parallels to AS through B cut CD in C'
- so, ABCD is transformed into $ABC'D'$.

Note:
for $h'_b = a$ one obtains a rectangle as solution,

for $h'_b > a$ there is no solution.

As one sees, this exercise pre-supposes the Thales Theorem, and provides a good opportunity to review it in an interesting context. The skills classes are a good place to carry this out; at the same time you can review the Inscribed Angle and the Central Angle Theorems.

2. Transformation of a given parallelogram into another that has the same area, a new side a' and a new angle α':

   Case 1: $a' \geqslant h_b$

   Transformation of a given parallelogram into one of the same area, with the same side a and a new altitude h'_b:

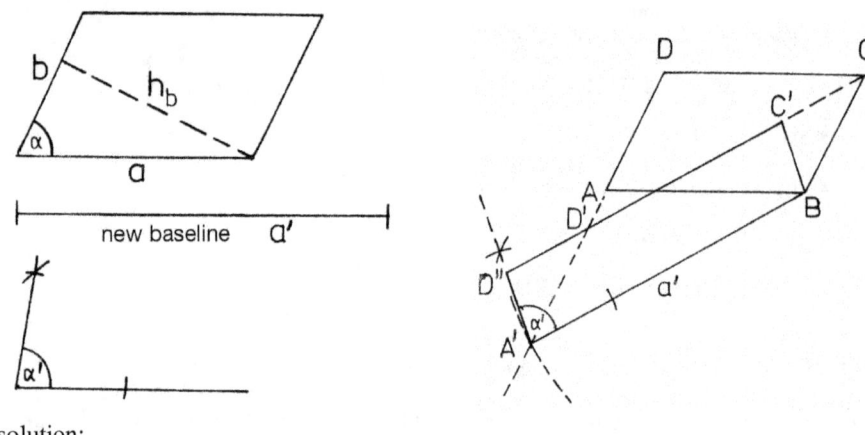

   solution:

   - Circle with radius a' centered on B cuts AD below in A'

   - The parallel to $A'B$ through C cuts AD in D'

   - so, ABCD is transformed into $A'BCD'$

   - Copy α' onto A' using $A'B$ as one side; the other side cuts CD' in D''

   - the parallel to $A'D''$ through B cuts CD' in C'

   - So, $A'BCD'$ is transformed into $A'BC'D''$

   Case 2: $a' < h_b$

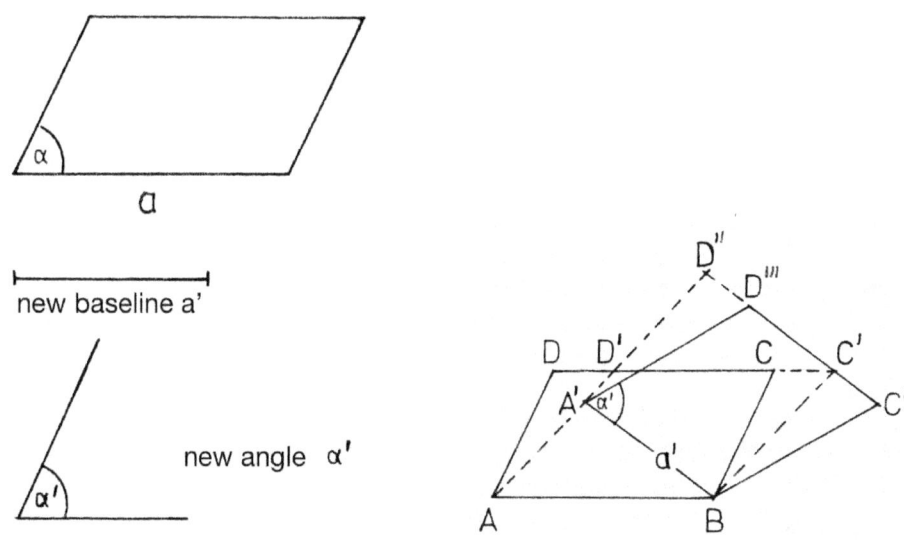

Solution:

- Draw a new baseline $\overline{A'B}$ at an angle to $\overline{AB}$.
- AA′ cuts CD in D′, the parallel to AA′ through B cuts CD in C'.
- So, ABCD is transformed into ABC′D′.
- The parallel to A′B through C′ cuts AA′ in D″
- So, ABC′D′ is transformed into A′BC′D″.
- Copy α' onto A′ using A′B as the lower side; the other side cuts C′D″ in D‴.
- The parallel to $A'D'''$ through B cuts C′D″ in C″.
- So, A′BC′D″ is transformed into A′BC″D‴.

Similar material can be found in *Hermann von Baravalle, "Geometrie als Sprache der Form"*, *A. Bernhard, Geometrie für 7. ind 8. Klasse an Waldorfschulen*, and in old school books from before 1960.

Another type of figure transformation is given by the so-called

2.2.3 Supplementary parallelograms

Through an arbitrary point of a diagonal of a parallelogram draw the parallels to the sides. This gives rise to four sub-parallelograms. Compare the area of the two sub-parallelograms which do not cross the diagonal. These two "supplementary parallelograms" have the same area. Why? (Hint: show that the diagonal cuts the other two parallelograms into triangles of equal area.)

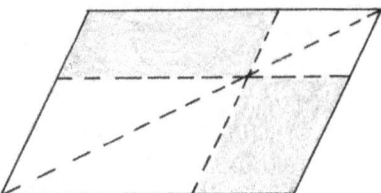

"Gnomon diagram"

This observation leads to the solution of the following exercise: transform a given parallelogram, while preserving its angle, into another of equal area but with an different base.

The application of this to a special case (the Altitude Theorem) can be found on the following pages. The book by Bernard cited above contains a detailed discussion of this theme.

In light of the constancy of the area demonstrated by this figure, one can at this juncture discuss and/or develop the possibility of using the supplementary parallelograms as an additional way to recognize or generate figures with equal areas. Naturally one can bring the figure into motion by letting the point move along the diagonal. The underlying aspect of motion, however, arises through the shearing. In my opinion, one can enunciate the following *orientation principle* in this regard:

> Bringing rigid figures into motion by shearing appears to provide a good counter-weight to the more technical nature of calculating plane and spatial figures. It requires a mobile imagination and provides the pupil an easy entrance into the thought-forms of projective geometry, as they are developed, for example, in *A. Bernard, Projektive Geometrie, Stuttgart, 1984.*

One more observation: later, in the study of solid geometry, the principle of shearing will be carried over into 3D space, in order to apply the principle of Cavalieri in an understandable way. Therefore, one should be careful not to handle shearing in plane geometry in a superficial way.

Transformation of a square into a rectangle of the same area, with a given side

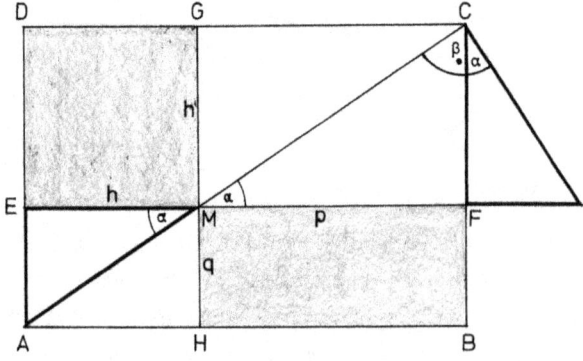

- Draw the square EMGD with side length h
- Draw the given rectangle side $\overline{MF} = p$
- Complete this to the "Gnomon diagram"
- HBFM is the sought-for rectangle.

The triangles AEM and MFC can be glued together along the sides $\overline{EM} = h = \overline{CF}$ to obtain a large right triangle. Going the other direction, we could start with such a right triangle, cut it along the altitude belonging to the right angle, and construct a gnomon diagram. In this way one obtains the Altitude Theorem of Euclid:

The altitude theorem of Euclid

$$h^2 = p \cdot q$$

Returning to the instruction period

Besides "plowing up" the shearing problem, the pupils can also, as needed, make notes of the solution of the Homework Exercise 3 which is still on the board. During this phase, the teacher draws examples of shearings of a figure, that follow one upon the other in easy steps, without necessarily revealing the solution of the exercises, which also serve as a homework assignment.

2.3 Period 3

Mental reckoning unit 2 (with visualization exercises)

Square numbers and square roots: after some reckoning, one can extend the table (see Unit 2).

Mental reckoning of areas, that arise by cutting a square:

We imagine a square whose base line is horizontal. Now we imagine a line running from the upper left corner to the midpoint*of the right side. What figures arise? How much is the area of the lower region, if we cut away the upper part? What fraction of the total area does it represent?

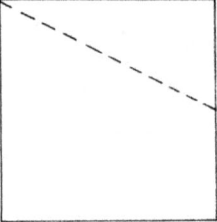

Figure 1

This is followed by further, more complicated, questions, always however keeping the original picture for a while but changing, for example, the location of the right point to be one-third of the way down from the top side, then one-fourth, etc. Then one can give the exact side length of the square and calculates then various (difficult) cut-away areas. Then one turns Figure 1 "on its side"

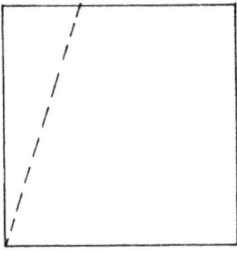
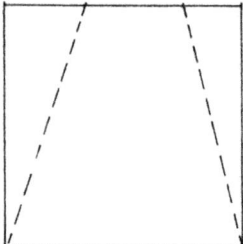

Figure 2   Figure 3

(Figure 2) and cuts off a second triangle on the other side (Figure 3). Or, one takes a rectangle instead of a square, etc.; how far one can go here depends on how much time one has.

Finally, the teacher draws such a trapezoid on the board with left and right "completion" figures and then develops (or simply recalls) in discussion with the students the area formula for a trapezoid. A sample of how to do this is given below:

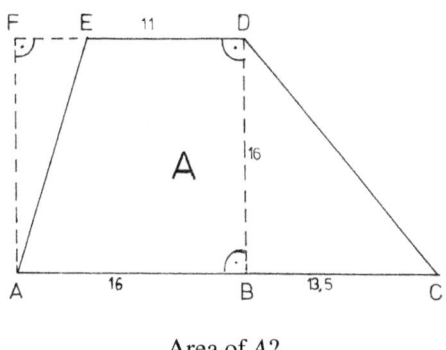

Area of A?

On the basis of what has been worked out in the previous two units, one should be able fairly quickly to sketch out a solution – and probably several – all of which should be able to be sketched on the board. The following board drawing shows one of these solutions, along with one way that the figure can be brought to speak for itself, at a level even a weak pupil can grasp.

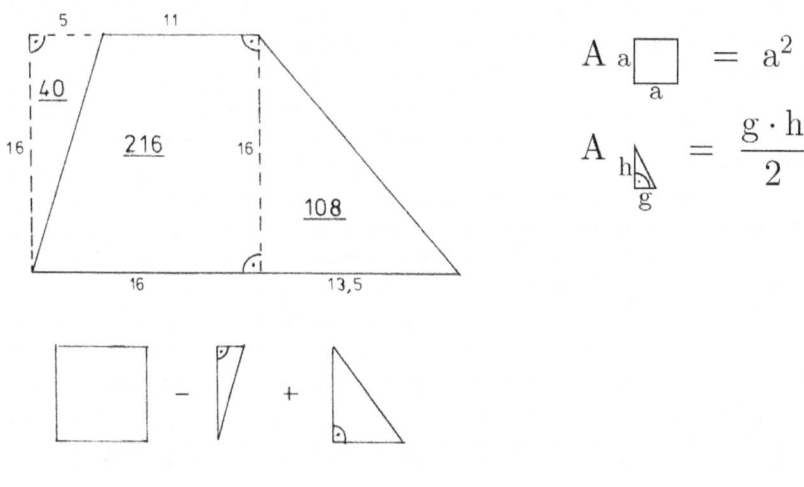

$$16^2 - \frac{5 \cdot 16}{2} + \frac{13{,}5 \cdot 16}{2}$$

$A = 256 - 40 + 108 \quad \underline{\underline{A = 324}}$

This board drawing should be preserved until the next meeting of the class.

Regarding the treatment of units goes, (see also p. 32), in this context I reach an agreement with the pupils, that one does not fix any particular unit of length, what's important, is that a measurement of area has a very different quality from a measurement of length. Of course one can write the relevant unit of measurement in every expression from start to finish; that however seems to me, in the case of auxiliary and intermediate calculations, too time-consuming and not worth the trouble. Mixing these two modes within a single chain of equations, for example," $\frac{3+5}{2} = \frac{8}{2} = 4\,\text{cm}$", should however never happen; it contradicts the meaning of the equals sign.

In this way one arrives at a derivation or justification of the formula for the area of a trapezoid. Both ways of looking at the problem should be given their due:

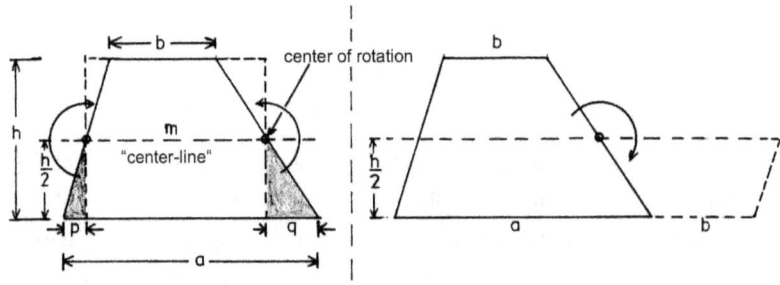

One the one hand, $m = a - p - q$,
on the other $m = b + p + q$.
Twice the middle edge is therefore:
$2m = a - p - q + b + p + q = a + b$,
so $m = \frac{a+b}{2} \cdot h$.

Hence we obtain

$$A_{\text{trapezoid}} = \frac{a+b}{2} \cdot h$$

Since the area of a parallelogram is base times height, we get:

$$A_{\text{trapezoid}} = (a+b) \cdot \frac{h}{2}$$

The students now have at their disposal a variety of approaches – including cutting into smaller pieces, shearing, or applying formulas – for calculating the areas of figures bounded by straight line segments. Now the Homework Sheet 1 can be distributed, and the students can work on it as soon as they have entered the figure on the board into their own notebooks. A minimum number of these exercises should be completed by the next meeting. This results in an automatic differentiation within the class, assuming the students have some experience here. Most students learn, in the course of working with such homework sheets, to estimate their own capacities accurately and generally seek out the appropriate exercises. Otherwise one needs to provide some guidance, for example, when a pupil has too little self-confidence, or is too lazy. I also recommend providing guidelines such as: "These... are easy; these... are a little more difficult; and these... are brain-teasers for specialists." Before this, ask the class, who wants to draw a solution for the shearing exercises on the board (one per exercise). (One is seldom disappointed, the exercises are just too fascinating.) Before the end of the period, the teacher draws a "Pythagorean Diagram" on the board.

Remarks on Homework Sheet 1 (see pp. 46 and 47):

1. This is a good opportunity, as a foreshadowing of studying solid geometry, to bring *thickness* into play (or in the 9th grade one still identifies the thickness with the specific gravity and works instead with it), see exercises 23 and 24. One often finds pupils have no concept of the weights of different substances. "How heavy is this iron clump? or this wood board?", etc. To confidently master such practical concepts and calculations, also provided by other exercises on the sheet, gives the young person of this difficult age, the feeling that he knows something of the "'real world"' and can find his way around there, which is something they need to experience. See also below, under Mental Reckoning Unit 6, p. 47

2. It's good when the teacher can compose his own exercises. Otherwise there are many exercise collections to buy with a variety of choices available.[13] Also, the figure itself is scanned into the article so has german directions and labels.

---

[13]The exercises on this sheet come from *Kusch: Mathematik Bd. 2, Geometrie, Cornelsen Verlag, Essen 1974, S. 110 – 11*.

Exercise Sheet 1a

Editors remark: We decided to leave these exercise-sheets in the original state, similar sheets should be available in most languages.

8.

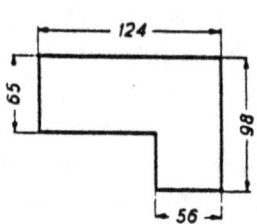

Berechne U in cm
A in cm²

9.

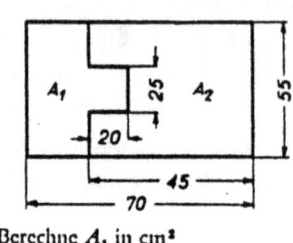

Berechne A_1 in cm²
A_2 in cm²

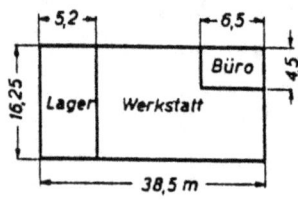

10. Berechne Werkstatt, Lager, Büro in m²

11.

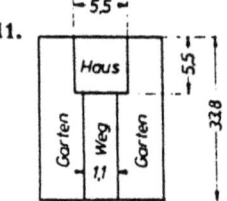

Berechne
1. das ganze Grundstück,
2. das Gartenhaus,
3. den Weg,
4. den Garten.

12.

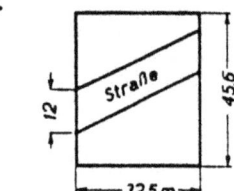

Berechne
1. das ganze Grundstück,
2. den Verlust durch die Straße,
3. den Rest des Grundstückes,

13. Berechne die fehlenden Größen eines rechtwinkligen Dreiecks:

	a	b	A
1.	2 m	1,5 m	
2.	3,6 m	2,75 m	
3.	6,24 m		15,6 m²
4.		3,97 m	7,98 m²

14.

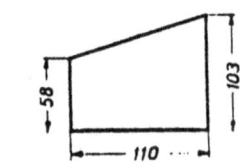

Berechne A in cm².

Exercise Sheet 1b

15.

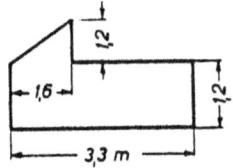

Berechne A in m²

16. Berechne die fehlenden Größen eines Trapezes:

A	a	c	h
	5,25 m	3,6 m	4,6 m
	8,7 m	6,5 m	5,25 m
8,75 cm²	40 cm	30 cm	
3240 cm²	75 cm	60 cm	
0,86 m²		0,95 m	0,8 m
3,815 m²	2,5 m		1,75 m

17.

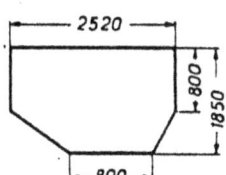

Berechne A in m²

18.

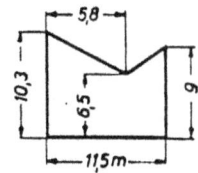

Berechne A in m²

19.

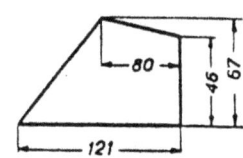

Berechne A in cm²

20.

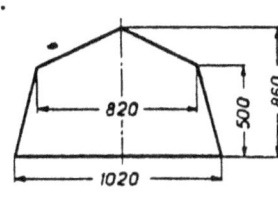

Berechne A in cm²

21.

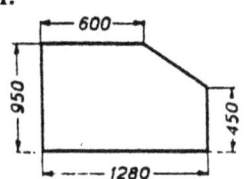

Berechne A in m²

22.

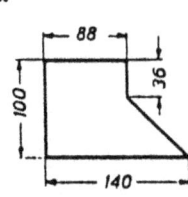

Berechne A in cm²

23.

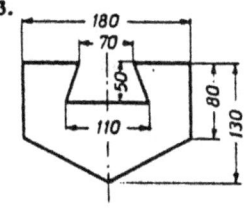

Berechne
1. A von 12 Blechen in m²
2. Gewicht der Bleche in kg
   (1 m² ≙ 16 kg)

24.

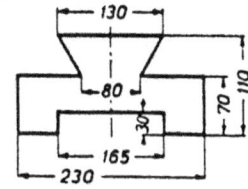

Berechne
1. A von 25 Blechen in m²
2. Gewicht der Bleche in kg
   (1 m² ≙ 7,8 kg)

2.4 Alternative beginning

The preceding main lesson plan is continued on p. 51. Here I offer an **alternative beginning** for the main lesson, with detailed descriptions of the instructional content.

It begins with the mental reckoning part of the 2nd unit (Mental Reckoning Unit 1) on p. 30. Then the board is flipped over, revealing the following figure:

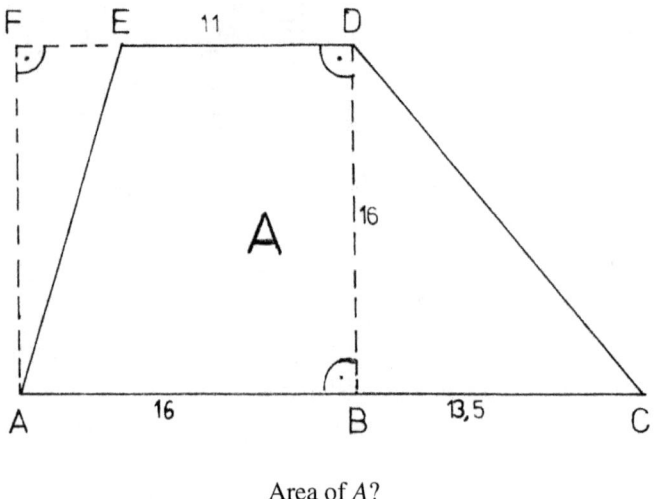

Area of *A*?

Depending on the mood and circumstances, one can give a short description (for example, a garden behind a house), or let the question speak for itself. I tend to favor the latter option in this situation. One can recognize what the class already has learned on the answers that they give, since at least some pupils will remember. Other questions naturally arise, for example, how long is FE or FA, or what good is $\triangle$EFA, since it doesn't have anything to do with the area in question. The teacher writes the answers to the original question on the board, perhaps the correct answer (324) is among them. The answers to the question "How'd you get that?" can now be very revealing. Or, no answers come. Then one can canvas for ideas for a solution. Regardless of what comes, they should be taken up in the classroom discussion and with (minimal) help from the teacher (Socratic method!) directed towards a solution, as the following illustrates:

1. If there are no suggestions, one can ask whether it isn't possible to give at least part of the desired area.
   Here one quickly sees the point of the square ABDF, from which one can easily separate off the triangle AEF. The triangle BCD is also quickly taken care of, so that the desired area can be produced by combining the component areas. For this, one should draw, no later than during the quiet work phase, an appropriate solution diagram on the board, which is a big help for the weaker students. (Only those that want, need to copy it.) A possible board

drawing is given below.

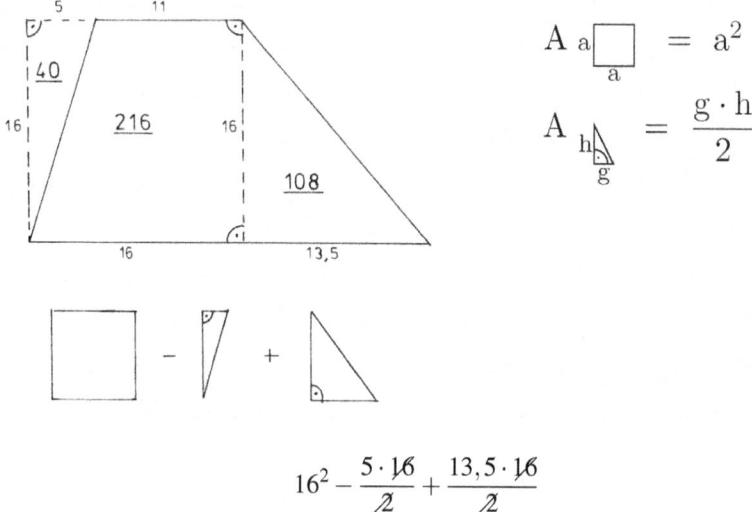

$$16^2 - \frac{5 \cdot \cancel{16}}{\cancel{2}} + \frac{13{,}5 \cdot \cancel{16}}{\cancel{2}}$$

$A = 256 - 40 + 108 \quad \underline{\underline{A = 324}}$

This board drawing should stay until the next class meeting. WIth regard to choice of units, see pp. 32 and 43.

2. One often receives suggestions that move in the direction of 1).

3. It may be that someone actually states the area formula for a trapezoid. This can be illustrated on the board, and then the teacher can ask for a justification for the formula.

4. Even when this doesn't occur, one can, on the basis of what has been done in (1) and (2), ask what the name of the figure in question is, and let the pupils search further for insights and ideas.

In the end, one invariably meets with ideas that have with to do with "cutting and re-attaching". In any case, you should collect a lot of suggestions, enter them by jotting them on the board or in the pupils' notebooks. In this way one arrives at the unfolding, or – if it's already been stated as in (3) – at the justification of the area formula. Both of the following derivations should be taken into account:

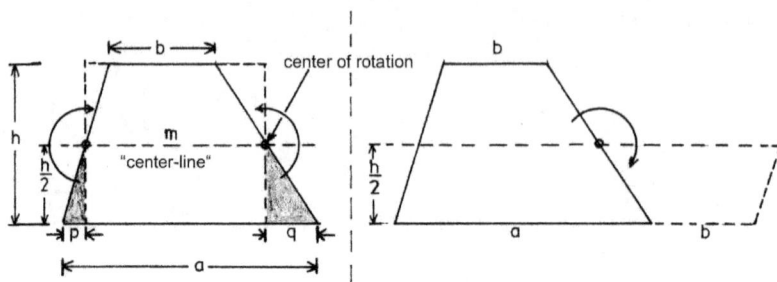

One the one hand, $m = a - p - q$,
while on the other, $m = b + p + q$.
Twice the middle edge is therefore:
$2m = a - p - q + b + p + q = a + b$,
also $m = \frac{a+b}{2}$. Hence we get:

$$A_{\text{trapezoid}} = \frac{a+b}{2} \cdot h$$

Since the area of a parallelogram is the base times the height, one obtains:

$$A_{\text{trapezoid}} = (a+b) \cdot \frac{h}{2}$$

If one of the ideas for a solution involves the shearing of triangles, the teacher can feel satisfied, and immediately take this up and apply it to difficult shearing problems (see below). Usually, however, there is no longer an awareness why the area of a parallelogram arises as shown in the figure above; in this case, one has to convert the parallelogram into a rectangle by a) shearing, and b) "cut and re-attach". This can be quickly done. Homework Sheet 1 (pp. 45 to 47) shows possible homework exercises, that give confidence in calculating the area of figures bounded by line segments. Two further discussion themes come up now:

1. The clarification of the question, what one understands by the "area" of a given figure, as distinct from the figure itself with its unique shape quality, along with its physical qualities such as roughness, etc.

2. The conversion of length and area measurements (from one unit to another).

I'll return to these issues below. **In the next class meeting** one can connect the mental reckoning with the question of area as follows:

A square has side length $a = 14$. What's its area A? Handle then a variety of other squares. One meets again in this way the square numbers. Then one continues with rectangles. A rectangle has a base of $g = 14$ and a height of $h = 15$. How big is A? Further rectangles follow, then parallelograms. At this point one should stay with the mental reckoning and use the occasion to discuss how one can produce from a parallelogram, a rectangle of the same area. The pupils share their thoughts, and reveal thereby whether they are familiar with "shearing" or "cutting and re-attaching"; in either case, one illustrates either case immediately on the board with a clear sketch.

One discusses why shearing can't change the area of a *parallelogram* ("for any parallelogram, I could cut off and sew back on"), shows this briefly on the board (or possibly with a prepared board drawing), and then goes on to triangles. Note that in completing the triangle to a parallelogram, the corresponding behavior is immediately obvious. In this way, the area formulae, which are often simply mechanically repeated like a mantra, become once more comprehensible.

Now one can turn to shearing problems. For this purpose the teacher has prepared a board drawing, that should be transformed into some *arbitrary* rectangle with the same area. As a next step, one can require that the square be transformed into a rectangle with the same area and a given base, see p. 35.

> Here one should encourage the pupils to come to the board to sketch any ideas and insights, even partial ones. A solution will gradually reveal itself in the course of the discussion. It sometimes happens, that several pupils are able to present different solutions immediately.

In any case, all the various student solutions should be documented on the board, and, if necessary, made transparent by the teacher by appropriate extensions, for example, by a series of drawings showing different situations. The teacher can also present a further solution to complete the picture, but this should be done modestly, and on the same level as the student solutions. Then it's time to pose further optional shearing exercises.

At this point, a phase of stabilizing the obtained results is in order. One can review the already calculated exercises from Exercise Sheet 1, compare the answers for the first exercises, respond to questions and problems, and then, circulating through the class, proceed to a phase of quiet work on the rest of the sheet.[14] The board drawing with the shearing stays until the next class meeting.

In the next period on the next day one takes up the mental reckoning with areas once more and extends the questioning to trapezoids: a trapezoid is created from a square by adjoining a right triangle. It has an lower edge of length 16 and an upper edge of length 12 (the parallel edges). What is its area? Continue with more exercises of the this type. In the main lesson one discusses the exercises on Sheet 1 and then continues with quiet work on the sheet, perhaps one discusses the shearing problem again. Before the end of the period the teacher draws the "Pythagoras Diagram" on the board.

This alternative path for the main lesson this returns to the original path at this point; both approaches now run together.

2.5 Period 4

Mental Reckoning Unit 3

More practice with the square numbers, during which the memory board (see p. 30) is covered up. One also works on square roots, "approximately": between which whole numbers lies $\sqrt{185}$?

---

[14] See p. 27, A Remark on "'Quiet work'"; as well as p. 52

Between 13 and 14. Calculate! $13^2 = 169$ and $14^2 = 196$., etc. Finally, work with the sum of square numbers. In the previous period the teacher drew a "Pythagoras Diagram" on the board, and can now introduce a connection with the question: What does the adding square numbers have to do with the figure on the board? The explanation of this question leads to mental reckoning of the following sort, with the table of square numbers now once more exposed to view: in a right triangle the two sides have length 12 cm and 5 cm. How long is the hypotenuse?, etc.

> Be sure after each answer to verbally go through the calculation, so that pupils who have difficulties with the mental picture, can follow the path of the solution.

At first the search for Pythagorean triples is limited to the possibilities contained in the table of square numbers. Later, one can extend the problem to include the search for the side of a right triangle when one side and hypotenuse is given; one can also allow problems whose solution is not a whole number, but an "approximate" square root. Such exercises go beyond merely repeating the Pythagorean Theorem and prepare the way for calculating the perimeter of figures which include "skew" sides. You can even discuss this possibility with the students now.

> The contents of the mental reckoning unit just described can be stretched out over several days; it's anyway important to deepen these skills.

Next, one can turn to discuss some of the solutions of the shearing exercises handled in the previous period. The teacher retreats to one of the back rows and leaves it up to the students to justify their solutions. The other pupils pose questions as they see fit.

> There's a certain threshold for participation that has here to be overcome, that gradually lessens through "cultivating" such situations. If the student presentations become too inert, the teacher can inject a "stupid" question, in order that the weaker students also really understand the solution. This phase comes to an end after two or three student presentations.

The next order of business is the discussion of some of the exercises on Homework Sheet 1, for example, from 8 to 12, then give a detailed solution for 17; the latter can then be presented as a "sample" solution on the board. Then one shifts over to quiet work on Sheet 1 and any remaining undone shearing exercises. Students are given the choice to copy the sample solution into their books. This, on the one hand, leads away from the stereotype of collective copying from the board; on the other, it avoids the dismaying situation of forcing students to copy down something which they regard as self-evident. Whoever needs it, will write it down! During this quiet work time, the teacher circulates in the classroom, letting the students show him what they have done during the period, giving help and tips, and clearing away any possible unclear points. (There may also be a need for a personal remark in particular cases.) The homework consists of continued work on Homework Sheet 1 and the shearing exercises. One can also begin now to work on the calculation of perimeter. As he goes around, the teacher can individualize the exercises for particular students, making them either more general or more restricted:

- "Work out these ... exercises; and when you have problems with these ... exercises, work on these ..."

- "If you wish, just work on the perimeter exercises, but then do all these ... exercises."

- "If you can do these ... difficult exercises, then you can leave these ... simpler exercises alone."

Such an internal differentiation of the class can have a very beneficial effect on the motivation to learn:

- The young person feels his abilities to be properly evaluated, and is prepared to achieve the minimum (and more) that corresponds to his possibilities.[15]

- He feels himself perceived as an individual, and senses: This adult is interested in me, he's concerned about me.

Herein lies the tremendous significance and potential of the quiet work phase, which for this reason shouldn't be shortened at the expense of the other phases. The foregoing detailed descriptions of the course of the instruction period should have made clear my approach, at least in the case that one uses mental reckoning as entrance into the main lesson.

In any case I think it's completely reasonable to expect, that by a good working pace, the pupil can complete at least the majority of the assigned work in the quiet work phase. And if he completes all the assigned work, there should be further exercises available that extend the assignment in interesting ways.

When one seeks the common structure of the instructional units which have been described, one can approximately represent it with the following schematic layout:

2.6 Structure of the main lesson period presented here

| First part: 10-20 min. | (Speech exercises or recitation) Mental reckoning, visualization exercises, connect to previous day's work | "rhythmic phase" | Strong leadership from teacher |

– possibly seamless transition –

---

[15] In *this* sense, the Waldorf school can be an "'achievement school'".

Second part:	Continuation and deepening of the previous day's content, development of new content	"primary phase"	Development through questioning ("Socratic method"), classroom discussions with student presentations

– noticeable transition –

Third part: at least 30 min.	Work on entries of main lesson book, independent work on exercises, also preparatory to being discussed and generalized on following day	"quiet work phase"	Students work on their own, or in groups, helping one another. *A crucial part of the period!*

It's my experience that a consistent application of this organization of the period has a harmonizing effect on the pupils of a 9th grade class. This is also valid for the 10th grade. In the higher grades, due to the contents and method of the main lesson, it can make sense to deviate significantly from the above plan. By paying attention to the atmosphere in the class, one can judge after a short time whether the indicated structure is fitting. A valuable reference here is *the methodological remarks to lesson organization*, made by Rudolf Steiner in the third lecture of the so-called ["Supplementary course"] lecture cycle.[16] The structure which is there proposed and justified, on the basis on deep considerations of human nature, is essentially valid for all main lesson units. Hints regarding the function of the rhythmic part and the so-called "alternation of methods" within a single instructional period can be found in an indirect but very illuminating form in R. Steiner, Meditativ erarbeitete Menschenkunde, 4. Vortrag, S. 58 ff (in: "Erziehung und Unterricht aus Menschenerkenntnis", GA 302a, Dornach 1977). In english: "Balance in teaching – 9 lectures, Stuttgart, sept - oct. 1923, lecture 4, published by Steiner Books). There Steiner speaks about the therapeutic effect of particular subjects of instruction and of particular measures, for example, "Achieving the integration of the ego in the human organization", and "Avoiding that the ego is too strongly absorbed by the rest of the organization". GA 302a also contains the lecture "Educational questions in puberty", important for the high school teacher, particularly in relation to the transition from middle to high school.

In the following I will describe the further course of the main lesson in a briefer form, without giving each segment in detail as I have up until now.

2.7 Mental reckoning units, which lead into the main part of the lesson

At the same time a presentation of further instructional theme

---

[16]R. Steiner: Menschenerkenntnis und Unterrichtsgestaltung, GA 302, Dornach 1978^4, S. 46 unten - S. 49 oben, Waldorf Education for Adolescence – 8 lectures, published by Steiner School Fellowship, 1980

Mental reckoning unit 4: *right triangles*

Here the aim is to practice the calculation of the third side of a right triangle given two of the sides, with the help of the Pythagorean Theorem (see Mental Reckoning Unit 3). This can lead into one of the following 5 themes:

2.7.1 Review of the extraction of square roots using pencil and paper.[17]

1. Regarding the technique for extracting square roots
   One can actually expect, that this has been thoroughly treated in the 8th grade. It is however for most of the 9th graders no longer consciously present and has to be recalled to mind. The technique in question, and its justification, is presented in a pedagogically-sound form in *A. Bernhard: Geometrie für die 7. und 8. Klasse an Waldorfschulen* and *E. Bindel: Die Arithmetik*[18]. If these have, in fact, already been handled in the middle school, then the teacher can carry out a root extraction on the board, bringing the pupils along by asking appropriate questions. He then asks the pupils repeat the process, and formulates the computation scheme as a "recipe" on the board. This will not just be gratefully accepted by the weaker students, they will probably require it to be able to successfully carry out the technique without extra help.

   The justification of the process can be given at a later time. It's also necessary to do so – the high school student is making the step from "How" to "Why"; the power of judgement has to be educated!

   > Here one further remark regarding inner differentiation among the class: it's a good idea here to give each pupil an individual exercise, tailor-made for him – naturally some are attracted by the challenge of solving more difficult exercises – and then to collect the solutions and look through them. The advantages are obvious.

2. Some students are grateful for "brain-teasers". In order not to punish noteworthy engagement and achievement, a certain number of the ordinary $\sqrt{}$-exercises can then be skipped. Here's one such interesting exercise, not completely simple, that requires intensive logical thinking:

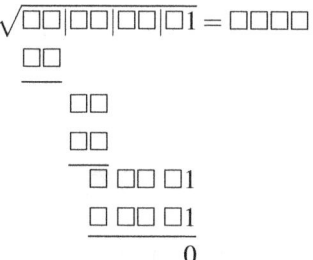

   One possible path to a solution is as follows:

---

[17] See also the article by Fr. Hartmann and the algorithms given on p. 130 and p. 136
[18] These books are currently only available in german.

- The last digit of the answer has to be a 1 or a 9, since otherwise the last digit of the subtrahend can't be a "1". We show now it can't be a 1. Notice that the last dividend is 5-digit. That means that twice the first 3 digits of the answer is a 4-digit number, which can only happen if the first digit is at least 5. But the first divisor is 2-digit, meaning that twice the first digit of the answer is a single digit, which is clearly impossible if the first digit is 5. So the last digit can't be a 1, hence it must be a 9.

- The ten's digit of the answer must be 0, otherwise one wouldn't have brought down the digit pairs twice in a row (to obtain the five-digit dividend). So we arrive at this:

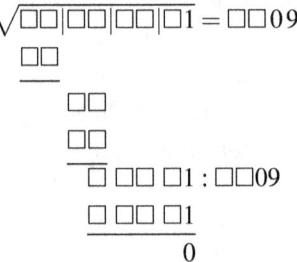

This means that the tens digit of the last remainder must be 8 (since $9 \cdot 9 = 81$):

$$\begin{array}{r} \square\,\square\square\,81 \\ \square\,\square\square\,81 \\ \hline 0 \end{array}$$

- the thousands digit of the answer has to be at least 4, since otherwise its square wouldn't be 2-digits (first subtrahend). Since however the first divisor is 2-digits, it can't be more than 4; hence it is exactly 4, and the tens place of the divisor is 8..

- Since the first remainder including the carry-in is 2-digits, the hundreds digit of the answer has to be 1; this yields:

$$\sqrt{16|\square\square|\square\square|81} = 4109$$
$$\begin{array}{r} 16 \\ \hline \square\square : 81 \\ \square\square \\ \hline \square\,\square\square\,81 : \square\square 09 \\ \square\,\square\square\,81 \\ \hline 0 \end{array}$$

- Therefore the second divisor has to be 8209, leading to a value of 73881 for the final subtrahend.

- Calculating backwards yields the final solution:

$$\sqrt{16|88|38|81} = 4109$$
$$\begin{array}{r} 16 \\ \hline \end{array}$$

$$88 : 81$$
$$\underline{81}$$
$$\overline{7\ 38\ 81} : 8209$$
$$\underline{7\ 38\ 81}$$
$$0$$

2.7.2 Proof of the area formula for a right triangle with the aid of the shearing principle.

This proof should be developed with the students themselves in classroom discussion. At this point it will be clear if the students' familiarity with shearing has ripened into a reliable skill.

> The experience of being able to prove such significant and practically-useful mathematical theorems, and to do so without external assistance, can support the pupils' trust in their own thinking, and consequently contribute to self-reliance at an age in which such self-reliance is often problematic.

To save time and also to be able to work at home, it's good to have some prepared sheets as shown on the following pages. It's possible to supplement the traditional historical proofs; the corresponding proof diagrams often speak for themselves. It's also a good opportunity to bring in stories and anecdotes. Lots of relevant material can be found in *H.v. Baravalle: Geometrie als Sprache der Formen, A. Bernhard: Geometrie für die 7. und 8. Klasse an Waldorfschulen* und *G. Ott: Geometrie für Klassenlehrer der 6., 7. und 8. Klassen*[19], and in books about the historical development of mathematics.

---

[19] These books are not available in english at the moment

The Geometric mean leg Theorem (Mean proportion leg theorem) (homework sheet 1)

Proof: By means of the sequence of shearings 1) to 2):

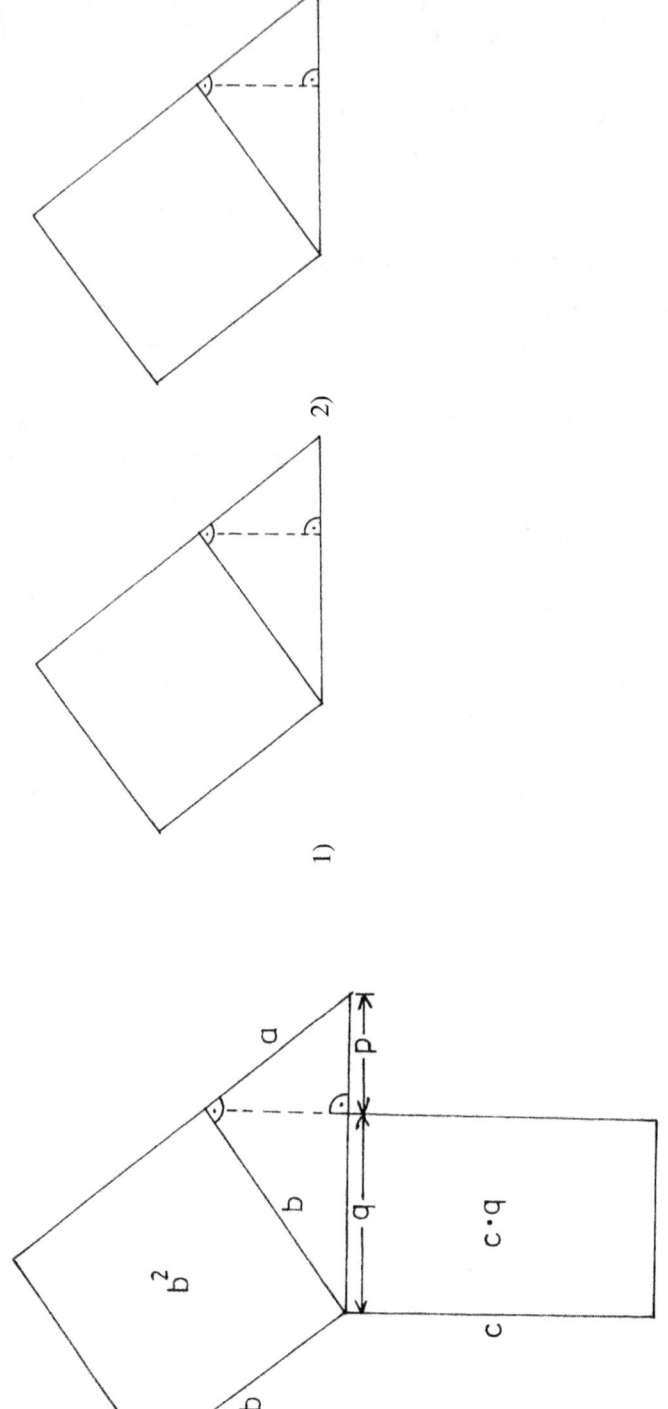

In a right triangle, the square on one side the same area as the rectangle constructed from the hypoteneuse and the orthogonal projection of that side onto the hypotenuse.:

$b^2 = c \cdot q$

bzw. $a^2 = c \cdot p$

The Altitude Theorem of Euclid (homework sheet 2)

Proof: By means of the sequence of shearings 1) to 3):

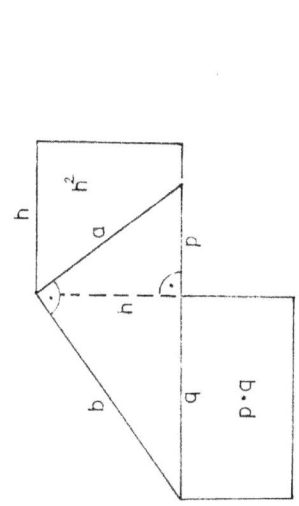

In a right triangle, the square on the altitude to the hypoteneuse is the product of the rectangle constructed from the two segments which this altitude divides the hypoteneuse.

$$h^2 = p \cdot q$$

2.7.3 Discussion of the connection between consecutive square numbers[20]

What's meant here is: the difference of consecutive square numbers is an odd number. What's more: the sequence of the difference of consecutive square numbers is the sequence of the odd numbers.

When one calculates this, one can then derive the binomial formula from first principles:

$$(n+1)^2 - n^2 = n^2 + 2n + 1 - n^2$$
$$= 2n + 1.$$

I consider such "outings" not only interesting in the sense of a diversion; they also serve the purpose of creating a sense of fullness, and letting important topics flow into the instruction, without seeming to make an effort. Even more harmless material, as shown in the following on p. 61, is a source of enjoyment and provides practice for "seeing".

---

[20] see also the contribution from Fr. Hartmann on p. 128 of this volume.

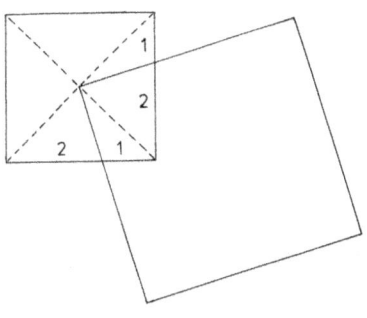

How big is the area of overlap of the two squares?

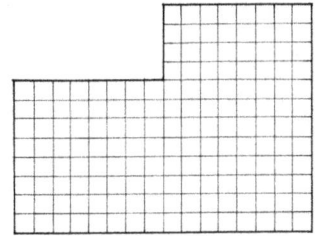

Using three line segments, divide the figure into two pieces which are mirror images of each other.

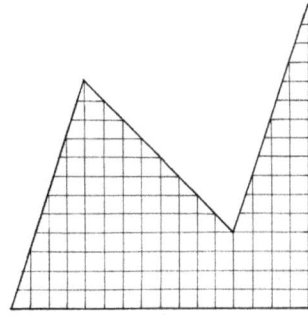

Divide the figure into two identical pieces using two line segments.

Solutions

1. As long as the corner of the large square occupies the center of the small square, the overlap of the two square always equals $\frac{1}{4}$ of the area of the small square.

2)   3)

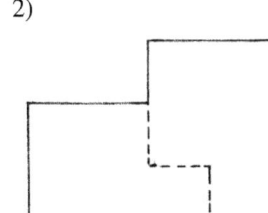   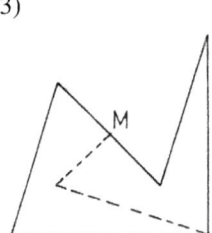

From: *Pierre Berloquin: Mathematische Kopfspiele, München 1983*

2.7.4 Investigation of the isosceles right triangle

Single steps:

- Calculate its hypotenuse.
- Consider the hypotenuse as a side of a square.
- This is "twice as big" as the square obtained by forming a square on one of the identical sides of the triangle.

The questioning of Menon by Plato leads in the same direction (in the dialog "Menon"), in a fashion that adapts well to inclusion in the classroom. (Hence the term: "Socratic method"). Indeed, one can read the dialog "Menon" together in class. The students enjoy it. Also for this topic, one is well-advised to have some historical anecdotes ready.

2.7.5 Investigation of the isosceles triangle

Single steps:

- Split it into two right angle triangles.
- The unknown side of the smaller triangles can be calculated; it is also the altitude of the isosceles triangle.
- Calculate then the area.

The material included in this and the previous theme will be later applied in calculating the area of a circle; it shows up, furthermore, in many other contexts. If one thinks it worthwhile, one can even begin to investigate the circle at this juncture.

Mental reckoning unit 5

The calculation of large square numbers in one's head, with help from the binomial formulae; each day a separate formula; at the same time work out on the board a detailed example; mental reckoning of a variety of examples. For example:

$$63^2 = (60+3)^2 = 60^2 + 2\cdot 60\cdot 3 + 3^2 = 3969$$
$$(a+b)^2 = a^2 + 2\cdot a\cdot b + b^2$$

On the next day:

$$58^2 = (60-2)^2 = 60^2 - 2\cdot 60\cdot 2 + 2^2 = 3364$$
$$(a-b)^2 = a^2 - 2\cdot a\cdot b + b^2$$

Simultaneously, fill in the table of square numbers on the memory board. Finally, one can practice the following calculation as an extension of the previous work:

$$43 \cdot 37 = (40+3) \cdot (40-3) = 40^2 - 3^2 = 1591$$
$$(a+b) \cdot (a-b) = a^2 - b^2$$

In this way, the binomial formulae and their applications, after a while, become reliably committed to memory.

All three binomial formulae can be so represented graphically, that the elements of the sum each correspond to an area. We illustrate the first binomial formula in the figure on the right.

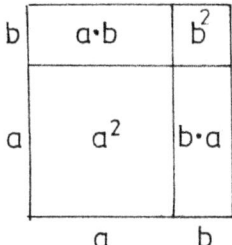

In this context one should note that products of pairs of numbers and areas are two qualitatively different objects. That needs to be discussed in the class if it hasn't already been. However, these diagrams can help some weaker students understand the binomial formulae, by providing an overview of it. Or, consider the problem "$(a+b)^2 \neq a^2 + b^2$" that often shows up even in upper grades; the diagram provides a more obvious and convincing rebuttal than does multiplying out the expression $(a+b) \cdot (a+b)..$

Mental reckoning unit 6

Calculating areas, also remainders obtained by removal.
These can be easily connected to the visualization exercises (see, for example, Unit 3). One can then shift over to alternating length and area units. This can flow into:

(1) Conversion of length and area units

For this, you should prepare a table of conversions. The units "Acre" and "Hectar" should also be used. Areas of agricultural and other sorts of real estate parcels can then be calculated in different units. Also, begin from the area and form of the parcel and work back to the lengths of its sides[21].

Many students have a difficult time to imagine the actual size of a piece of land with given dimensions; this provides a further, necessary field for practice, which is also useful for further mental reckoning units.

---

[21] The exercises should just give an impression and might be adopted to the units used in the different countries

The following Homework Sheet 3, designed for the whole class, and Homework Sheet 4, containing 12 different exercises – each of which can be assigned based on the varying ability levels present in the class – train skills in converting among units of area and generate thereby the desired confidence.

(2) Discussion/review of mass, weight, density, etc.

This is connected to exercises 23 and 24 of the first exercise sheet (p. 46). One considers here volumes of boxes. If circumstances permit, you can bring the above concepts into sharper focus using irregular bodies (rocks, iron weights, etc.) with the aid of overflow vessels and table balances; the effect is very enlivening!

Conversion of area units (Homework Sheet 3)

→ See our table!

1. $350 \text{ mm}^2 =$ ___ cm^2
2. $150 \text{ mm}^2 =$ ___ cm^2
3. $1537 \text{ mm}^2 =$ ___ cm^2
4. $3{,}56 \text{ dm}^2 =$ ___ cm^2
5. $153 \text{ dm}^2 =$ ___ cm^2
6. $0{,}56 \text{ dm}^2 =$ ___ cm^2
7. $3{,}526 \text{ m}^2 =$ ___ cm^2
8. $0{,}0291 \text{ m}^2 =$ ___ cm^2
9. $3{,}00 \text{ m}^2 =$ ___ cm^2
10. $0{,}00125 \text{ a} =$ ___ cm^2
11. $1{,}562 \text{ m}^2 =$ ___ cm^2
12. $17{,}25 \text{ dm}^2 =$ ___ cm^2
13. $1567{,}8 \text{ mm}^2 =$ ___ m^2
14. $36700 \text{ mm}^2 =$ ___ m^2
15. $1765 \text{ mm}^2 =$ ___ m^2
16. $1567{,}6 \text{ cm}^2 =$ ___ m^2
17. $98765 \text{ cm}^2 =$ ___ m^2
18. $1565 \text{ cm}^2 =$ ___ m^2
19. $354{,}3 \text{ dm}^2 =$ ___ m^2
20. $3670 \text{ dm}^2 =$ ___ m^2
21. $136 \text{ dm}^2 =$ ___ m^2
22. $15{,}67 =$ ___ m^2
23. $3{,}68 \text{ ha} =$ ___ m^2
24. $0{,}027 \text{ km}^2 =$ ___ m^2
25. $3987{,}4 \text{ m}^2 =$ ___ ha
26. $3650 \text{ m}^2 =$ ___ ha
27. $1675{,}62 \text{ m}^2 =$ ___ ha
28. $0{,}789 \text{ km}^2 =$ ___ ha
29. $1{,}764 \text{ km}^2 =$ ___ ha
30. $15{,}684 \text{ km}^2 =$ ___ ha
31. $10{,}374 \text{ a} =$ ___ ha
32. $1376 \text{ a} =$ ___ ha
33. $9{,}806 \text{ a} =$ ___ ha
34. $3156{,}4 \text{ m}^2 =$ ___ dm^2
35. $15000 \text{ m}^2 =$ ___ dm^2
36. $346{,}5 \text{ a} =$ ___ dm^2
37. $1{,}095 \text{ a} =$ ___ dm^2
38. $0{,}156 \text{ ha} =$ ___ dm^2
39. $13{,}674 \text{ ha} =$ ___ dm^2
40. $0{,}05 \text{ km}^2 =$ ___ dm^2
41. $1{,}009 \text{ km}^2 =$ ___ dm^2

another example

	21700000000	mm^2
=	217000000,00	cm^2
=	2170000,0000	dm^2
=	21700,000000	m^2
=	217,00000000	a
=	2,17	ha
=	0,0217	km^2

Homework Sheet 4a

315 mm² =	cm²	88 700 mm² =	m²
2508 mm² =	cm²	1425 mm² =	m²
44,7 dm² =	cm²	147,5 cm² =	m²
0,774 dm² =	cm²	60 560 cm² =	m²
2,721 m² =	cm²	4560 dm² =	m²
0,086 m² =	cm²	0,85 dm² =	m²
1,34 a =	cm²	14,7 a =	m²
0,045 a =	cm²	22 700 a =	m²
15,6 m² =	cm²	0,135 ha =	m²
4,5 cm² =	cm²	2,76 ha =	m²
0,56 ha =	cm²	0,076 km² =	m²
0,027 km² =	cm²	14 km² =	m²
0,58 km² =	cm²	8,75 km² =	ha
1,76 km² =	ha	156 m² =	cm²
8,875 km² =	a	8,7 a =	cm²
0,15 ha =	a	66,56 m² =	cm²
270,8 ha =	a	0,05 a =	cm²
0,0076 ha =	dm²	7,93 dm² =	cm²
7,786 a =	m²	1,7 dm² =	cm²
0,658 m² =	dm²	88,9 ha =	m²
0,0001 km² =	dm²	0,75 ha =	m²
13,507 m² =	mm²	6,58 a =	m²
145 dm² =	mm²	13 a =	m²
13,8 cm² =	mm²	150,7 a =	ha
0,756 dm² =	cm²	3337 ha =	a
3,85 m² =	dm²	27,5 ha =	a
7,6 ha =	m²	127 653 dm² =	a
22,85 ha =	m²	276,5 ha =	dm²
9800 ha =	km²	0,65 a =	dm²
14 760 ha =	km²	2257,6 m² =	km²
44 760 mm² =	cm²	1 476 561 cm² =	km²
1 776 544 mm² =	cm²	16,7 cm² =	mm²
8795,8 mm² =	dm²	2,654 cm² =	mm²
13,75 km² =	ha	0,07 cm² =	dm²
4,767 km² =	ha	38 517 cm² =	dm²
127 km² =	a	217 653 cm² =	m²
2766 m² =	a	3929 cm² =	m²
2766 m² =	ha	2,701 km² =	m²

Homework Sheet 4b

732 km² =	ha	142,61 mm² =	cm²
5,13 km² =	ha	4478 mm² =	m²
33,76 a =	ha	227 228 mm² =	m²
2,58 a =	ha	14,7 a =	m²
0,0036 a =	km²	3,9 a =	m²
37 500 a =	km²	19 ha =	m²
22 777 000 m² =	km²	8,6 ha =	m²
1043 m² =	km²	125 ha =	a
980 ha =	km²	25,6 ha =	a
4,78 ha =	km²	21,5 m² =	dm²
9999 mm² =	dm²	0,76 m² =	dm²
14 786 mm² =	dm²	225,6 cm² =	dm²
223,4 mm² =	cm²	33,75 cm² =	dm²
7785 cm² =	mm²	4444 mm² =	cm²
864,45 cm² =	mm²	273 896 mm² =	m²
2763 cm² =	m²	14 005 mm² =	m²
1 273 456 cm² =	m²	15,6 a =	m²
237 dm² =	m²	3,45 a =	m²
21,7 dm² =	m²	2,7 ha =	m²
49,86 dm² =	cm²	14,8 ha =	m²
0,0513 dm² =	cm²	33 ha =	a
0,00051 dm² =	mm²	2170 ha =	a
6,82 dm² =	mm²	16 m² =	dm²
0,0071 km² =	m²	1,76 m² =	dm²
2,56 km² =	m²	2276 cm² =	dm²
0,000256 km² =	mm²	43,567 cm² =	dm²
8875 cm² =	mm²	237 km² =	ha
445,86 cm² =	mm²	6,14 km² =	ha
33 950 cm² =	m²	44,15 a =	ha
200 240 cm² =	m²	6,67 a =	ha
21,7 dm² =	m²	0,0048 a =	km²
417 dm² =	m²	477 469 a =	km²
0,056 dm² =	cm²	22 528 715 m² =	km²
95,8 dm² =	cm²	16 217 m² =	km²
0,0059 dm² =	mm²	891 ha =	km²
20,681 dm² =	mm²	7,42 ha =	km²
700,27651 km² =	m²	8848 mm² =	dm²
14,7 km² =	m²	13 270 mm² =	dm²
0,00076 km² =	mm²	432,5 mm² =	cm²

Mental reckoning unit 7

Perimeter of figures. You can gradually shift over to difficult figures, those with a "slanting" side. The table of square numbers on the memory board may be used for this. This leads to: lengths of fences around pieces of land, the length of the floor molding in a living room, etc. This can be further developed into:

(1) Calculation of perimeters using the Theorem of Pythagoras

Appropriate figures are like those on Exercise Sheet 1. You can work on the problems following suggestions of students, and write sample solutions on the board. Analogous text exercises are also to be recommended, and abundantly available in the standard exercise collections and textbooks. Some such exercises can be found on the following pages. As a matter of necessity, what has already been worked out in Exercises 4 and 5 of Mental Reckoning Unit 4, finds its way into these exercises, particularly #3 on p. 70.

In this connection the question arises: how many digits does one have to calculate, when one has to do with some concrete situation (measured lengths, accuracy of measurement, etc)? In the 9th grade I present the following reasoning: it's pointless to have more digits in the answer than the number of reliable digits of the numbers which define the problem in the first place. (At the most one extra digit for rounding.) In the 10th grade I bring in more precise observations in connection with surveying/trigonometry/logarithms. A very stimulating resource in this regard is Chapter 30 (pp. 224-232) of the book "Arithmetik und Algebra" by Louis Locher-Ernst, Dornach 1984, a book that, on account of its technical virtuosity and its didactically sound concept formation (to name just two of its virtues) should be kept in mind as a source of fresh ideas and as a reference book.

Remark: the following exercises do not have yet the form of a polished exercise sheet.

1. The steepest cable car in the world runs on the Pilatus (Switzerland). On a path of length s, it rises uniformly a vertical distance of h. How long does this path appear on a map with scale 1:25000?

    a) s = 1130 m   b) 2150 m   c) 10232 m
        h = 489 m   650 m   123 m

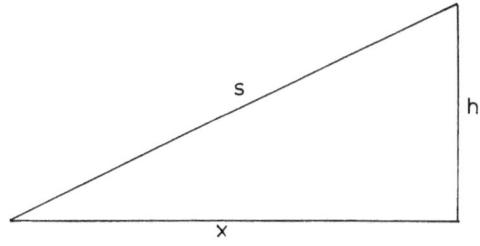

1) We have

$$x^2 = 1130^2 - 489^2$$
$$= 1276900 - 239121$$
$$= 1037779$$

also

$$x \approx 1018,71 \text{ cm}$$

On the map:

$$1018,71 \text{ m} \cdot \frac{4}{100.000}$$
$$= 0,0101871 \text{ m} \cdot 4$$
$$= 0,0407484 \text{ m}$$
$$\approx 4,07 \text{ cm}$$

2) Given s = 2150 m, h = 650 m

$$x^2 = 4622500 - 422500$$
$$x^2 = 4200000$$
$$x = 2049,39$$

On the map:
8,2 cm (8,197)

3) Given s = 10232 m, h = 123 m

$$x^2 \approx 104690000 - 15129$$
$$x^2 \approx 104670000$$
$$x \approx 10231,26$$

On the map:
40,93 cm (40,925)

2. The cross section of a coastal dike is shown in the figure. Calculate the height h and the length l of the gradual descent on the side of the ocean.

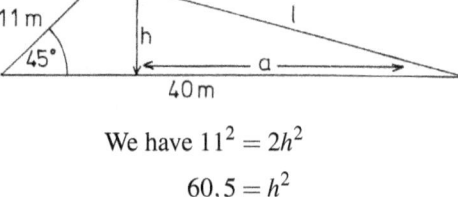

We have $11^2 = 2h^2$

$$60,5 = h^2$$
$$h \approx 7,78$$

with $a = 40 - 7,78 - 4$

$$= 28,22$$

Hence: $l^2 = h^2 + a^2$

$$= 7,78^2 + 28,22^2$$
$$= 60,5 + 796,37$$
$$= 856,87$$

and thus $l \approx 29,27$ m

3. In the symmetric beam structure shown in the figure, the triangle BCD is equilateral and the triangles ABD and CDE are isosceles. Calculate all the angles and lengths, assuming the total length is 8 m.

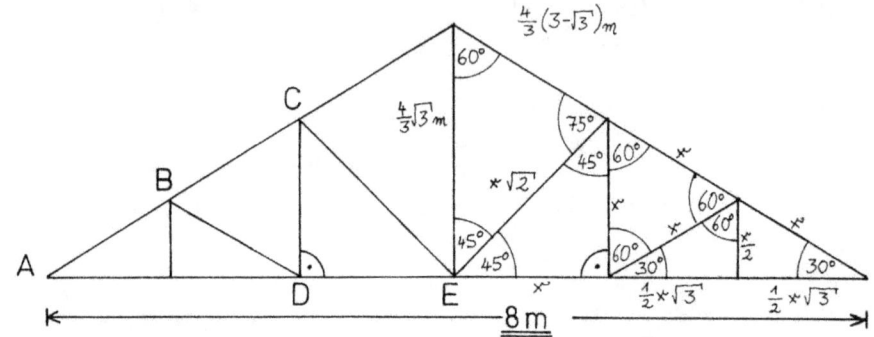

Solution:

$$8 = 2x\sqrt{3} + 2x$$
$$4 = x\sqrt{3} + x$$
$$x = \frac{4}{\sqrt{3}+1} \approx 1,464$$
$$x\sqrt{2} \approx 2,07$$
$$(x\sqrt{3} \approx 2,54)$$

Solution!

4. On the basis of the figure, determine the distance of the inaccessible point B from A by measuring the distances AC and AD. Explain the process.

$$\overline{AC} = 64\,\text{m} \ (36\,\text{m})$$
$$\overline{AD} = 28,8\,\text{m} \ (18\,\text{m})$$

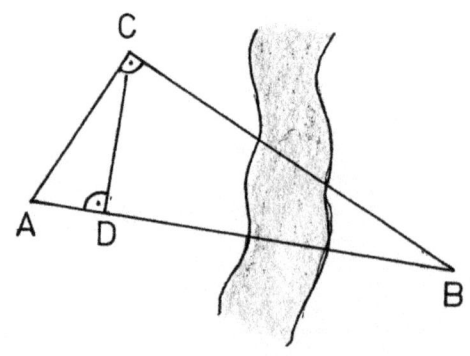

We know $\dfrac{AC}{AD} = \dfrac{AB}{AC}$:

$$\frac{64}{28,8} = \frac{AB}{64}$$

$$\overline{AB} = \frac{64^2}{28,8}$$

$$\approx 142,22$$

$$(72\,\text{m})$$

(2) Calculation of circle properties

We omit a detailed account of the possible approaches to handle this problem, due to the availability of existing works devoted to this theme. In *Ernst Bindel, Die Arithmetik*, one finds a worthy approach, that has been didactically thought-out and supplemented by historical material. *H. Baravalle, Geometrie als Sprache der Formen*, also contains a lot of relevant material. Both authors essentially build upon the method of Archimedes[22]. Beginning with an inscribed equilateral triangle, the number of vertices of the figure is successively doubled to a maximum of 96, thereby covering more and more of the area of the circle. Each step is carried out both by drawing and by calculation; in the process one obtains approximations for both the circumference and the area of the circle. One can spend quite some time on the number π, but the actual calculation should wait until grade 10.

> The "irrational", as a new problematic in the phase of puberty and beyond, is in any case a theme in the 9th grade, as well as the mathematics curriculum (π, square roots that never end).

In this context, some possibilities suggest themselves:

1. **The "Buffon needle problem"** leads "experimentally" to the number π and furthermore can be used as a "contact point" to discuss the birth of probability theory. I've let the pupils collect data for the problem and generate an associated table of values; some have event spent hours, with enthusiasm bordering on obsession, focused on the task of obtaining a large number of throws, in order to verify the assertion with the highest possible accuracy. The following book excerpts help to bring the Buffon problem in sharp focus; the ethnic-nationalistic undertone is naturally repulsive to the contemporary reader. [23]

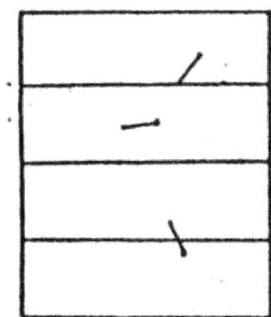

2. Various approximative constructions of the number π.
   Particularly note-worthy is the beautiful construction by Kochanski (see *H.v. Baravalle:*

---

[22] Archimedes Werke, Wissenschaftliche Buchgesellschaft, Darmstadt 1972
[23] There is an english translation of the article available at https://link.springer.com/chapter/10.1007%2F978-3-642-13983-3_15

Geometrie als Sprache der Formen; E. Bindel: *Die Arithmetik*)). This makes it possible to bring in the properties of the isosceles triangle and the Pythagorean Theorem; using these one can then construct the segment corresponding to the approximation $\frac{22}{7} \approx \pi$.

3. Various numerical formulas that provide approximations of π. (See as in b) *H. v. Baravalle* and *E. Bindel*.) In this context, one can also introduce first observations regarding different domains of numbers and irrational numbers.

Mental reckoning unit 8 : *Circle calculations* **(repeatedly!)**

A wide variety of area and perimeter problems related to the circle; remainder surfaces, remainder perimeter, composite figures. Here π should be handled as "a little more than 3":

- "The area of a circle is a bit more than 75 cm^2 What is its radius?"

- "one forms a circle from a thick rope of length 20 m. What is the diameter?"

- "A square of area 16 cm^2 is cut out of a circle. A little more that 60 cm^2 remains. What is the diameter of the circle?", etc.

Once again, the memory board can be used. This can lead into:

2.7.6 Calculating properties of the most diverse figures

On the accompanying exercise sheets on pp.73-75, choose some representative problems. The exercises are largely taken from the textbooks mentioned above. The solutions should be calculated with $\pi \approx 3{,}14$. It's important to keep in mind, that as a *matter of principle* one should always first solve the problem in terms of the concrete values given, and only *then* move on to a general solution. One has to develop a sense for whether the latter makes sense, in each particular case. At least the better students can be encouraged to work on the general solution and present it on the board.

At this stage, it's appropriate to handle the "lune of Hippocrates" and similar problems:

1)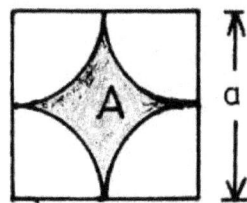

Calculate A

a) for a = 70 cm

b) in general

2)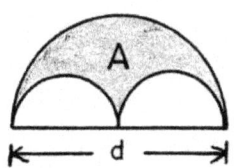

Calculate A

a) for d = 70 cm

b) in general

3)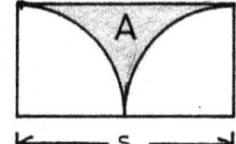

Calculate A

a) for s = 16 cm

b) in general

4)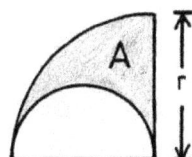

Calculate A

a) for r = 32 cm

b) in general

5)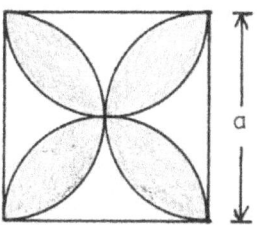

Calculate A

a) for a = 40 cm

b) in general

6)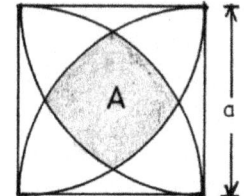

Calculate A

a) for a = 20 cm

b) in general

7)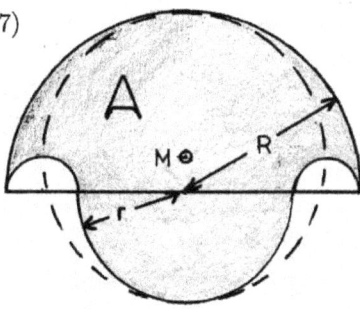

Calculate A

a) for R = 70 cm r = 8 cm

b) in general

c) Compare A with the area of the circle centered on M.

8)

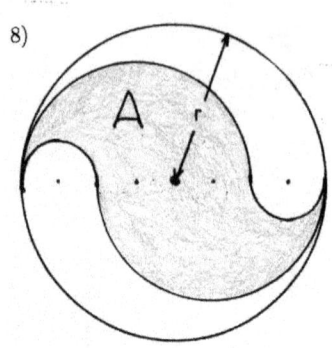

Calculate A

a) for r = 28 cm
b) in general

9)

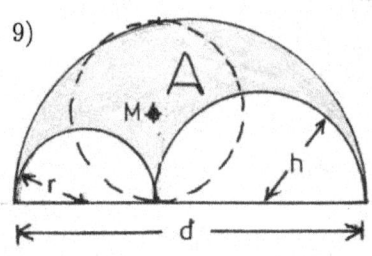

Calculate A

a) for d = 10 cm, r = 2 cm
b) in general
c) Compare A with the area of the circle centered on M.

10)

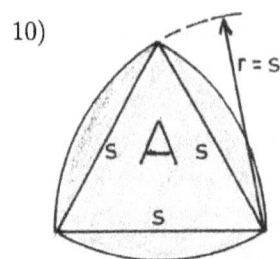

Calculate A

a) for s = 5 cm
b) in general

11)

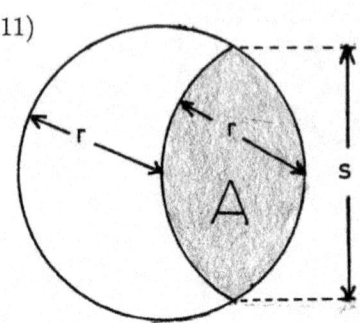

Calculate A

a) for r = 35 cm
b) in general

12)

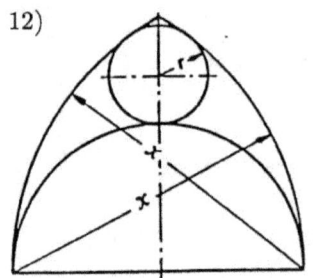

Calculate x at first for r = 3,2 cm and then in general.

13)

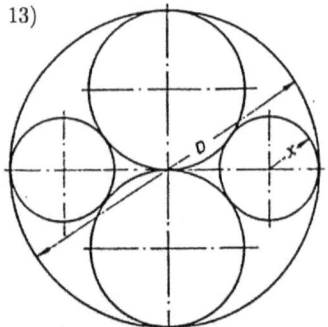

Calculate x at first for r = D = 12 cm and then in general.

14)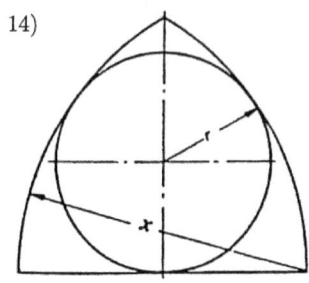

Calculate x at first for r = 1,9 cm and then in general.

17)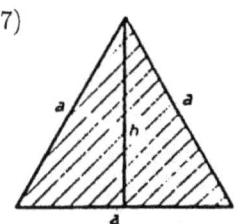

A steel rod has a triangular cross-section with height h. Calculate the area of the cross section A from this height.

15)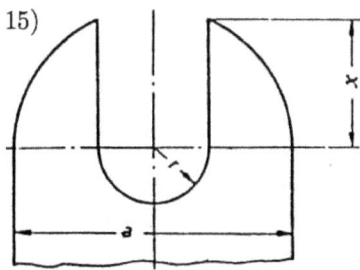

Calculate the length x of the cut-out channel, first for a = 46 mm and r = 15 mm and then in general.

18)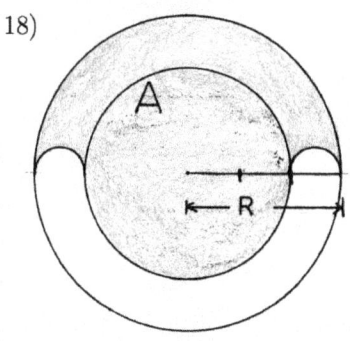

Calculate A

a) for R = 3 cm
R = 6 cm, R = 12 cm

b) in general

16)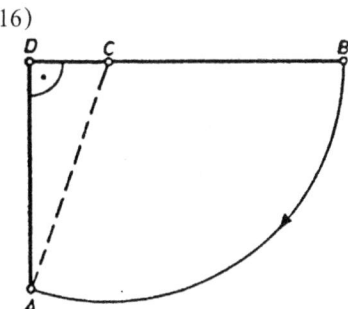

A right-angled framework consists of the rods $\overline{AD}$ and $\overline{DB}$. A joint is to be constructed in point C, so that when the joint closes, point B coincides with A. Calculate $\overline{DC}$ at first for $\overline{AD} = 52$ cm and $\overline{DB} = 80$ cm and then in general.

19)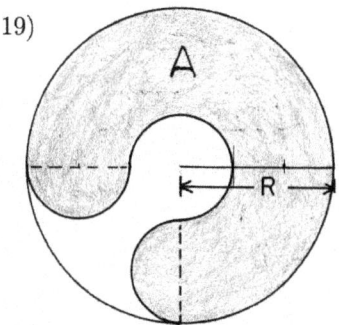

Calculate A

a) for R = 3 cm

b) in general

Solutions to the homework sheets page 73 – 75:

Formulas

Circle $\quad A_\circ = \pi r^2 \quad U = 2\pi r$

Circular sector $A_\triangleleft = \pi r^2 \cdot \dfrac{\alpha}{360°} = \dfrac{r \cdot b}{2}$

Slice of circle $A_\flat = \dfrac{r \cdot b}{2} - \dfrac{s \cdot (r-h)}{2} \approx \dfrac{2}{3} s \cdot h$

because $\dfrac{A_{sector}}{A_{circle}} = \dfrac{\alpha}{360°}$ and $\dfrac{\alpha}{360°} = \dfrac{b}{2\pi r}$

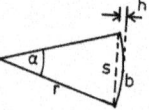

1) $A = a^2 \left(1 - \dfrac{\pi}{4}\right) = 0{,}2145 a^2$

$A = 1051{,}05 \text{ cm}^2$

2) $A = \dfrac{d^2 \pi}{16} = 0{,}19625 d^2$

$A = 490{,}625 \text{ cm}^2$

3) $A = \dfrac{s^2}{2}\left(1 - \dfrac{\pi}{4}\right) = 0{,}1075 s^2$

$A = 27{,}52 \text{ cm}^2$

4) $A = \dfrac{\pi r^2}{8} = 0{,}3925 r^2$

$A = 401{,}92 \text{ cm}^2$

5) $A = a^2 \left(\dfrac{\pi}{2} - 1\right) = 0{,}57 a^2$

$A = 912 \text{ cm}^2$

6) $A = a^2 \left(1 + \dfrac{\pi}{3} - \sqrt{3}\right)$

$= 0{,}315 a^2$

$A = 126 \text{ cm}^2$

7) $A = \pi \left(\dfrac{R+r}{2}\right)^2$

$= 0{,}785 (R+r)^2$

$A = 615{,}44 \text{ cm}^2$

The two areas are the same

8) $A = \dfrac{\pi r^2}{2}$

$A = 1231{,}5 \text{ cm}^2$

bei $\pi = 3{,}14$:

$A = 1230{,}88 \text{ cm}^2$

9) $A = \dfrac{\pi}{2} r(d - 2r)$

$= 1{,}57 r(d - 2r)$

$A = 18{,}84 \text{ cm}^2$

The two areas are the same

10) $A = \dfrac{s^2}{2}(\pi - \sqrt{3}) = 0{,}704 s^2$

$A = 17{,}6 \text{ cm}^2$

11) $A = \dfrac{r^2}{6}(4\pi - 3\sqrt{3})$

$= 1{,}227 r^2$

$s = r\sqrt{3}$

$A = 1503 \text{ mm}^2$

$s = 60{,}62 \text{ mm}$

12) When the radius r goes through the center of the small circle it also goes through the tangential contact point with the small circle

13) $x = 6r$
$x = 19,2\,\text{cm}$

14) $x = \dfrac{D}{6}$
$x = 2\,\text{cm}$

$x = \dfrac{8}{3}r$
$x = 5,07\,\text{cm}$

15) $x = \sqrt{\dfrac{a^2}{4} - r^2}$
$x = 17,4\,\text{mm}$

16) $\overline{DC} = \dfrac{\overline{DB}^2 - \overline{AD}^2}{2\overline{DB}}$
$\overline{DC} = 23,1\,\text{cm}$

17) $A = \dfrac{h^2}{\sqrt{3}} = \dfrac{h^2}{3}\sqrt{3}$

18) $A = \dfrac{25}{36}R^2\pi$

$R = 3$: $A = \dfrac{25}{36} \cdot 9 \cdot 3,14$
$= 78,5 : 4$
$A = 19,63\,\text{cm}^2$

$R = 6$: $A = \dfrac{25}{36} \cdot 36 \cdot 3,14$
$= 25 \cdot 3,14$
$A = 78,5\,\text{cm}^2$
$x = 6r$
$x = 19,2\,\text{cm}$

$R = 12$: $A = \dfrac{25}{36} \cdot 144 \cdot 3,14$
$= 100 \cdot 3,14$
$A = 314\,\text{cm}^2$

19) $A_{\bigcirc} = \dfrac{3}{4} \cdot R^2 \cdot \pi$

$A_{\bigcirc} = \dfrac{3}{4} \cdot \dfrac{1}{9} \cdot R^2 \cdot \pi$

$A_{\bigcirc} = \dfrac{1}{9} \cdot R^2 \cdot \pi$

$A = A_{\bigcirc} - A_{\bigcirc} + A_{\bigcirc}$

$= \left(\dfrac{3}{4} - \dfrac{1}{12} + \dfrac{1}{9}\right) R^2\pi$

$= \dfrac{27 - 3 + 4}{36} R^2\pi$

$= \dfrac{28}{36} R^2\pi$

$A = \dfrac{7}{9} R^2\pi$

$R = 3$:

$A = \dfrac{7}{9} \cdot 9 \cdot \pi$
$= 7 \cdot \pi$
$\approx 7 \cdot 3,14$
$A \approx 21,98\,\text{cm}^2$

The following mathematical puzzle lends itself well for a transition to the main part of the lesson. Many students will have the feeling that the solution is paradoxical, but it deepens the understanding of the relation between circumference and radius: "How does the diameter grow, as the circumference of the circle grows?", or, the same question with the roles reversed.

As a next step, inspired by a similar goal, one can discuss the connection between the growth of the diameter and the growth of the area, and thereby work out the fundamental difference between length and area growth.

Suppose we tie a rope tighly around the Earth's equator. Now we add 1 extra meter of lenght. All around the earth the rope is raised up uniformly as high as it is possible. Would a mouse be able to slip under this rope?

The answer is surprising: it is possible, not only a mouse but even a cat would be able to fit under the rope.

It is possible to widen the question, i.e. to ask what would happen, if we would tie the rope around our waist and add the same length...

2.8 Outlook

At this point one can make a transition to the exposition of solid geometry. This can be done in a way that immediately makes use of, both with respect to method and content, what's been developed in the planar case, but applied instead to the situation in space. A supplementary article devoted to this theme is intended.

3 Remarks on effective teaching habits

I prefer to have the usual two skills classes per week as a double-period, since the required alternation of techniques otherwise leads to feeling "short of breath", and the students don't have sufficient stillness to follow a train of thought, including the associated "stabilization" and – most importantly – practice phases.

I'm happy to handle geometric, arithmetic, and algebraic content together in a single instructional period, or in a sequence of periods. Whereby I always try my best not to mix up the distinctive thought-forms appropriate for each domain. In the 9th grade, one should be particularly alert here.

Now and again, I develop in parallel some themes, that appear not to have anything to do with each other, until gradually a connection can be dimly perceived, and finally reveals itself, so that the intended content, illuminated from different sides, attains sufficient density and fullness.

In the first meetings of an instructional unit I attempt, moving slowly, to create a solid foundation. This makes it possible for weaker students to find a connection, or a re-connection, to the material. The time spent at the beginning in the way allows one to avoid the time-consuming eradication of deficits later on, and the weaker students also gain self-confidence again. This careful beginning shouldn't mean, that more gifted students don't have plenty to keep them busy. The posing of problems and the level of the exercise sheets have to display an accordingly wide spectrum. On the other hand, the more gifted students are expected to furnish the more difficult formulations, provide overviews of themes, and explanations, as needed.

It's important to me, to lead the pupils as often as possible into self-initiated activity. So, in addition to extensive practice, they should have the chance to discover much on their own, and present results in their own way.

I also enjoy bringing in other knowledge of varied sorts: biographical, intellectual-historical, development of consciousness, anecdotal, and just plain interesting; sometimes to introduce it, sometimes just to point to it, sometimes in more detail, depending on the situation.

In the first part of the main lesson, after the morning verse, speech exercises, and a recitation, I make mental reckoning and/or visualization exercises. Then the pupils are awake and receptive; I often shift over then seamlessly to the main theme.

Regarding the amount of homework: most pupils have a certain "exercise-excess" from the main lesson, which has to be worked off; I supplement these with difficult exercises that also tend to be more interesting, which can be worked on as alternatives or supplements.

Any board drawing, if it's not to be too "sketchy", has to be absolutely precise and well laid-out, logically constructed, and expressive of its meaning. The pedagogical effect of such a board drawing can scarcely be over-estimated.

I need lots of board area, so that usually I work with extra movable boards whose content can be left unchanged for several days at a time, without disturbing other instruction in the same room. I also find it good to use a large paper pad (a "flip chart", standing on an easel), for writing out important statements, examples, formulas, and tables; the resulting sheets are then hung up around the room and serve as a "memory on display".

3.1 Remarks on student notebooks:

1. If you have to put a new 9th grade class to work for the first time, I recommend the following procedure: *2 homework notebooks* for working out homework exercises. When the one is collected by the teacher, the other is still available to the student. It may be the case, that in order from the beginning to guarantee a regular work ethic, one or the other of these notebooks has to be collected each class meeting. Students who leave the notebook or homework assignments at home, have to bring it to me at my home the same day. For most students that is so inconvenient that he chooses the more comfortable path, that is, he does his homework every day. Laxity on the part of the teacher at this point often leads later to difficulties, related to the work habits of the students.

2. "*good notebook*", which is kept continuously up-to-date with the contents of the main lesson and the general results and noteworthy details of the practice sessions, not however every completed exercise. The entries should be neat and clean. I prefer the use of binders, as opposed to pre-stapled books, that allow for example the inclusion of supplementary sheets and exercise sheets. These "'good'" books are collected by the students in a safe place and at the end of the high school provide a compendium of our mathematical work together, which can be then referred to when needed, for example, by reviews or other exam-related occasions.

In Lübeck we start using a pocket calculator first in the 10th grade *after* the two main lessons (the higher number operations and trigonometry), just for interest calculation and on the surveying field trip; from then on, it is the appropriate, contemporary tool for numerical calculations. The students are quite convinced by the reasons which we give for this policy:

- One quickly forgets how to calculate, or becomes very slow at it – particularly mental reckoning – when one uses a pocket calculator.
- One must first understand and master a calculation, before it makes sense to use a pocket calculator to carry it out.
- At the end of his school career, a young person should be equipped with a maximum of individual reckoning skills.

Furthermore, from contact with students transferring in from state schools, who currently bring severe reckoning weaknesses with them (even the more gifted ones), our students experience that early and intensive use of pocket calculators also has its shadow-side.

3.2 Books referred to in the text

Unfortunately these books are not available in english, we will still provide you with the source

BARAVALLE H.V.: Geometrie als Sprache der Formen, Verlag Freies Geistesleben, Stuttgart 1980^3

BERLOQUIN P.: Mathematische Kopfspiele, München 1983

BERNHARD A.: Geometrie für die 7. und 8. Klasse an Waldorfschulen, Verlag Freies Geistesleben, Stuttgart 1993

BINDEL E.: Die Arithmetik, Verlag Freies Geistesleben, Stuttgart 1967

EIGENMANN P.: Geometrische Denkaufgaben, Ernst Klett Verlag, Stuttgart 1981

LOUIS LOCHER-ERNST: Arithmetik und Algebra, Dornach 1984

OTT G.: Geometrie für Klassenlehrer der 6., 7. und 8. Klassen

3.3 Further Literature

- ULIN, BENGT: Finding the Path, AWSNA, 1991.
- Historical sources, given in the text.
- We close with a pointer to a magnificent work which presents the development of mathematics in a fascinating way, using a genetic and historical approach, a book from which teachers (and not just teachers!) can gather a multitude of new ideas and knowledge for the classroom, some may even have the feeling they really get to know mathematics for the first time through the book.
- LANCELOT HOGBEN, Mathematics for the Millions, Norton, New York, 1983 (original 1937)

A remark on geometric locus

Uwe Hansen

The concept of geometric locus plays a central role in mathematics. Every student ought to be acquainted with the following geometric loci: perpendicular bisector of a segment, angle bisector of two intersecting lines, parallel to a line, circle, ellipse, parabola, hyperbola, Cassini curves – especially the lemniscate, and the circles of Apollonius ("division circles"[24]).

The understanding of the concept of geometric locus can be extended through the following examples:

Example 1: Two intersecting lines g_1 and g_2 are given. The distance of a point P from g_1 is d_1, and from g_2 is d_2. Describe the location of P satisfying, under the following conditions:

$\quad$ a) $d_1 + d_2 =$ constant $\qquad$ b) $d_1 - d_2 =$ constant
$\quad$ c) $d_1 \cdot d_2 =$ constant $\qquad$ d) $d_1 : d_2 =$ constant?

In case a) one obtains a rectangle with diagonals g_1 and g_2.. In case b), one obtains a "negative" rectangle: all its four sides intersect the "line at infinity" of the plane, and g_1 and g_2 are once again diagonals. In case c) one obtains hyperbolas with asymptotes g_1 and g_2, and in case d) one obtains lines that pass through the intersection point of g_1 and g_2.

Example 2: A point G and a line l, not passing through G, are given. d_1 and d_2 are the distances of an arbitrary point to G and l, resp. Where does P lie, under the following conditions:

$\quad$ a) $d_1 + d_2 =$ constant $\qquad$ b) $d_1 - d_2 =$ constant
$\quad$ c) $d_1 \cdot d_2 =$ constant $\qquad$ d) $d_1 : d_2 =$ constant ?

In case a) one obtains a curve consisting of two parabolic that meet on the line l. Also in case b) one obtains a curve consisting of one or two parabolic arcs, both of which pass through infinity. If there are two, they also meet on line l. In case c) one obtains curves shaped like mussel shells (viewed from the side), while case d) yields the conic sections: ellipse, parabola, and hyperbola. Cases c) and d) can be drawn in a single drawing, by letting the distances d1 and d2 take values from a geometric series. See the figures on the next page , which show the geometric loci for a range of values of the constant value.

---

[24] Locus of points whose distances to two given points have a constant ratio

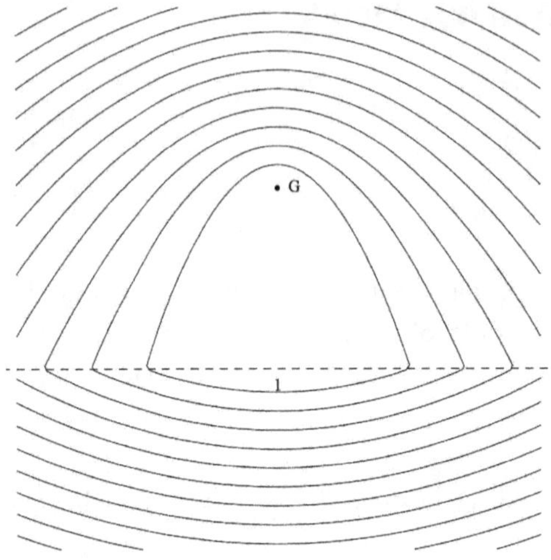

case a)

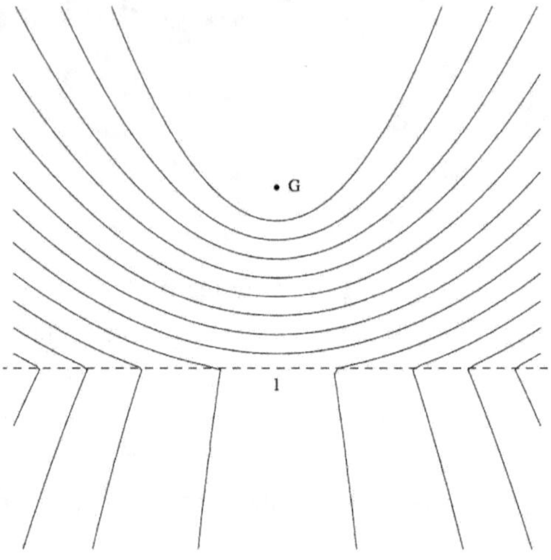

case b)

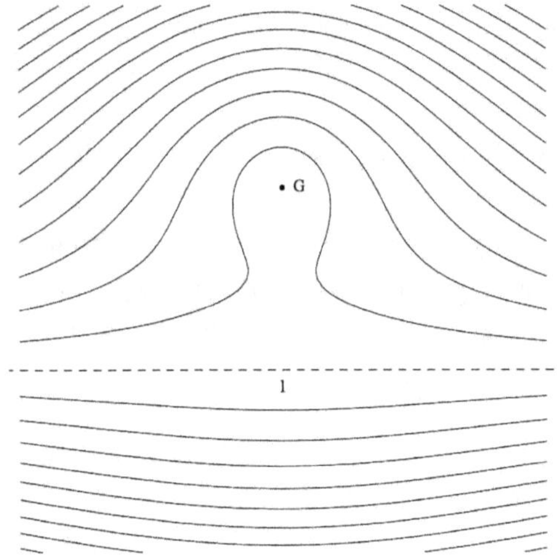

case c)

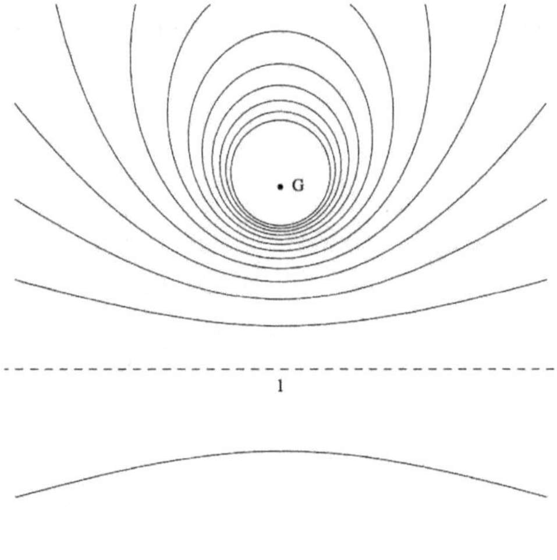

case d)

Example 3: Which points P lie the same distance from the line g and the sides of the angle? The solution curve is pieced together from a parabolic arc and two half-lines (angle bisectors). The measurement of the angle doesn't have to be 90°.

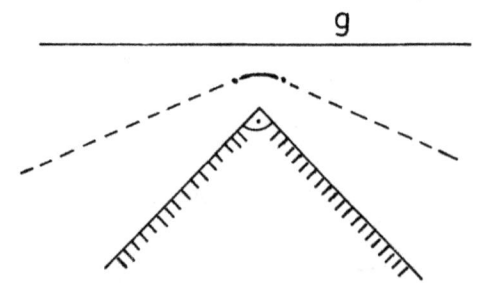

Example 4: Which points P lie the same distance from the sides of the two angles? The solution curve consists of two parabolic arcs and two half-lines.

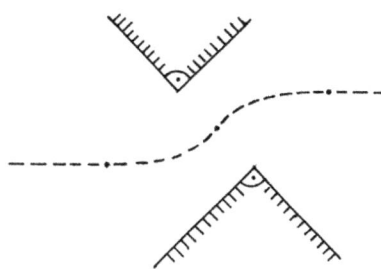

Example 5: On which curve do the points P lie, that are the same distance from the two half-lines a and b? The solution curve consists of a line segment and two half-parabolas.

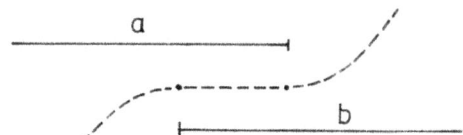

Example 6: Which points P lie exactly the same distance from the sides of the angle as from point A? As solution one obtains a curve made up of two parabolic arcs.

On this example we want to demonstrate how one can go about solving such problems. With A as center, a circle spreads out with a certain constant speed; this is intersected with the geometric locus, of all points whose distance to the sides of the angle is the current radius of the circle. As the radius changes, the intersection points run through the desired curve.

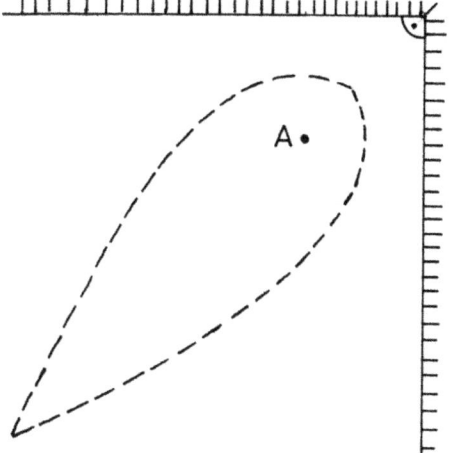

Example 7: Which points P lie the same distance from the half-line h, as from the circle k? The solution is pieced together from one hyperbolic arc and two parabolic ones.

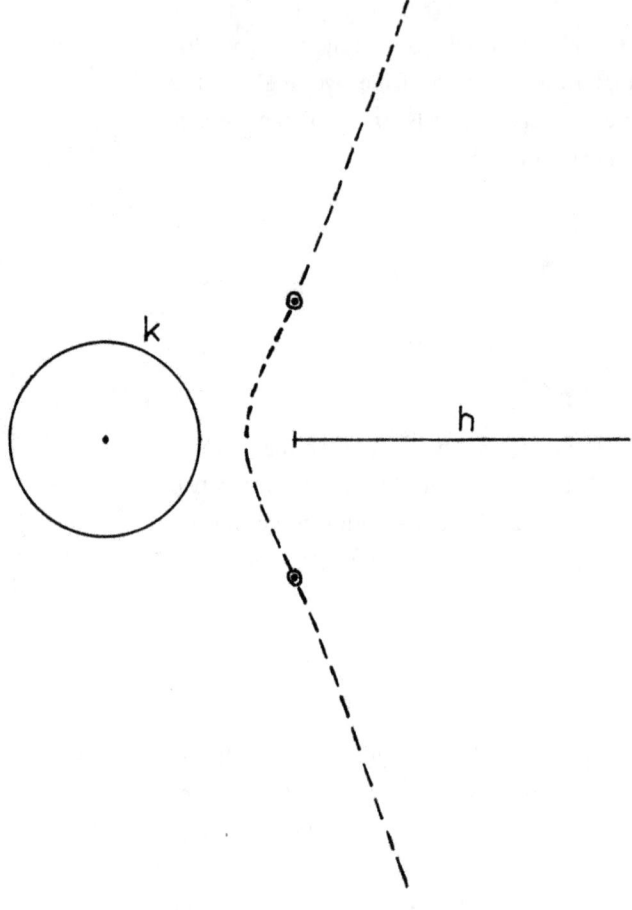

Curves as Loci

A contribution concerning the metamorphosis of curve forms

SIGURD BINDEL UND KLAUS LABUDDE

"The Curriculum of the Independent Waldorf School", edited by Caroline von Heyebrand, gives the following theme for the 9th grade: the treatment of conic sections and selected curves of higher degree, based on the theory of geometric locus. The concept of geometric locus belongs to the fundamental foundations for teaching geometry in the middle grades. Thus it certainly makes sense for class teachers to handle conic sections already in the 8th grade, whereby they will naturally place a different emphasis than the high school teacher in the 9th grade.

The aim of the current article is, on the basis of our own experiences, to present some ideas and impulses related to selected examples of higher-degree curves describing geometric loci. For brevity's sake, we refer henceforth to such curves as *locus-curves*. High school teachers may object, that there's no time to handle this theme in their geometry classes; the main lessons of the 9th grade are already full. In answer, one can point out that for every grade in the high school, there is more suitable material than one has time available to present. Furthermore, one can also – speaking here from experience –introduce locus-curves in the subject "Descriptive geometry"[25]. Also here there are traditional themes, but it's by no means rigidly fixed. After all, it's the task of the teacher to discover what themes are important, what needs attention, in his 9th grade. In this sense, this article is intended as a possible offering for the geometry instruction in the 9th grade. As a path leading into the material I have usually used:

4   Three Problems of Delos[26]

The Pythia of Delos, the oracle of Apollo, posed three problems for the human being: Construct using compass and straight edge[27]:

1. Squaring the circle

2. Doubling the cube

3. Trisecting the angle

---

[25] In German-speaking lands, there has been a tradition of teaching descriptive geometry (that is, careful drawing of 2- and 3D views of objects) in the math skills classes of the 9th and 10th grades of the high school.

[26] Delos, now known as Delopulo or Mikra Dilos, one of the smallest islands of the Aegean See, completely consisting of granite. In antiquity: temple of Apollo, sacred site of all Ionic sea states, main slave market.

[27] Unmarked ruler, solely for drawing straight lines

All three tasks are, however, insoluble with compass and straight edge. A variety of constructions and insights in the history of mathematics owe their existence to the attempt to solve these problems. Here I want to present two examples that have led to new curve forms. First we give a short description of the three tasks.

4.1 Squaring the circle

The surface of a circle is to be transformed into a square of the same area.

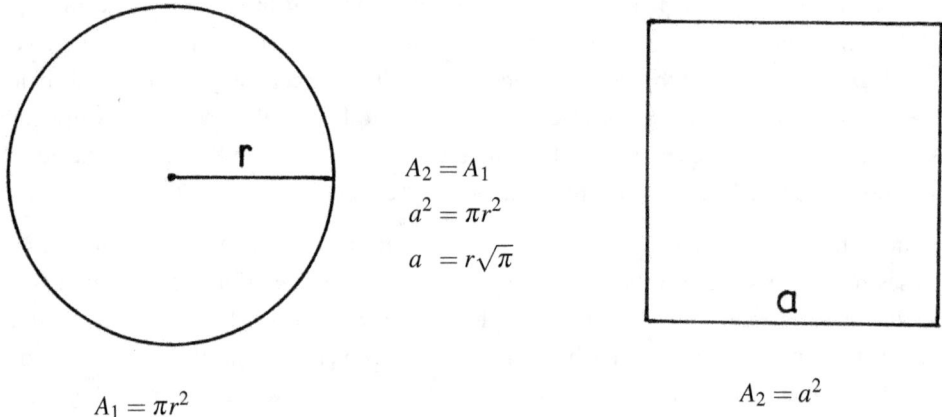

$A_2 = A_1$
$a^2 = \pi r^2$
$a = r\sqrt{\pi}$

$A_1 = \pi r^2$

$A_2 = a^2$

4.2 Doubling the cube

Two identical cubes are to be transformed in a single cube of the same (combined) volume.

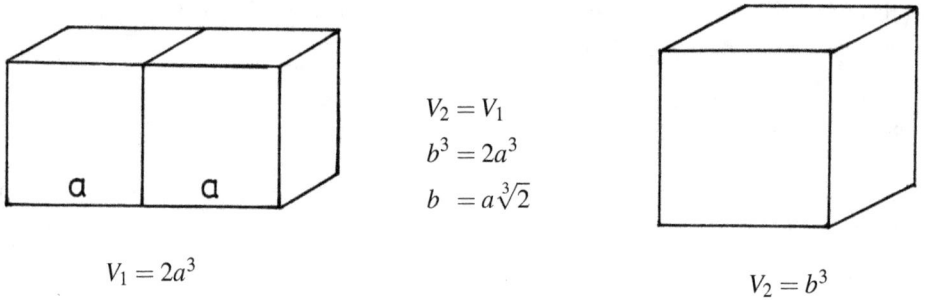

$V_2 = V_1$
$b^3 = 2a^3$
$b = a\sqrt[3]{2}$

$V_1 = 2a^3$

$V_2 = b^3$

4.3 Angle trisection

An arbitrary angle is to be divided into three equal angles.

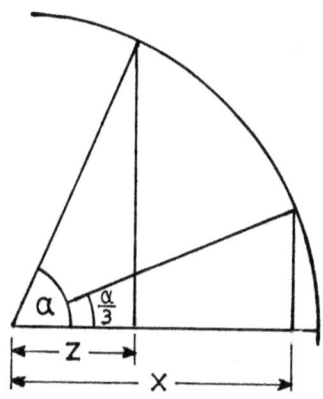

$\cos 3\alpha = 4\cos^3 \alpha - 3\cos \alpha$
$\cos \alpha = 4\cos^3 \frac{\alpha}{3} - 3\cos \frac{\alpha}{3}$
$x = \cos \frac{\alpha}{3} \qquad z = \cos \alpha$
Cubic equation:
$z = 4x^3 - 3x$
oder x aus: $4x^3 - 3x - z = 0$

5 The Conchoid

The conchoid was discovered by the Greek mathematician Nicomedes (circa 150 B. C.); using this curve he was able to solve the angle trisection problem.

The solution he found will be shown at the end of the chapter. First, we describe the conchoid.

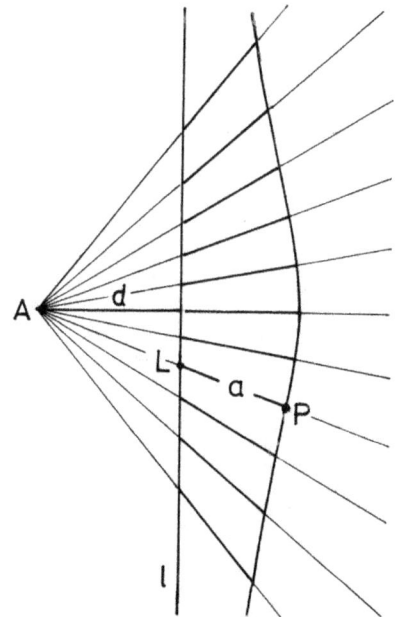

Definition:
One constructs a line pencil[a] in the point A, the "pole" point. The "'guide"' line l, lying the distance d from A, cuts this line pencil in the points L. From each L-point, one measures off the constant length a away from the pole to obtain the point P. These P-points create the *conchoid*, also known as mussel-curve (on account of its shape).

---
[a]The *line pencil* in a point A is the set of all lines passing through P

Instead of measuring the length a in the direction away from A, one can also measure it in the direction towards A. The drawing on the following page shows conchoids for which the guide line lies 6 cm from the pole A. Conchoids are drawn for $a = 2; 4; 6;$ cm in the outer direction, and for $a = 2; 4; 6; 8; 10$ cm in the inner direction. For the "inner" conchoids there are three different form principles:

Wave forms for	$0 < a < 6\,\text{cm}$
Cusp forms for	$a = 6\,\text{cm}$
Loop forms for	$a > 6\,\text{cm}$

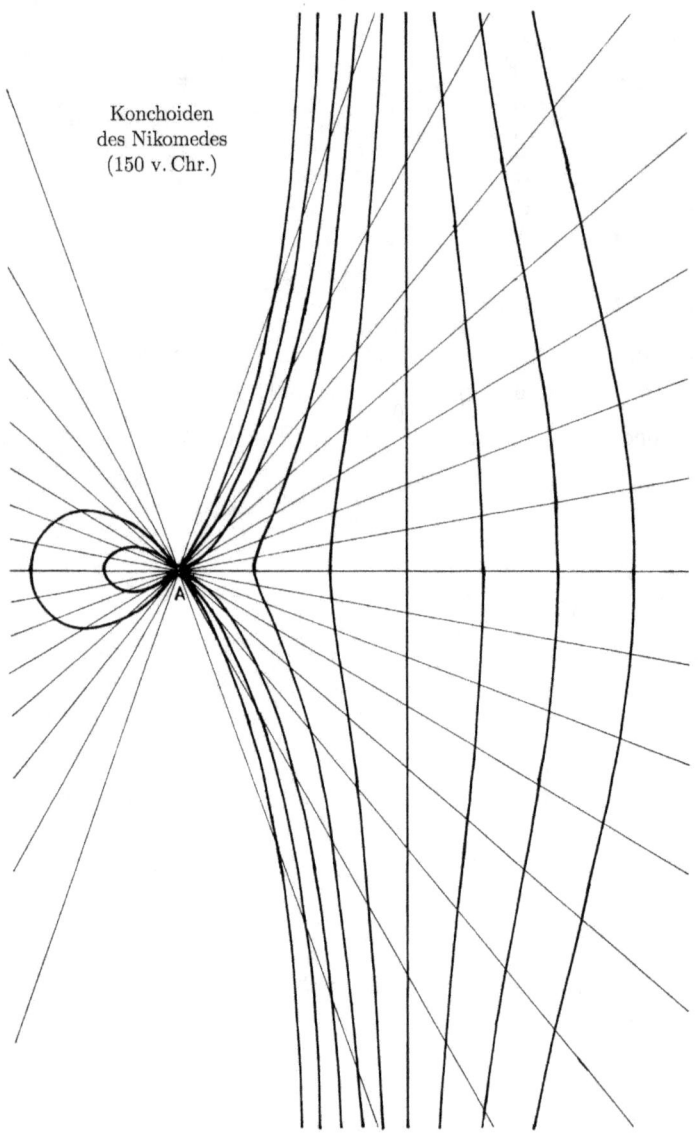

Konchoiden des Nikomedes (150 v. Chr.)

The three types of conchoid shapes are shown below, separately drawn:

Wave form

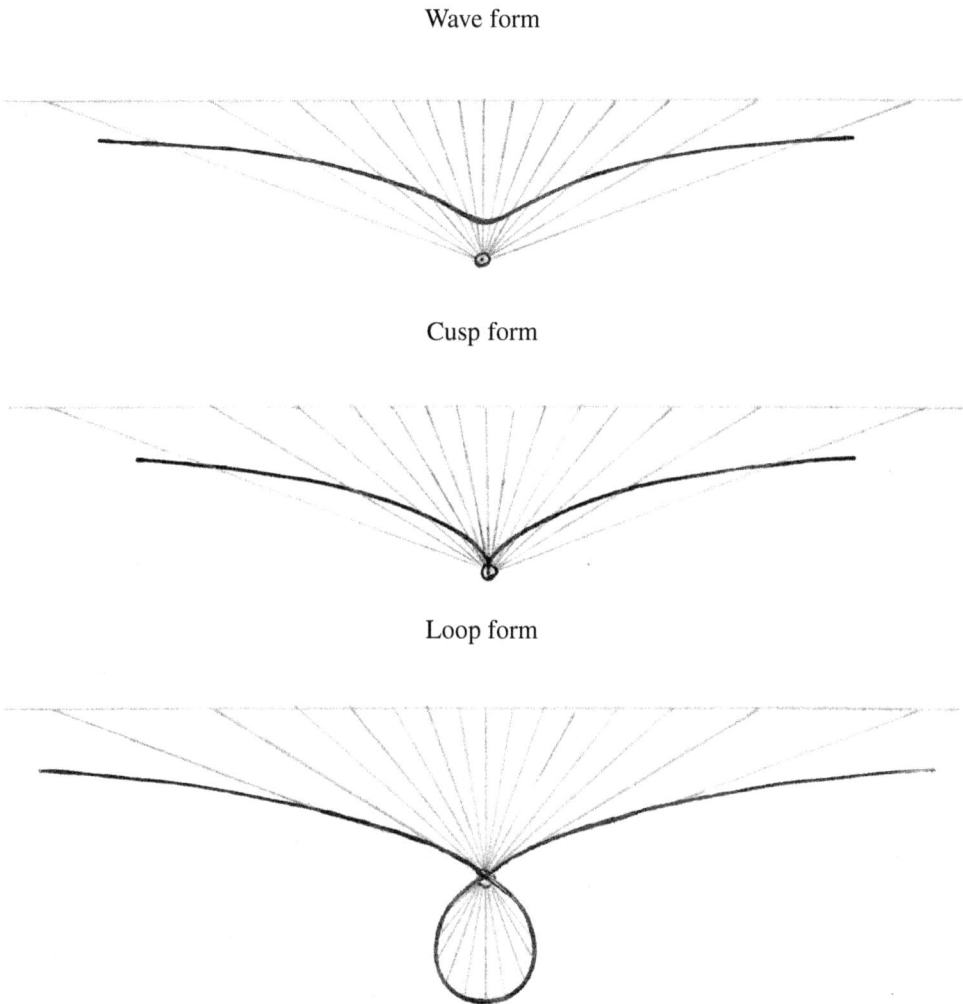

Cusp form

Loop form

It's worth noting, that all conchoids have the guide line as asymptote. After this introduction, we turn now to a rich application domain:

Conchoids from polygons
(triangles, quadrilaterals, etc.)

One starts with a *polygon*[28], chooses a pole point A either centered or asymmetric, produces the line pencil in A, cuts the given polygon with the lines of the pencil to produce the L-points. If one now interprets each line segment of the figure as a piece of a guide line, one can then draw the inner (or outer) conchoids corresponding to the polygon. This gives rise to curved forms displaying a rich interplay of forms.

Remark: If you want the students to get acquainted with the richness of these forms by drawing them, it's possible to reduce their work load by providing sheets on which the polygonal figure and selected lines of the line pencil have already been drawn.

Conchoid of an equilateral triangle

---

[28] a curve consisting of a sequence of line segments joined pairwise at their endpoints

Conchoid of a square

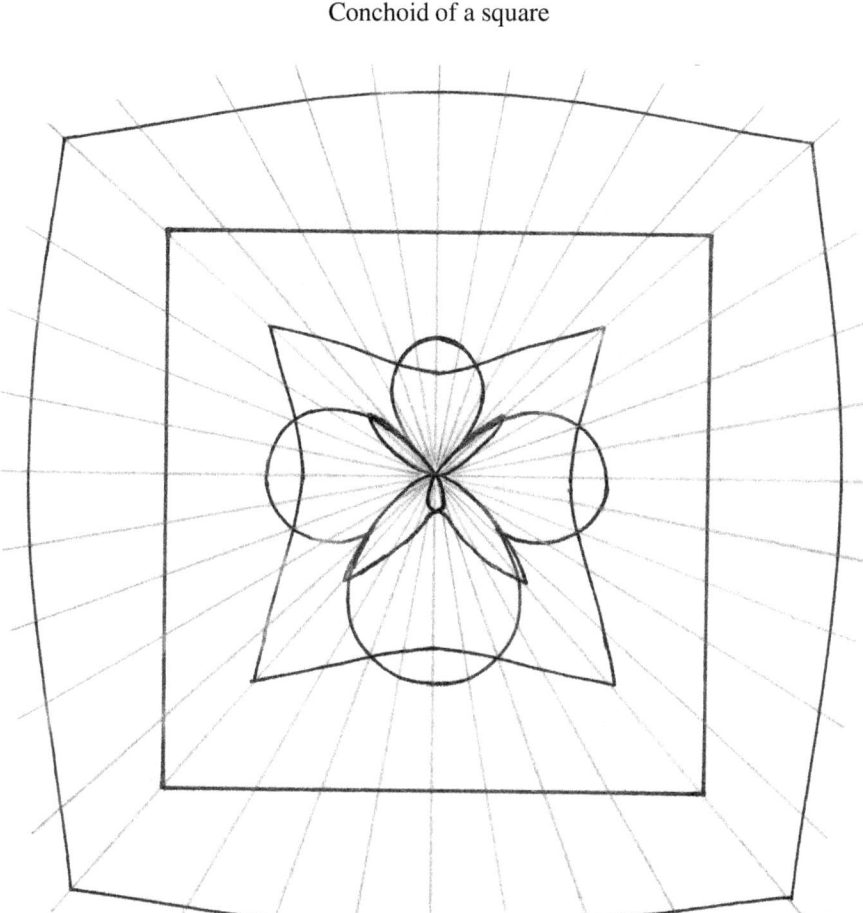

Remark: Another variation of conchoid can be obtained by replacing the polygonal figure by a circle.

Construction of angle trisector

following Nicomedes

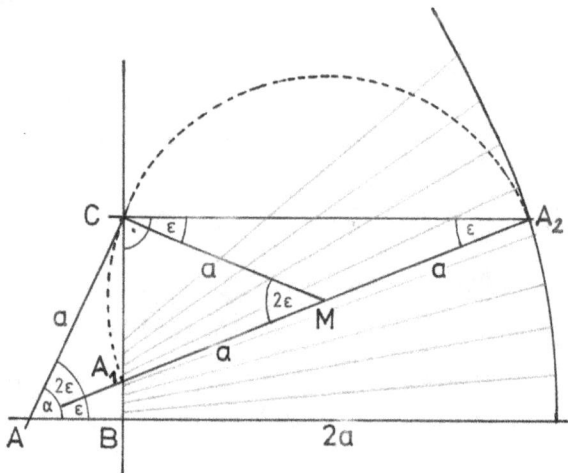

Konstruktion:

1. Construct angle α in the pole A.
2. Measure off from A, on one side of the angle, the segment $\overline{AC} = a$.
3. Drop the perpendicular from C, it meets the other side of the angle in B.
4. Draw the outer $2a$-Conchoid, with pole A and guide line BC.
5. Draw the parallel to AB through C, this meets the conchoid in the point A_2.
6. AA_2 cuts the guide line BC in A_1.
7. The angle $A_1 AB = \frac{\alpha}{3}$.

Proof:

1. Let M be the midpoint of $A_1 A_2$. Then $\overline{A_1 M} = \overline{MA_2} = a$ (on account of the conchoid construction).
2. The Thales circle with center M and radius a passes through C, since $A_1 C \perp CA_2$.
3. In the isosceles triangle MCA_2 let the basis angle be ε. Then the exterior angle at M is 2ε.
4. In the isosceles triangle ACM the base angles are both 2ε.
5. The angles $CA_2 A$ and $A_2 AB$ are alternating angles of two parallel lines, hence equal.

Hence, the angle at A satisfies: $\alpha = 2\varepsilon + \varepsilon = 3\varepsilon$,
and consequently $\varepsilon = \frac{\alpha}{3}$ q.e.d.

The proof is ingenious, but the construction can't be carried out with compass and straight edge, as it requires finding the intersection of a line with a curve, that has either to be constructed point-by-point, or, as already was done in antiquity, drawn with a special "conchoid compass".[29]

Remark: The proof is almost certainly not appropriate to present to the whole class. One can however entrust it to a gifted individual students or a small group to work on, possibly to be followed later by a report to the class.

6 The Cissoid

In the search for a solution to the second Delos problem, doubling the curve, the Greek Diocles (circa 150 B. C.) found a curve construction that leads to a solution of this problem: the cissoid, also known as the "ivy curve" due to its shape. To begin with, we construct some cissoids, based on various initial conditions. At the end, Diocles' proof will be presented, showing how one can solve the doubling of the cube using this curve.

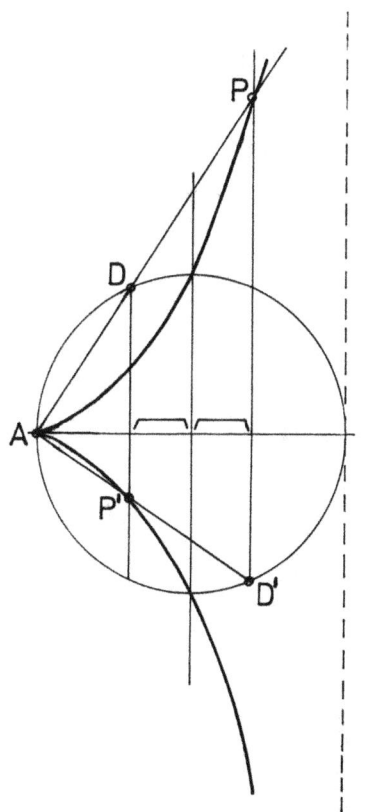

Definition: Draw a horizontal and a vertical diameter in a circle. At the left end of the horizontal diameter lies the fixed pole A. Symmetric on either side of the vertical diameter, draw two vertical chords. Connect the pole A with an end-point D of one of the chords. Then the intersection of the line AD with the line of the other chord lies on a curve, the *cissoid of Diocles*.

Description: The cissoid has a cusp at the pole A, passes through the endpoints of the vertical diameter, and approaches asymptotically the tangent to the circle at the right endpoint of the horizontal diameter.

In the following drawings (p. 94) one sees conchoids that arise as the pole moves along the line of the horizontal diameter, away from the circle. Each of these cissoids runs its course in a bounded

---

[29] See *Egmont Colerus*: Vom Punkt zu vierten Dimension – Geometrie für Jedermann, Paul Zsolnay Verlag

area of the plane. The further the pole moves away, the more the cissoid approaches the circle, in a wave-like manner.

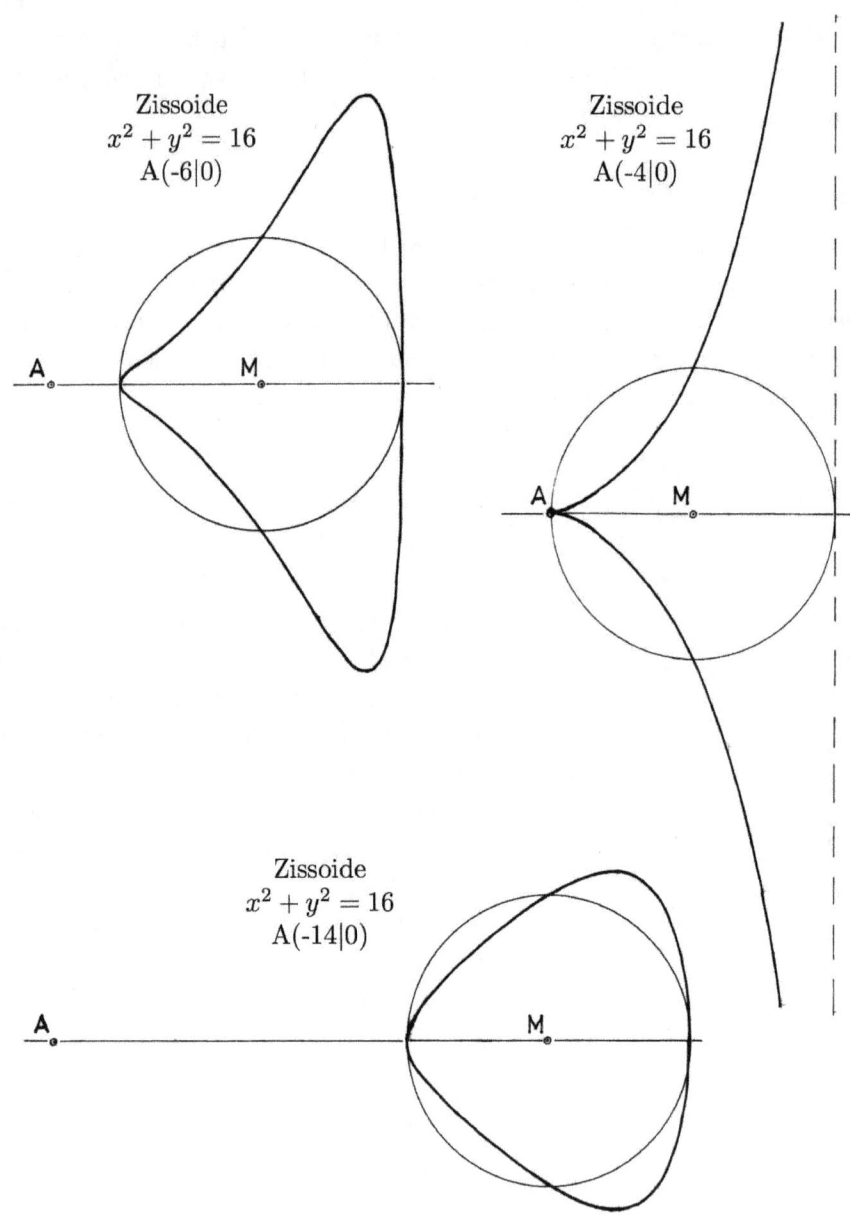

Next come cissoids, in which the pole A moves along the horizontal diameter towards the center of the circle. This gives rise to *looped* cissoids. Each of these features an asymptotic line located symmetrically, on the opposite side of the circle center, to the pole point. The further the pole moves towards the center point, the more the curve approaches a circle plus a vertical line passing through the circle's center.

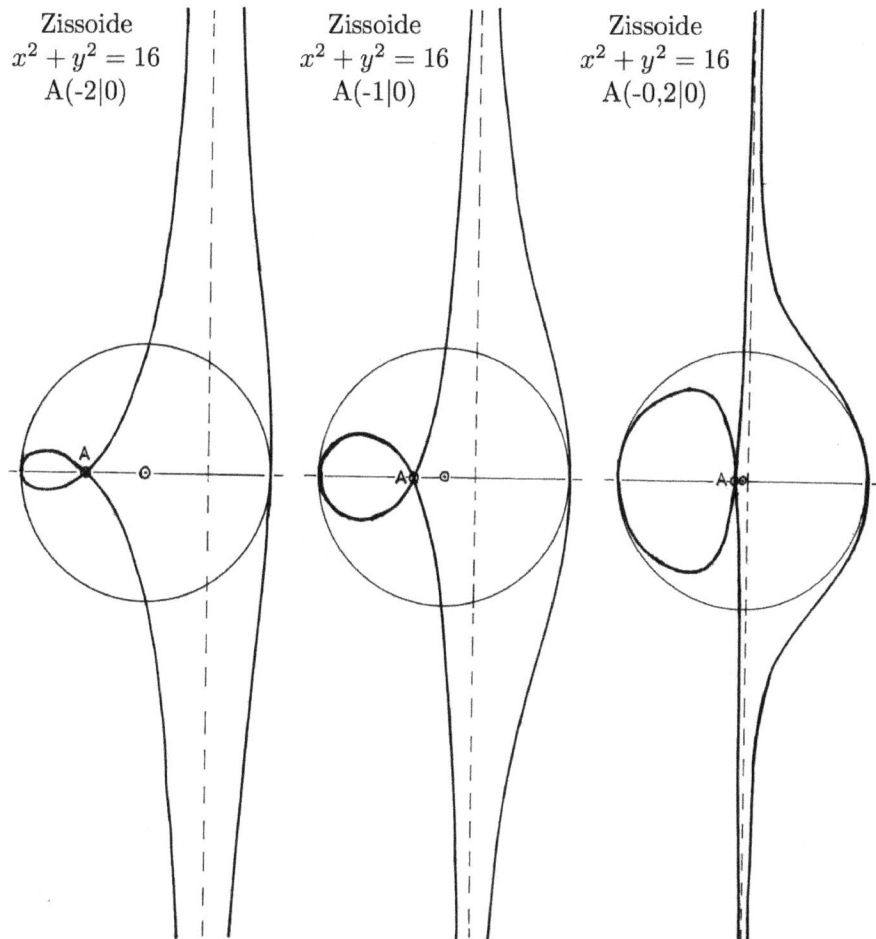

Solution of the problem of doubling the cube

using the cissoid of Diocles (150 B.C.)

We seek as two edges of cubes, a pair of segments a and s, whose third powers stand in a proportion of 2:1 with each other: $a^3 = 2 \cdot s^3$. Draw a cissoid in a circle with the diameter $AB = d = 2 \cdot r$, with pole A lying on the circle. Mark off the vertical segment $AP_1 = 2 \cdot r$. Connect P_1 with B and intersect this line with the cissoid to obtain P. Intersect AP with the circle to obtain C. Let the perpendiculars from C and P to the horizontal diameter meet this diameter in H, resp., Q, and be of length a, resp. t.

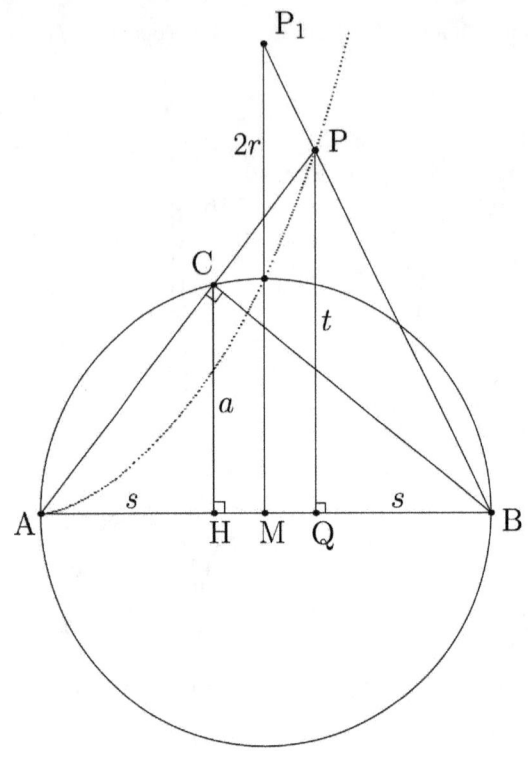

Claim:

$$a^3 = 2 \cdot s^3 \text{ hence } \left(\frac{a}{s}\right)^2 = 2 \cdot \frac{s}{a}$$

Proof:

By the construction of the cissoid AH = QB = s and AQ = HB = $d - s$. The right triangle AHC is similar to both triangles AQP and CHB, so that corresponding sides are proportional:

$$\frac{a}{s} = \frac{t}{d-s} \quad (1)$$

$$\frac{a}{s} = \frac{d-s}{a} \quad (2)$$

From this follows

$$\left(\frac{a}{s}\right)^2 = \frac{t}{d-s} \cdot \frac{d-s}{a} = \frac{t}{a} \quad (3)$$

Since the triangles MBP_1 and QBP are similar, $t = 2 \cdot s$. Through substituting in (3) one arrives at the claim:

$$\left(\frac{a}{s}\right)^2 = \frac{t}{a} = 2 \cdot \frac{s}{a}$$

1. Cube: $V_1 = s^3$

2. Cube: $V_2 = a^3$

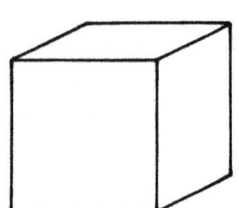

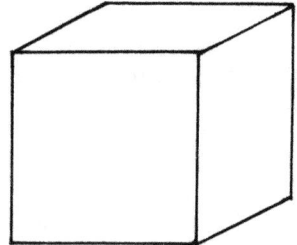

If one wants to transform a particular cube with $s = s_1$ cm, then one has to construct a_1 using similar figures:

$$s_1 : a_1 = s : a$$

Remark: See the remark at the end of the construction of the angle trisection discussion!

A generalization of the conchoid construction

The linear trifolium

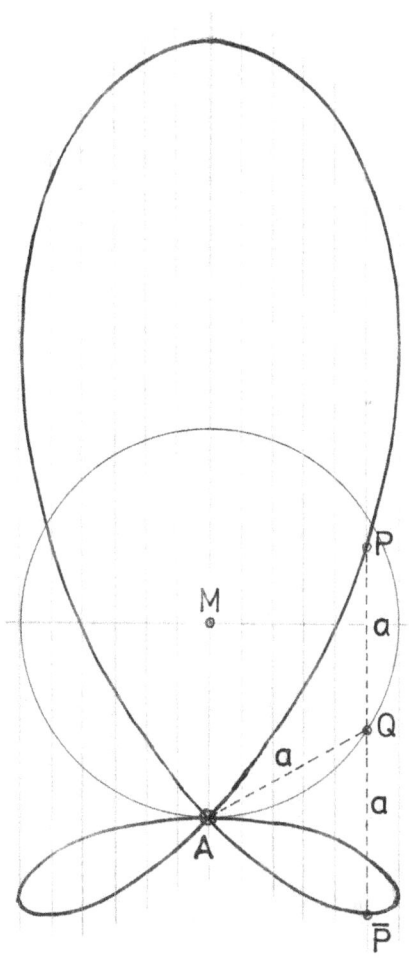

The construction of the conchoid featured in the first section can be generalized as follows: *A line pencil centered on a point S cuts a given curve k. At each point Q where a line of the line pencil intersects the curve, one measures from Q a line segment of length a, in both directions. The resulting points P and $\overline{P}$ lie on the (generalized) conchoid.*

When the curve k is a line and a is a constant, one obtains thereby the conchoid of Nikomedes. When k is a circle and a a constant, one obtains the circle conchoid. Depending on the position of S in respect to the circle k, and the length a of the segments to be measured off, there arise a variety of interesting conchoid forms which deserve their own discussion.

A further generalization suggests itself: the length a is not constant, but is determined for each line of the pencil through a further construction. In the following discussion, a fixed point A is chosen, and then $a = AQ$.

If, in particular, A lies on the circle with center M and one chooses a line pencil that is parallel to the line AM, one obtains thereby a 3-leaved curve form, that was investigated first in 1890 by B. de Longchamps and H. Brocard, who named it originally *trifolium droit*; today it is known as the *torpedo curve*.[30]

---

[30] See Dennis Lawrence, A Catalog of Special Plane Curves, Dover, New York, 2014. There, the torpedo curve is shown to be the pedal curve of Steiner's curve (three-cusped hypocycloid).

Two-leaved forms

If the pole A is chosen on the horizontal diameter, one obtains a 2-leaved form, that – depending on the position of the pole – can appear as a figure-eight, as a two-leaved form with cusp, or as two separated ovals,

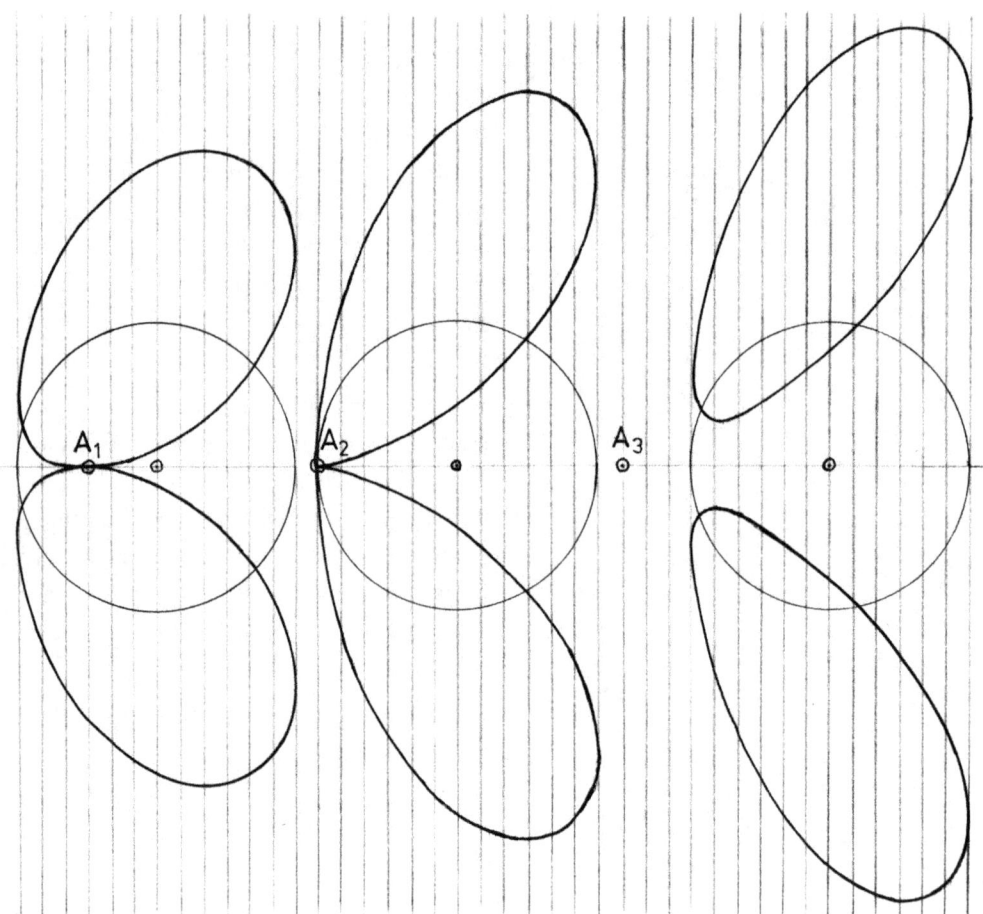

If the pole A_2 lies on the left edge of the circle (as in the middle figure), one gets the two-leaved form, where a cusp from inside meets the leaf transition in the pole point.

If the pole A_1 lies inside the circle (left figure), then two ovals meet in a figure-eight form in the pole point.

If the pole A_3 lies outside the circle (right figure), then the curve consists of two disconnected ovals.

Transition from two-leaved to three-leaved form

If you let the pole point A move along the lower half of the circle, one obtains a transition from two-leaved to three-leaved forms, as shown in the following figures.

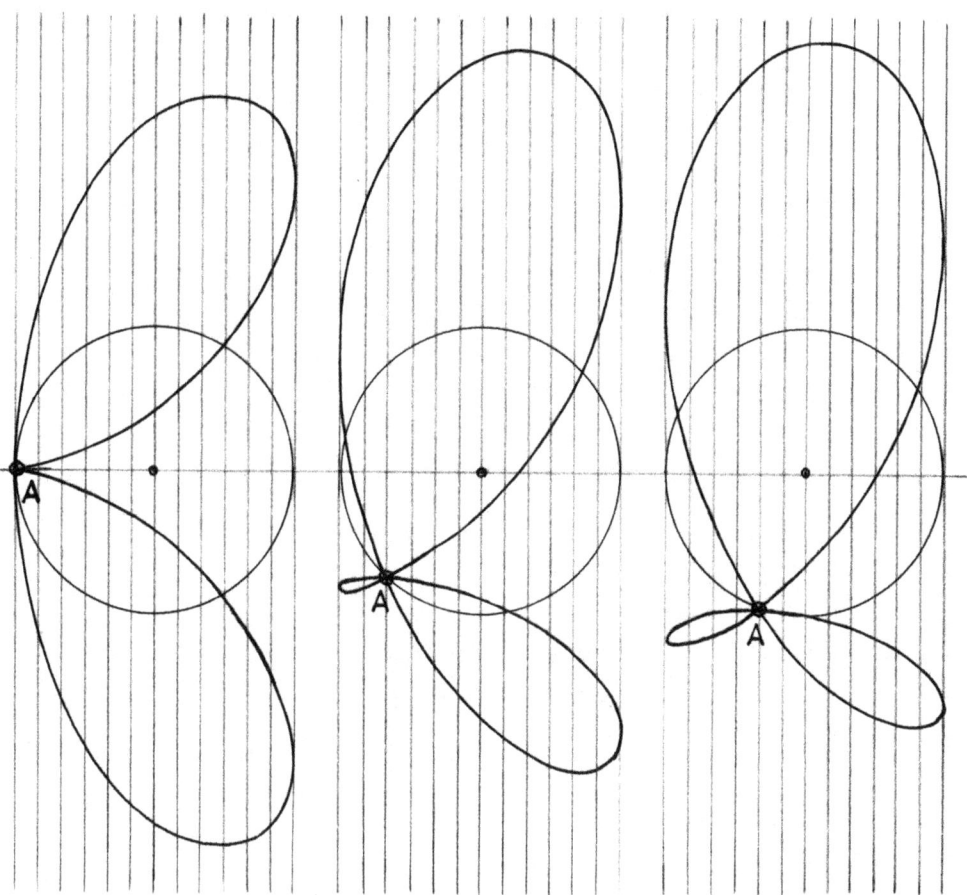

The cusp blows itself out into a small leaf loop and the what had been the lower leaf becomes smaller. The further the pole moves down along the circle, the large becomes the left lower leaf, while the right lower leaf shrinks further.

When the pole arrives at the lowest point of the circle, the two leaves have become the same size and symmetrical, one has arrived at the three-leaved form shown at the beginning of the discussion.

One can vary the curve in many ways, for example, one can move the pole A to new positions with respect to the circle. But it's also possible to replace the circle with other curves, for example, with a line. Or, one can replace the parallel line pencil with an ordinary one.

As beautiful as this family of curve forms is, one must nonetheless be careful not to get lost within it. The unified construction principle must always allow an overview of the curve, as well as insight into the inner connections. The same goes, of course, for the other families of curves treated here.

The treatment of locus-curves can be easily extended through many interesting types of curves: for example, the epicycles, the Ptolemy used to explain the path of the planets, also the Cassini curves including the lemniscate, that represents an important spiritual and corporeal formative principle.

Now I'd like to give hints to literature that deals with how to draw locus-curves.

The treatment of parabola, ellipse, and hyperbola is presented in a very accessible way in the book by Ernst Bindel, "Die Kegelschnitte. Ihre zeichnerische Gewinnung und ihre Beziehung zum Menschen". (Verlag Freies Geistesleben, Stuttgart).

An equally valuable treasure of the first rank is Louis Locher-Ernst: "Geometrisieren im Bereich wichtigster Kurvenformen". (New edition from Verlag am Goetheanum, Dornach, 1988). The conic sections, the Cassini curves, and the logarithmoid curves[31] are derived on the basis of geometric movements; additionally, spirals and cycloids are dealt with.

Finally, the following works include valuable material:

Arnold Bernhard: "Projektive Geometrie, aus der Raumanschauung zeichnend entwickelt"' (Verlag Freies Geistesleben, Stuttgart), individual chapters.

Louis Locher-Ernst: "Geometrische Metamorphosen" (Philosophisch-Anthroposophischer Verlag am Goetheanum, Dornach), individual chapters.

Louis Locher-Ernst: "Einführung in die freie Geometrie ebener Kurven" (Verlag Birkhäuser, Basel)

7 Concluding observation

What needs to be taken into account, to ensure that the constructive treatment of locus-curves takes place within a healthy working process? The task fortunately lends itself immediately to a learning process in which doing and thinking alternate in a lively way. The precise construction of the individual curve points demands a secure overview of the growing network of lines, circles, and points, and furthermore a calm hand. If the individual points constructed in this way are to be connected in the end to form the desired locus-curve, this activity will be accompanied by fine, almost imperceptible sensory processes. In addition to sight, the sense of self-motion and the sense of equilibrium are the principle senses involved. With "equilibrium" one has in mind of course something more general than the concept as it appears in statics. "Balance" in the widest sense of the word expresses better the intended meaning here. One has only to observe oneself in drawing, as one attempts to connect as precisely as possible with a freehand curve a series of previously-constructed points. With practice, one develops gradually a secure sense for the "right

---

[31] The logarithmoid curves in fact were first introduced by Locher-Ernst in this book.

path", along which the point moves, as it runs along the curve. Deviations from this correct path call forth the necessity of corrections, in order to remove the "imbalances" in the drawing. The sense of balance speaks in this way to the student. – Hence, the practical side of activity in such a course is also a field for training the senses.

All action focuses on the incomplete and is therefore oriented on the future. In contrast, observation focuses on what has become. It is oriented on the past. In this context, the opposition "Expansion – Concentration" can be understand as the double gesture of such a course of study, in the sense of Goethe's poem that begins, "In every breath we breathe two graces share..."[32]

A further process that plays an important role in this course is the creation of inner mental pictures, whereby in this case we are concerned primarily with mobile, not static, pictures.

In connection with our theme, two sorts of mobile mental pictures need to be distinguished. The simpler type is concerned with a single curve, that arises as the trace of a single point moving in a lawful way. Beyond this, one has the other, more difficult type of mental picturing. If for example for a conchoid the distance d of the pole to the guide line remains constant but the length a continuously changes, then the task arises to create an inner picture of how the curve as a whole continuously changes. The fundamental principle of curve-construction remains the same throughout. Such processes lead into the domain of curve metamorphoses. It is too challenging, in general, for 9th graders. It ought to be reserved for the upper classes in the high school, where the theme "metamorphosis" plays also an important role, not only in geometry. Even when drawing several curves according to the same construction principle on a single sheet of paper (p. 88), the emphasis here should be on the individual curve and not on the whole family of curves obtained as the result of transforming a *single* curve. Hence, the treatment of locus-curves in the 9th grade can be seen as a preparation for later comprehension of the concept of metamorphosis in the upper grades.

Finally, we want to consider a peculiarity in the form principle we encountered: the threefold sequence of wave, cusp, and loop. The question is, whether this threefold structure can be seen as a symbol of a reality that extends beyond geometry alone. Not as just an analogy, but as a reality experienced within. Ernst Bindel presented in his book on conic sections a relation between the three characteristic conic section forms and the threefold human being.

Can one find something comparable for the threefold structure of wave, cusp, and loop? With the conchoids, one can connect the wave with the approaching towards a goal, the cusp with the attainment of the goal, and the loop – pushing forward on the other side – with complete penetration, on the one hand, and the appearance of something completely new, on the other.

At the beginning of the human cognition process stands the wrestling with a goal. One has a feeling that it exists. Its exact form lies still in darkness. Then the goal is reached – in *one* moment. The situation, so to speak, "comes to a point". What comes next is an essential crossing-through, and in this something new appears. The loop as a symbol of streaming out from a point,

---

[32] J.W. Goethe "West-Eastern Divan"

along with the appearance of something completely new.

Only to the extent that the teacher him-/herself has found a way, through careful and tentative seeking, to experiencing a real correspondence in this direction, can (or should!) this theme find its way into the classroom instruction. A precondition for this, is that this seeking has led to a genuine inner certainty.

The Irrational in Arithmetic and Geometry

Alternating subtraction and the euclidean algorithm, commensurability, extraction of roots, and continued fractions.

PETER BAUM

1 Preliminary remarks

In the ninth grade, one has, as a general rule, two mathematics main lessons available. One is devoted to arithmetic and algebra, the other to geometry. In many Waldorf schools it's usual that the geometry main lesson concerns conic sections (parabolas, ellipses, and hyperbolas), following a path like that laid out in the book with the same name by Ernst Bindel. I've usually handled conic sections in the context of descriptive geometry [33] and have laid the focus of the main lesson on similarity theory, beginning with the congruence theorems, that follow from the uniqueness of the solution of the corresponding triangle constructions, and leading on to the important theorems (a group centered on the Pythagorean Theorem, the inscribed angle theorem, secant-tangent theorem, the Theorem of Ptolemy). The following article doesn't present the content of a single main lesson, but rather handles partial domains from both main lessons, that are thematically connected and are historically significant. The connection between Pell's Equation and the extraction of square roots is presented in an appendix.

2 An entryway into euclidean geometry

The richer and more varied experience that the pupils made with geometric drawing the the middle school, the clearer can the teacher in the ninth grade work out the conceptual framework of the subject, applying an economy of word and expression necessary for the task. As in other subjects, for example, history and biology, one takes hold of material already handled in the 8th grade, but under a new aspect.

I like to begin the main lesson with a review of constructions with compass and straight edge. What can one achieve with these two drawing aids? To begin with, they allow one to connect two points with a line, and to draw a circle of a given radius centered on a given point. As a description these two statements suffice:

> "I draw a line g through the points A and B."
> "I draw a circle with radius r centered on the point M."

One can strengthen the organizing power of geometry in the student, when in the formulation of such descriptions, one omits all accessory expressions, which served in the middle school the purpose of making the pupil conscious of his activity, in favor of the pure concept of the

---

[33] In many German Waldorf schools it has been traditional to learn descriptive geometry (similar to 2D and 3D technical drawing but laying particular emphasis on perspective drawing) in the skills classes in the 9th and 10th grades.

construction (for example, "I take my compass and put the tip on the point M and rotate it around to draw a circle...", etc.). Of course one can never draw a line completely, but it should always be thought of as a complete whole, in order that one doesn't lose track of possible intersection points. The same goes for circles, one should always keep the complete circle in mind, even when one can or will only draw it only partly on the paper. What gets drawn is in any case only an approximation to what is meant: the objects of geometry (lines, circles, points) are pure objects of thought, that as sense perceptions don't exist. What you might take for an excellent point, carefully brought onto the paper using a freshly sharpened H7 pencil, reveals itself, under magnification, as a mountain of graphite of considerable dimensions. Naturally it isn't our goal here to cultivate philosophical speculations in this direction. But the question of what is a point, what is a line, should be nonetheless brought to the students' attention, in order to awake in them a consciousness for problems involving human cognition.

How one names what one draws is also important. One should use as few different terms and symbols as possible. A collection of tried and tested symbols is found in Figure 1.

The main lesson instruction in a Waldorf school can develop to its full potential, only when the teacher observes the principle of repetition. Thus, the teacher in the ninth grade should also review the basic constructions (perpendicular bisector, perpendicular from a point to a line, parallel lines, angle bisector), which have already (hopefully) been taught in the sixth grade. If a magnitude is given in a basic construction, that means to begin with nothing more than it's given in the drawing. Once you've discussed how to copy a segment and an angle without using a marked ruler or a protractor, just using compass and straight edge, and these constructions been practiced thoroughly, then students can be allowed to use marked rulers and drafting triangles.

The classical triangle constructions involving three given magnitudes offer a rich field for practicing. Comparing real solutions to illusory solutions makes clear the difference between a construction and producing a beautiful drawing. Once a construction has been understood, students can make use of other drawing aids. The precision of a drawing is independent of this. For example, from a point outside a circle one can draw a tangent to the circle very exactly by careful sighting, without constructing it via the Thales circle, but to do so the pupil should first know the construction. Important here is to clarify the concepts of drawing, construction, and precision, which in the previous grades have received hardly any attention.

The amount of time you spend on triangle constructions depends on how thoroughly the class teacher pursued this topic in the middle school. They provide rich material for homework brainteasers, especially for the more gifted students. It's important that one doesn't assign any exercises that don't in fact have solutions. A book providing a systematic overview of triangle constructions with many example exercises has been published by the Klett Verlag .[35]

---

[35] K. Herterich: Die Konstruktion von Dreiecken, Klett Verlag

A, B, C, ...	Points
a, b, c, ...	Segments or lines
ABC	Triangle
abc	Trilateral[34]
ab=C	Intersection point of lines a and b
AB=c	Joining lines of points A uand B
$\overline{AB}$	Segment between points A and B
∠ab	Angle between the rays a and b
α, β, γ, ...	Angles
∠ABC = β	The angle in triangle ABC with apex B
$a \parallel b$	Parallel lines
$a \perp b$	Line a is perpendicular to line b
P ∈ g	Point P lies on the line g
g ∈ P	Line g passes through the P
P ∉ g	Point P does not lie on the line g
g ∉ P	LIne g does not pass through the point P
M_a, M_b, M_c	Midpoints of the triangle sides a, b, c
m_a, m_b, m_c	Perpendicular bisectors of triangel sides a, b, c
$w_\alpha, w_\beta, w_\gamma$	Angle bisectors of triangle
s_a, s_b, s_c	Medians of triangle
h_a, h_b, h_c	Altitudes of triangle
H_a, H_b, H_c	Bases of altitudes of triangle
△ABC ≅ △DEF	Triangles ABC and DEF are congruent
△ABC ∼ △DEF	Triangles ABC and DEF are similar

Figure 1: Notation

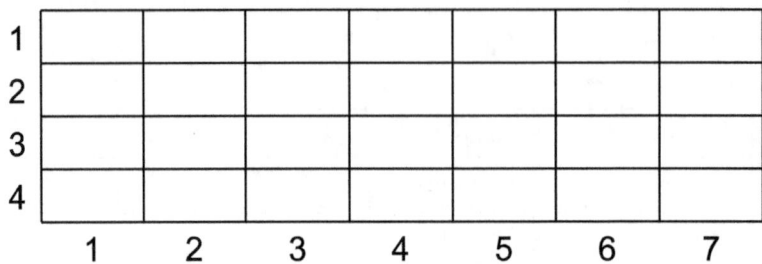

Figure 2: Area calculation

3 Measurement

In the ninth grade one also carries out calculation of surface areas and volumes of solid bodies. Before or after, it's a good idea to discuss measurement *per se*.

What is measurement? What exactly is measured?

It turns out that a measurement, reduced to essentials, is a kind of counting. You count how often a particular chosen magnitude, the unit measurement, can be fitted into a magnitude of the same type. In general, one wants to compare two magnitudes of the same type with the help of a third. Lengths have to be measured with lengths, weights with weights, areas with areas, etc. With regard to the measurement of surface areas and volumes of solid bodies, there is a common misconception, that you measure these by measuring lengths, and that the surface area is then the product of two of these lengths; and the volume, the product of three. In reality, however, also in this case one counts how often a standard area – the unit area – fits into the surface to be measured, and how often the standard volume fits into the solid body to be measured. That the unit of area is typically a square means that to find the area of a rectangle one can shorten the counting process by multiplying the number of rows (or fitted-in squares) by the number of columns. Measuring the side lengths of the rectangle serves then only to arrive at the number of columns and the number of rows. This is obvious when one chooses a rectangle rather than a square as the unit area:

Also here (Figure 2) is the measurement of the surface area (the number of unit areas) given by the product of the number of columns and the number of rows – here $4 \cdot 7 = 28$ – and, in fact, not a "product" of lengths, which is erroneously suggested by the standard written form $m \cdot m = m^2$. That one can "calculate" in this way in physics with units of measurement, requires a special justification and will not concern us here further.

How exact can a measurement be?

When you measure a segment, the unit of length is fitted into the segment as often as it goes, say, four times. Then, in general, a segment is left over, smaller than the unit of length. Thus, the segment to be measured is larger than four and smaller than five meters. This result is for most applications not good enough: hence, one measures the remainder with a smaller unit of length, the centimeter. But also here the same problem arises: there is usually a segment left over that is shorter than a centimeter. For some situations the precision may be enough, for example, for the length of a garden bed. But in many cases one measures the remainder again, with a smaller unit of length, the millimeter. But also here, it's often the case that a segment is left over, this time smaller than a millimeter. We notice: the situations in which the unit of length fits exactly into the segment to be measured, are actually exceptional. For practical measurement, this doesn't make any difference: one uses smaller and smaller fractions of a meter as units of length, until the precision is sufficient for the particular application. In measurement technology, one arrives in any case eventually at a limit, beyond which the measurement becomes meaningless. The smallest unit of measurement, that is technically feasible, then fits a whole number of times into the magnitude to be measured, with an insignificant remainder.

Is this also theoretically so? Given two segments, is it always possible to find a third segment – a unit of length – such that both segments are a whole-number multiple of the unit of length?

If one constructs a rectangle from the two given segments (as the rectangle's sides), then this question can be so phrased: is there a square which can be used to tile the rectangle (cover it completely without overlap)?

If such a square exists, one says that the two segments are *commensurable*, that is, they have a common measure. If such a square doesn't exist, one says the sides of the rectangle are *incommensurable*.

For example, the segments $a = 3,40$ m and $b = 4,10$ m have the common measure $c = 0,1$ m = 1 dm, since $a = 34c$ and $b = 41c$, and the rectangle's area can be covered with $34 \cdot 41 = 1394$ squares with side-length $c = 1$ dm. Of course, any fraction of the form $c:n$ is also a common measure of a und b.

After making the problem clear to the pupils by discussion of further examples, one can search for a procedure to find the largest square which tiles a given rectangle. Use a piece of graph paper to develop the procedure of "alternating subtraction" on these examples:

$$a = 12\,\text{cm},\ b = 5\,\text{cm} \qquad a = 12\,\text{cm},\ b = 7\,\text{cm} \qquad a = 20\,\text{cm},\ b = 12\,\text{cm}$$

The smaller rectangle side b is laid out along the longer side a as often as it fits. This produces a remainder c mit $c < b$. This remainder c is then laid out along b as often as possible, until there remains a segment d mit $d < c$, etc. On the graph paper, at some point there won't be any remainder left. The square with side-length given by the last non-vanishing remainder is then the desired largest square with tiles the rectangle.

In order that weaker students understand the "recipe", the teacher should carefully prepare a figure on the board in which the individual segments are represented with different colors. A slow treatment will prove to be the most economical in the long run.

Once several appropriate examples have been constructed from beginning to end, then the pupils will be convinced that the remainder has to vanish at some point, and therefore that it's always

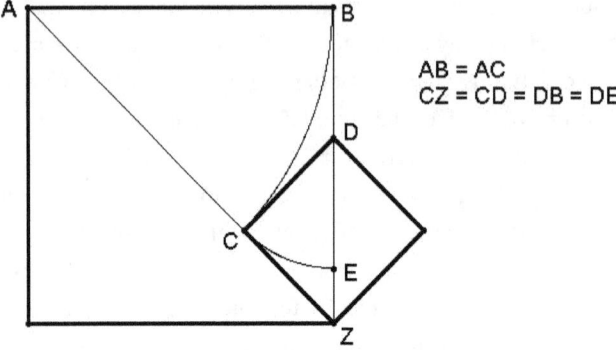

Figure 3: Incommensurable

possible to find a square which fills out the rectangle. They find themselves in good company with the ancient Greeks in this opinion.

It's now possible to clarify the concept of the proportion of two commensurable segments a and b.

If they have two a common measure c, then $a = m \cdot c$ and $b = n \cdot c$, where m and n are whole numbers. The proportion of a to b is then the fraction $\frac{m}{n}$, hence a purely numerical proportion.

Which proportion characterizes then the side of a square and the diagonal of the same square?

To answer this question, we have to seek a common measure. For this, we carry out the process of alternating subtraction: first we lay out the side AD of the square along the diagonal AZ and obtain point C. The perpendicular at C to the diagonal cuts the side of the square in point D. One can then show that the triangle $\triangle CDZ$ is right-angled and isosceles, therefore can be extended to a square, and that $\overline{CD} = \overline{DB}$. The pupils should prove this themselves, for example, using triangle congruence theorems that they already know.

The continuation of the "alternating subtraction" leads to laying out the diagonal remainder $\overline{CZ}$ along the square side $\overline{BZ}$ as often as possible. By the previous remark, this leads at first to point D, a second laying out leads to point E. This second step can be described as "laying out the side of a square (CD) along its diagonal (DZ)" – this is obviously just a smaller version of the "alternating subtraction" that we began with (laying out side AD along the diagonal AZ). So we can never come to an end, there will always be a non-vanishing remainder. Consequently, there is no common measure of the side of a square and its diagonal; we say these lengths are incommensurable.

On the other hand, the diagonal can be calculated using the Pythagorean Theorem: for $a = 1$ m we obtain $d^2 = 2 \cdot a^2$ and $d = \sqrt{2} \cdot a$, so $d = \sqrt{2}$ m. Accordingly, $\frac{d}{a} = \frac{\sqrt{2}\,\text{m}}{1\,\text{m}} = \frac{\sqrt{2}}{1} = \sqrt{2}$ and it follows from the foregoing that it isn't possible to write $\sqrt{2}$ as an ordinary fraction.

A further example of incommensurable segments is provided by the regular pentagon, whose construction should have already been handled in the middle school. This can either be repeated now, or introduced for the first time. Less well-known, but more transparent and beautiful than the standard construction is the following construction of the pentagon from the circumcircle (see Figure 4):

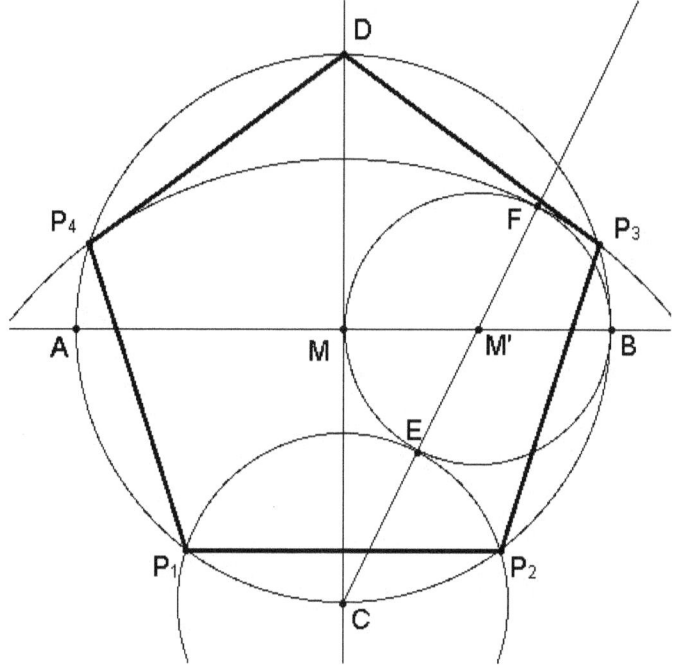

Figure 4: construction of the pentagon from the circumcircle

1. Circle centered on M of radius r

2. Diameters AB and CD with AB⊥CD

3. Radius $r =$ MB is bisected byM'

4. Line CM'

5. The circle centered on M' with radius $r' =$ MM' cuts the line CM' in E and F

6. The circles centered on C with radii $r_1 =$ CE and $r_2 =$ CF cut the circumcircle in the points P_1, P_2, P_3, P_4. The fifth point is D.

One can also draw the regular pentagon with the help of its characteristic angles: $\alpha = 36°$, $\beta = 2\alpha = 72°$, $\gamma = 3\alpha = 108°$. But first one should allow the pupils to discover that these are in fact the angles that occur. The following considerations are one possible way to do this (compare Figure ??):

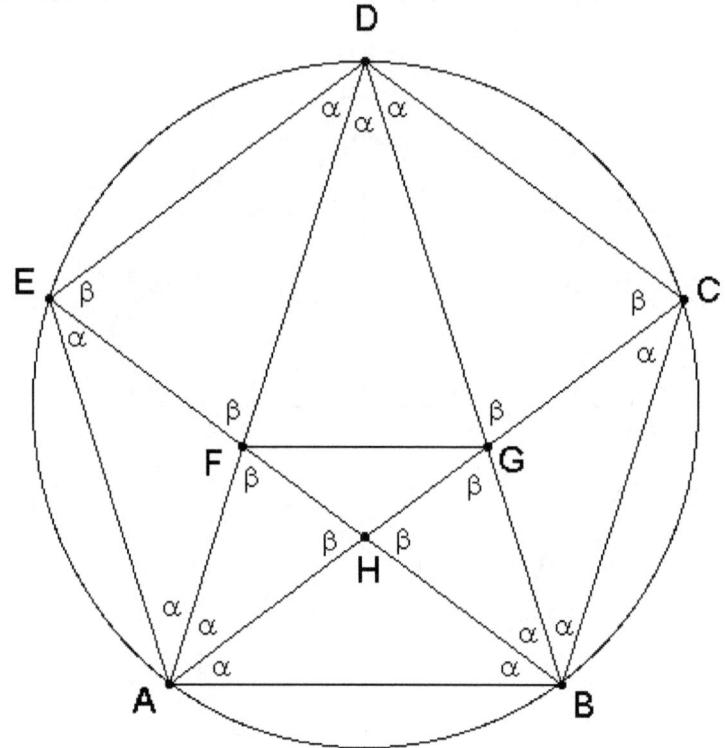

Figure 5: the angles in the pentagon

We draw four diagonals in the pentagon and obtain the intersection points F, G, and H. Let α denote the inscribed angles of the pentagon sides, while β and γ denote the inscribed angles on the pentagon diagonals. Then it is immediately clear that $\gamma = 3\alpha$ and $\beta = 2\alpha$. From the angle sum of a triangle it then follows that $5\alpha = 180°$, hence $\alpha = 36°$ and therefore $\beta = 72°$ and $\gamma = 108°$.

By the Exterior Angle Theorem, the angles at F, G, and H are also $\beta = 2\alpha$. Hence the seven triangles DEF, CDG, FGD, AHE, BHC, ABF, and ABG are isosceles and congruent, that is, DF, DG, HE, HC, AG, and BF have the same length as a pentagon side.

We now ask about the proportion of a diagonal of the pentagon to a side of the pentagon, and seek a common measure using the procedure of "alternating subtraction". Removing the side from the diagonal AD leads to the point F. The remainder AF has now to be removed from the pentagon side. Since $\overline{AF} = \overline{FG} = \overline{GB}$ and the angles at the vertices F and G equal 36° und 72°, the trapezoid ABGF can be extended by addition of a fifth point to a regular pentagon, in which AG is a diagonal. Then the task of laying off the remainder AF along a side of the original pentagon is a smaller version of the original task of laying out a pentagon side along its diagonal. Hence there is once again a remainder, for example, the segment HG, which, by the foregoing, will be the side of a smaller regular pentagon, in which the segment AF = FG is the diagonal. Since by this "alternating subtraction" there always is a non-vanishing remainder, the side and diagonal of a regular pentagon are incommensurable.

The geometric procedure of "alternating subtraction" has an arithmetic analogy that becomes obvious when one writes out the preceding three numerical examples (in Section 3 on p. 107):

$$12\,\text{cm} = 2 \cdot 5\,\text{cm} + 2\,\text{cm} \qquad\qquad 12\,\text{cm} = 1 \cdot 7\,\text{cm} + 5\,\text{cm}$$
$$5\,\text{cm} = 2 \cdot 2\,\text{cm} + 1\,\text{cm} \qquad\qquad 7\,\text{cm} = 1 \cdot 5\,\text{cm} + 2\,\text{cm}$$
$$2\,\text{cm} = 2 \cdot 1\,\text{cm} \qquad\qquad\qquad\;\; 5\,\text{cm} = 2 \cdot 2\,\text{cm} + 1\,\text{cm}$$
$$2\,\text{cm} = 2 \cdot 1\,\text{cm}$$

$$20\,\text{cm} = 1 \cdot 12\,\text{cm} + 8\,\text{cm}$$
$$12\,\text{cm} = 1 \cdot 8\,\text{cm} + 4\,\text{cm}$$
$$8\,\text{cm} = 2 \cdot 4\,\text{cm}$$

The measure of side length of the square obtained by this procedure is a common divisor of the measure of both rectangle sides, and, in fact, the largest such divisor.

4 The euclidean algorithm and continued fractions

The arithmetic procedure to find the greatest common divisor of two whole numbers (for example 854 and 679), is called the *euclidean algorithm*. It is described in the beginning of the seventh book of Euclid's "Elements", and should actually be handled in the middle school in connection with the greatest common divisor (GCD) and the least common multiple (LCM). It goes like this:

1. How often does 679 go into 854? 1 time, one writes the 1 above, between the 854 and 679.

2. What is the remainder? For this, write 1 times 679 underneath the 854, calculates the difference 175 and puts this remainder to the right of the 679. Then the process is repeated, with 679 and 175:

3. How often does 175 go into 679? 3 times, one writes the 3 above, between 679 and 175.

4. What's the remainder? 3 times 175 is 525, taken away from 679 leaves a remainder of 154, etc.

In this way one obtains the following layout:

$$
\begin{array}{cccccccccc}
& 1 & & 3 & & 1 & & 7 & & 3 \\
854 & : & 679 & : & 175 & : & 154 & : & 21 & : & 7 \\
-679 & & -525 & & -154 & & -147 & & -21 & \\
\hline
175 & & 154 & & 21 & & 7 & & 0 &
\end{array}
$$

The last non-zero remainder, in this case 7, is the largest common divisor of 854 and 679.

A second example: What is the greatest common divisor of 741 and 559?

$$
\begin{array}{ccccccccc}
& 1 & & 3 & & 14 & \\
741 & : & 559 & : & 182 & : & \mathbf{13} \\
-559 & & -546 & & -182 & \\
\hline
182 & & 13 & & 0 &
\end{array}
$$

The corresponding equations with remainders are as follows:

$$741 = 1 \cdot 559 + 182 \qquad 559 = 3 \cdot 182 + 13 \qquad 182 = 14 \cdot 13 + 0$$

The GCD of 741 and 559 is therefore 13.

From this one can write the following equations based on fractions:

$$\frac{741}{559} = 1 + \frac{182}{559} \qquad \frac{559}{182} = 3 + \frac{13}{182} \qquad \frac{182}{13} = 14 + 0$$

The pupils discover:

- the first fraction of an equation is the inverse of the last fraction of the previous equation, and

- the last fraction of an equation is always reduced to simplest terms.

Since

$$\frac{13}{182} = \frac{1}{\frac{182}{13}} = \frac{1}{14}$$

and

$$\frac{182}{559} = \frac{1}{\frac{559}{182}} = \frac{1}{3 + \frac{13}{182}} = \frac{1}{3 + \frac{1}{14}}$$

one obtains

$$\frac{741}{559} = 1 + \frac{1}{3 + \frac{1}{14}}.$$

These "continued fractions" can be calculated starting on the right to get:

$$3 + \frac{1}{14} = \frac{42}{14} + \frac{1}{14} = \frac{43}{14}$$

$$1 + \frac{14}{43} = \frac{43}{43} + \frac{14}{43} = \frac{57}{43}$$

thus $\frac{741}{559} = \frac{57}{43}$. This is the fraction obtained when you divide through by the common factor 13. If you want a fraction of about the same value with a smaller numerator and denominator, you can replace $3 + \frac{1}{14}$ with 3 to get $\frac{741}{559} \approx 1 + \frac{1}{3} = \frac{4}{3}$. In fact, $\frac{741}{559} = \frac{57}{43} = 1,32558$ and $\frac{4}{3} = 1,3\overline{3}$ are almost exactly the same.

An interesting application for continued fractions is provided by the comparison of temporal rhythms. Here are the average values of the year and month rhythms[36]:

Tropical solar year:	365,242 199 d
Sidereal solar year:	365,256 366 d
Synodic month:	29,530 588 d
Sidereal month:	27,321 661 d
Tropical month:	27,321 582 d
Draconic month:	27,212 220 d
Anomalistic month:	27,554 550 d
Period of moon nodes:	6.793,50 d

The tropical solar year is the time it takes for the seasons to return, hence the time between two spring or fall equinoxes or two summer or winter solstices. A calendar year should ideally be just so long that such seasonal points always occur on the same date of the calendar. But a calendar year can only have a whole number of days, that is, either 365 – which is too short – or 366, which is too long. The question arises, how can one find a regular rhythm of interleaving short and long years, so that in the long run the dates of the seasons don't shift around?

In this context it's appropriate to make a short astronomical side-tour in order to understand the calendar better.

If we are located in the Northern Hemisphere of the earth and follow the path of the sun in the heavens on March 21, we see it rises almost exactly in the east at 6 am, and moves during the course of the day along the southern skies, before setting at 6pm almost exactly in the west. It moves on this day along a particular great circle of the celestial sphere, the *celestial equator*. In winter the sun moves below this great circle and in summer, above it. For this reason, in winter it rises in the south-east and sets in the south-west, the day is short and the night is long, while in summer it rises in the northeast, sets in the northwest, the days are long and the nights are short.

---

[36] Numerical values are taken from
W.Winnenburg: Einführung in die Astronomie, Mannheim 1990

Early in the year on March 20 or 21, there is a moment in which the sun is located exactly on the celestial equator. This position in the heavens is called the spring equinox. In 2014 the sun passed through the equinox point at 16:57 GT on March 20, and in 2015 at 22:45 GT on March 20.

The time it takes for the sun to return to the spring equinox point is called the *tropical solar year*. Since this time is almost six hours longer than 365 days, we can't let every year have 365 days. That would have the consequence, that after 4 years the sun would arrive at the spring equinox on March 22, and after $4 \cdot 30 = 120$ years it would arrive only 30 days later, that is, on April 21. That would mean that eventually every month would sooner or later arrive at the height of summer, which would make long-term planning quite impractical. Therefore, every four years one makes the year a day longer, this year is called a *leap year*, and contains a February 29. That would be the final solution of the calendar problem, if the tropical solar year was exactly 6 hours longer than 365 days. But, since it's actually somewhat shorter, one has to make a further correction after a while.

Which corrections come into consideration, can be discovered via the continued fraction and its approximating fractions.

Expressing the days in a tropical year as a fraction yields $365.2422 = \frac{3652422}{10000}$ and following the above scheme:

	365		4		7		1	
3652422	:	10000	:	2422	:	312	:	
-3650000		-9688		-2184		-238		
2422		312		238		74		

	3		4		1		1		1		2	
238	:	74	:	16	:	10	:	6	:	4	:	2
-222		-64		-10		-6		-4		-4		
16		10		6		4		2		0		

The continued fraction is hence:

$$365.2422 = 365 + \cfrac{1}{4 + \cfrac{1}{7 + \cfrac{1}{1 + \cfrac{1}{3 + \cfrac{1}{4 + \cfrac{1}{1 + \cfrac{1}{1 + \cfrac{1}{1 + \frac{1}{2}}}}}}}}}$$

This yields a series of fractions for the approximation of the fractional part of the solar year:

$$\frac{1}{4} \quad \frac{7}{29} \quad \frac{8}{33} \quad \frac{31}{128} \quad \frac{132}{545} \quad \frac{163}{673} \quad \frac{295}{1218} \quad \frac{458}{1891} \quad \frac{1211}{5000}$$

They represent, the fraction of a day which a solar year is longer than 365 days. One can read off from these values, how many extra days have to be inserted in how many years: in 4 years, one extra day or in 29 years, 7 extra days or in 33 years, 8 extra days, etc. The fourth approximation is pretty exact:

$$\frac{31}{128} = \frac{32}{128} - \frac{1}{128} = \frac{1}{4} - \frac{1}{128}$$

If one would use this value to arrange the leap years, then one would have to – just as in the Gregorian calendar – make every fourth year a leap year, but then after 128 years, leave it out, and it would last around 80,000 years before one would have to correct the calendar.

In the actual Gregorian calendar, the leap years are the years which are divisible by 4. But among the years which are multiples of 100, only every fourth one (those divisible by 400) are leap years, for example, 1600, 2000, 2400 (compare to DIN-1355). In this way one obtains the following length of a tropical year:

$$365 + \frac{1}{4} - \frac{1}{100} + \frac{1}{400} = 365 + 0,25 - 0,001 + 0,0025 = 365,2425$$

Hence the Gregorian year is, on average, $365,2425 - 365,242198 = 0,000302$ days too long, so that in 3311 years one has to replace a leap year with an ordinary year.

Another application example arises through the question, when solar and lunar eclipses repeat themselves. A solar eclipse can only occur when the moon passes in front of the sun, that is, when it's a new moon. A lunar eclipse can only occur when the earth passes between the sun and the earth, that is, when it's full moon. The time between the repetition of a given phase of the moon is called a *synodic month* (Synode = coincidence of sun and moon, for example, in a new moon) or *lunation*. It has the average value of $L = 29,530588$ days or $L = 29$ d 12 h 44 m $2,8$ s.

It's not always the case that at a new moon, the moon lies exactly on the ecliptic, that is, directly in front of the sun. The path of the moon in the heavens is sometimes above the ecliptic, sometimes below. The points, at which the moon crosses over the ecliptic, are called the *nodes* of the moon. At a rising node, the moon, viewed from the northern hemisphere on the earth, moves from below the ecliptic to above it, that is, from south to north, while at a falling node it moves from above to below, that is, from north to south. The repetition of the position of the moon node is called the *draconian month*, since only then can a lunar or solar eclipse (derived from *ecliptic*) can occur. The term draconian reflects the old belief that at an eclipse, a dragon swallowed the sun or the moon. The draconian month has an average value of $L = 27,21222$ days or $D = 27$ d 5 h 05 m 36 s. An eclipse can repeat when a whole number of synodic months and a whole number of draconian months have passed by. To arrive at this period, we calculate the proportion $L : D$ in a continued fraction:

	1		11		1		2		1
2953059	:	2721222	:	231837	:	171015	:	60822	:
-2721222		-2550207		-171015		-121644		-49371	
231837		171015		60822		49371		11451	

	4		3		4		1		3		10		6	
49371	:	11451	:	3567	:	750	:	567	:	183	:	18	:	3
-45804		-10701		-3000		-567		-549		-180		-18		
3567		750		567		183		18		3		0		

The continued fraction therefore is:

$$\frac{2953059}{2721222} = 1 + \cfrac{1}{11 + \cfrac{1}{1 + \cfrac{1}{2 + \cfrac{1}{1 + \cfrac{1}{4 + \cfrac{1}{3 + \cfrac{1}{4 + \cfrac{1}{1 + \cfrac{1}{3 + \cfrac{1}{10 + \frac{1}{6}}}}}}}}}}$$

The approximation fractions are:

$$\frac{L}{D} \approx \frac{12}{11}, \frac{13}{12}, \frac{38}{35}, \frac{51}{47}, \frac{242}{223}, \frac{777}{716}, \frac{3350}{3087}, \frac{4127}{3803},$$

$$\frac{15731}{14496}, \frac{161437}{148763}, \frac{984353}{907074}$$

The numerator represents the number of draconian months (D) and the denominator, the number of synodic months (S), after which a full moon (approximately) once again occurs on a moon node. We calculate this length of time for the first seven approximate fractions and put them into a table:

Z	N	S·Z (Days)	L·N (Days)	Difference (Days)	Difference (Hours)	S·Z (Years)
12	11	326.54664	324.83649	1.7102	41.045	0.894
13	12	353.75886	354.36708	-0.6082	-14.597	0.969
38	35	1034.06436	1033.57065	0.4937	11.849	2.831
51	47	1387.82322	1387.93773	-0.1145	-2.748	3.800
242	223	6585.35724	6585.32157	0.0357	0.857	**18.030**
777	716	21143.89494	21143.90244	-0.0075	-0.180	57.890
3350	3087	91160.93700	91160.93133	0.0057	0.137	249.590

The fifth approximation yields 18.03 years, called the Saros period, which was already known to the Chaldeans in 600 B. C. With this period, the lunar eclipse repeats itself, on average, 45 times, and the solar eclipse, 70 times. The eclipses of the Saros series begin as partial eclipses, become gradually better until they become total eclipses, then gradually disappear again after a partial phase. Within a Saros period, there are on average 42 different solar eclipses and 27 different lunar eclipses. Also the fourth approximation of 3.8 years provides cycles of eclipses, which however repeat much less often because the difference in the 6th column is almost 3 hours.

A third example is the question, when does the full moon return to exactly the same position with respect to the fixed stars? For this, one has to calculate the ratio of the synodic month $L = 29,530588^d$ to the sidereal month $S = 27,321661^d$ (the time it takes the moon to return to a fixed star):

	1		12		2		1	
29530588	:	27321661	:	2208927	:	814537	:
-27321661		-26507124		-1629074		-579853	
2208927		814537		579853		234684	

	2		2		8		17		1
579853	:	234684	:	110485	:	13714	:	773	:
-469368		-220970		-109712		-13141		-573	
110485		13714		773		573		200	

	2		1		6		2		2		5	
573	:	200	:	173	:	27	:	11	:	5	:	1
-400		-173		-162		-22		-10		-5		
173		27		11		5		1		0		

The continued fraction is thus:

$$\frac{29530588}{27321661} = 1 + \cfrac{1}{12 + \cfrac{1}{2 + \cfrac{1}{1 + \cfrac{1}{2 + \cfrac{1}{2 + \cfrac{1}{8 + \cfrac{1}{17 + \cfrac{1}{1 + \cfrac{1}{2 + \cfrac{1}{1 + \cfrac{1}{6 + \cfrac{1}{2 + \cfrac{1}{2 + \frac{1}{5}}}}}}}}}}}}}}$$

The approximating fractions are given by

$$\frac{L}{S} \approx \frac{13}{12},\ \frac{27}{25},\ \frac{40}{37},\ \frac{107}{99},\ \frac{254}{235},\ \frac{2139}{1979},\ \frac{36617}{33878},\ \ldots$$

The numerator represents the number of sidereal months and the denominator, then number of synodic months, after which the full moon once more appears in the same position with respect to the fixed stars. We calculate these values and combine them into a table:

Z	N	S·Z (Days)	L·N (Days)	Difference (Days)	Difference (Hours)	S·Z (Years)
13	12	355.181593	354.367056	0.814537	19.549	0.972
27	25	737.684847	738.264700	-0.579853	-13.916	2.020
40	37	1092.86644	1092.631756	0.234684	5.632	2.992
107	99	2923.417727	2923.528212	-0.110485	-2.652	8.004
254	235	6939.701894	6939.688180	0.013714	0.329	**19.000**
2139	1979	58441.032879	58441.033652	-0.000773	-0.019	160.006

The fifth approximation provides the Metonic cycle of almost exactly 19 years. After this length of time, the phases of the moon once again occur on the same dates. This cycle plays an important role in the determination of the date of Easter.

5 Calculation of square roots

The ability to have an overview of the various phases of a process and also to be able to identify the current phase, is helpful in every profession. It can be practiced particularly well in reckoning exercises. In the following examples this aspect stands in the foreground and not so much the practical application, which in the age of calculating machines has lost some of its significance.

Sometimes the pupils are acquainted with the standard procedure for calculating square roots from the middle school:

$$\sqrt{10'30'41} = 321$$
$$\underline{-9'00'00}$$
$$1'30'41 \quad 62 \cdot 2$$
$$\underline{-1'24'00}$$
$$0'06'41 \quad 641 \cdot 1$$
$$\underline{-06'41}$$
$$0$$

Applied to numbers of roughly this size, the procedure is usable and the students ought at some point to be acquainted with it.

The procedure gets to be quite tedious from around the 5th decimal place. There is a recursive formula that is more comfortable to use, that arises from a procedure of Rafaele Bombelli (1572), and which provides the average value of the Heron algorithm (an ancient method for calculating square roots).

Bombelli proceeded as follows, using the example of $\sqrt{13}$:
A first approximation is 3, let the remainder be x. Then $\sqrt{13} = 3+x$, hence $13 = 9+6\cdot x+x^2$.
From this follows $x = \frac{2}{3} - \frac{x^2}{6}$, and thus one obtains by ignoring x^2, the second approximation
$\sqrt{13} \approx 3+\frac{2}{3} = \frac{11}{3}$. Now one can repeat the procedure with this better approximation and sets
$\sqrt{13} = \frac{11}{3}+x$,, which leads to $13 = \frac{121}{9} + \frac{22}{3}\cdot x+x^2$ and $x = -\frac{4}{9}\cdot\frac{3}{22} - \frac{3x^2}{22}$, so the third approximation is $\sqrt{13} \approx \frac{11}{3} - \frac{2}{33} = \frac{119}{33}$.

The general recursive formula is obtained as follows:

Let z be the root, z^2 the given number, and z_1 the first approximation. Then

$$z = z_1 + x \qquad (4)$$
$$z^2 = z_1^2 + 2\cdot z_1 \cdot x + x^2$$
$$x = \frac{z^2 - z_1^2}{2z_1} - \frac{x^2}{2z_1}$$

Substituting for x in 4 leads to

$$z = z_1 + \frac{z^2 - z_1^2}{2z_1} - \frac{x^2}{2z_1} < z_1 + \frac{z^2 - z_1^2}{2z_1} = z_2.$$

From this follows

$$z_2 = \frac{z^2 + z_1^2}{2z_1} = \frac{z^2}{2z_1} + \frac{z_1}{2}$$

and in the next step through the substitution $z = z_2 + x$ repeating the same process gives

$$z_3 = \frac{z^2 + z_2^2}{2z_2} = \frac{z^2}{2z_2} + \frac{z_2}{2}.$$

One obtains the recursive formula

$$z_{n+1} = \frac{z^2}{2z_n} + \frac{z_n}{2}, \qquad (5)$$

with which one obtains better and better values. Then from $z < z_n$ for $n = 2, 3, \ldots$ it follows that $z_{n+1} < z_n$, as $z < z_{n+1} = \frac{z^2}{2z_n} + \frac{z_n}{2} < \frac{z_n^2}{2z_n} + \frac{z_n}{2} = z_n$.

The example $z^2 = 5$ provides the following approximations:

$$z_1 = 2$$
$$z_2 = \frac{5}{2\cdot 2} + 1 = \frac{9}{4}$$
$$z_3 = \frac{5}{2}\cdot\frac{4}{9} + \frac{9}{8} = \frac{161}{72}$$
$$z_4 = \frac{5}{2}\cdot\frac{72}{161} + \frac{161}{144} = \frac{51841}{23184}$$

Already the fourth approximation provides a very accurate result:

$$z_4 = 2,23606797791...$$
$$\sqrt{5} = 2,23606797749...$$

The derivation of the approximation solution following Bombelli has the advantage that it can be applied to arbitrary n^{th} roots:

$$z^n = (z_1 + x)^n = z_1^n + n \cdot z_1^{n-1} \cdot x + ... \tag{6}$$

$$\frac{z^n - z_1^n}{n \cdot z_1^{n-1}} \approx x$$

$$z = z_1 + x \approx z_1 + \frac{z^n - z_1^n}{n \cdot z_1^{n-1}} = \frac{z^n + (n-1)z_1^n}{n \cdot z_1^{n-1}}$$

$$z \approx \frac{z^n + (n-1)z_1^n}{n \cdot z_1^{n-1}}$$

Thus, for example, $\sqrt[3]{30} \approx \frac{30 + 2 \cdot 3^3}{3 \cdot 3^2} = \frac{28}{9}$ and $\sqrt[4]{60} \approx \frac{60 + 3 \cdot 3^4}{4 \cdot 3^3} = \frac{101}{36}$.

The formulas can be improved if one takes into account x^2:

$$x \approx \frac{z^n - z_1^n}{n \cdot z_1^{n-1}}$$

$$x^2 \approx \frac{z^n - z_1^n}{n \cdot z_1^{n-1}} \cdot x$$

If one uses these in the binomial formula6, one obtains the improved approximation

$$x \approx \frac{2z_1(z^n - z_1^n)}{(n-1)z^n + (n+1)z_1^n} \text{ and finally } z \approx z_1 \cdot \frac{(n+1)z^n + (n-1)z_1^n}{(n-1)z^n + (n+1)z_1^n}.$$

For $z^2 = 5$ and $z_1 = 2$, the first step using this formula gives $\sqrt{5} \approx 2 \cdot \frac{3 \cdot 5 + 2^2}{1 \cdot 5 + 3 \cdot 2^2} = \frac{38}{17} = 2.2352...$

These final remarks on higher roots will go over the heads of almost all ninth graders. I include them here, since more and more students ask how one can actually calculate higher roots. The treatment given here offers food for the more capable students and can serve as the basis for a classroom report, also in the higher grades.

6 Square roots and their continued fractions

In conclusion, we want to include some observations on the continued fractions of square roots (of whole numbers). When the pupils calculate the square roots of the natural numbers $n = 2, 3, 5, 6, 7, 8, 10, 11, 12, 13, 14, \ldots$ following the procedure described in the article by Friedrich Hartmann in this volume on page 128, they obtain

$$\sqrt{2} = 1 + \cfrac{1}{1+\sqrt{2}} = [1;\overline{2}] \qquad \sqrt{3} = 1 + \cfrac{1}{1+\cfrac{1}{1+\sqrt{3}}} = [1;\overline{1,2}]$$

$$\sqrt{6} = 2 + \cfrac{1}{2+\cfrac{1}{2+\sqrt{6}}} = [2;\overline{2,4}] \qquad \sqrt{7} = 2 + \cfrac{1}{1+\cfrac{1}{1+\cfrac{1}{2+\sqrt{7}}}} = [2;\overline{1,1,1,4}]$$

$$\sqrt{8} = 2 + \cfrac{1}{1+\cfrac{1}{2+\sqrt{8}}} = [2;\overline{1,4}] \qquad \sqrt{10} = 3 + \cfrac{1}{3+\sqrt{10}} = [3;\overline{6}]$$

$$\sqrt{11} = 3 + \cfrac{1}{3+\cfrac{1}{3+\sqrt{11}}} = [3;\overline{3,6}] \qquad \sqrt{12} = 3 + \cfrac{1}{2+\cfrac{1}{3+\sqrt{12}}} = [3;\overline{2,6}]$$

$$\sqrt{13} = 3 + \cfrac{1}{1+\cfrac{1}{1+\cfrac{1}{1+\cfrac{1}{3+\sqrt{13}}}}} = [3;\overline{1,1,1,1,6}]$$

$$\sqrt{14} = 3 + \cfrac{1}{1+\cfrac{1}{2+\cfrac{1}{1+\cfrac{1}{3+\sqrt{14}}}}} = [3;\overline{1,2,1,6}]$$

The pupils discover, based on these examples:

- The continued fraction has the form

$$\sqrt{n} = a_0 + \cfrac{1}{a_1 + \cfrac{1}{a_2 + \cfrac{1}{a_3 + \ldots + \cfrac{1}{a_{k-1} + \cfrac{1}{a_0 + \sqrt{n}}}}}}, \qquad (7)$$

hence is infinite.

- The continued fraction has a period, that is, there is a natural number k so that $a_k = 2a_0$, $a_{k+m} = a_m$.
- The period has a mirror symmetry, that is, $a_1 = a_{k-1}$, $a_2 = a_{k-2}$, $a_3 = a_{k-3}$ etc.

There remains to make a simple observation which the students are capable of understanding, and which establishes a connection between square roots and continued fractions.

Every natural number n lies between two consecutive square numbers $a^2 \leq n < (a+1)^2$, can therefore be written in the form $n = a^2 + b$ with $a, b \in \mathbb{N}$.

Let $z = \sqrt{n} = \sqrt{a^2 + b}$, that is, $z^2 = a^2 + b$. From this follows:

$$z^2 - a^2 = b$$
$$(z-a) \cdot (z+a) = b$$
$$z = a + \frac{b}{a+z}.$$

One can now substitute this formula for z on the right side and obtains:

$$z = a + \frac{b}{a + \left(a + \frac{b}{a+z}\right)} = a + \frac{b}{ab + \frac{b}{a+z}} \tag{8}$$

Continued substitution leads to the infinite continued fraction

$$\sqrt{n} = a + \frac{b}{2a + \frac{b}{2a+\dots}} \tag{9}$$

with the period $2a$. From this one can easily calculate usable approximations. The smaller that $\frac{b}{2a}$ is, the "better" are these approximations.

A general continued fraction has the form

$$z = a_0 + \frac{b_1}{a_1 + \frac{b_2}{a_2 + \frac{b_3}{a_3 + \dots}}}. \tag{10}$$

If all the partial numerators are the same ($b_i = b$), and if $a_i = 2a_0$, then it is clear that the continued fraction 9 represents the square root $\sqrt{a_0^2 + b}$.

The euclidean algorithm, as well as the procedure given by Friedrich Hartmann in this volume to calculate square roots, always leads to continued fractions in which all the partial denominators are positive whole numbers and all partial numerators b_i have the value 1. Such continued fractions are called *regular*, one can also write them in the more comfortable square bracket notation:

$$\sqrt{n} = a_0 + \frac{1}{a_1 + \frac{1}{a_2 + \frac{1}{a_3 + \dots + \frac{1}{a_{k-1} + \frac{1}{a_0 + \sqrt{n}}}}}} = [a_0, a_1, a_2, a_3, \dots]$$

For which values of b is then the continued fraction in 9 then regular? Apparently for $b = 1$, the period length is then $k = 1$:

$$\sqrt{a^2 + 1} = a + \frac{1}{2a + \frac{1}{2a+\dots}} = [a, \overline{2a}],$$

But also for $b = 2$ one obtains by cancellation a regular continued fraction, with the period length $k = 2$:

$$\sqrt{a^2+2} = a + \cfrac{1}{a + \cfrac{1}{2a + \cfrac{1}{a + \cfrac{1}{2a+\ldots}}}} = [a, \overline{a, 2a}]$$

When $a = b \cdot c$, $c \in \mathbb{N}$, then b and c are divisors of a, and by canceling one obtains a regular continued fraction with the period length $k = 2$:

$$\sqrt{a^2 + \frac{a}{c}} = a + \cfrac{1}{2c + \cfrac{1}{2a + \cfrac{1}{2c + \cfrac{1}{2a+\ldots}}}} = [a, \overline{2c, 2a}] \ .$$

With these formulas one can easily calculate the corresponding regular continued fractions for the square roots of 2, 3, 5, 6, 10, 11, 12, 17, 18, 20, 26, 27, 30, ... For example,

$$\sqrt{39} = \sqrt{6^2 + \frac{6}{2}} = [6; \overline{4, 12}]$$

7 Appendix

The material contained in this section is not intended for the classroom instruction of a 9th grade class, but rather as a compendium of background information for the teacher. Readers who wish to pursue continued fractions further are referred to the literature. [37].

Let n be a natural number, not a square, and $z^2 = n$. Then z can be written as an infinite, repeating continued fraction:

$$z = a_0 + \cfrac{1}{a_1 + \ldots + \cfrac{1}{a_{k-1} + \cfrac{1}{a_0 + z}}} = [a_0, \overline{a_1, a_2, \ldots, a_{k-1}, 2a_0}]. \tag{11}$$

We denote the approximating fraction of an infinite continued fraction as $\frac{p_n}{q_n} = [a_0, a_1, \ldots, a_n]$, yielding

$$\frac{p_0}{q_0} = [a_0] = \frac{a_0}{1}$$

$$\frac{p_1}{q_1} = [a_0, a_1] = a_0 + \frac{1}{a_1} = \frac{a_1 a_0 + 1}{a_1}$$

etc. The denominator and numerator of the approximating fraction satisfy the recursive formulas:

$$p_n = a_n \cdot p_{n-1} + p_{n-2} \tag{12}$$

$$q_n = a_n \cdot q_{n-1} + q_{n-2}. \tag{13}$$

The period sequence for the continued fraction 11 7.1 has a symmetry: $a_k = 2a_0$, $a_{k-i} = a_i$ for $i = 1, 2, \ldots, k-1$. One can also write the continued fraction:

$$z = [a_0, \overline{a_1, a_2, a_3, \ldots, a_3, a_2, a_1, 2a_0}].$$

If one solves the continued fraction equation $z = a_0 + \cfrac{1}{a_1 + \ldots + \cfrac{1}{a_0 + z}}$ beginning on the lower RHS, one obtains an equation of the form $z = \frac{p \cdot z + c}{q \cdot z + d}$ with natural numbers p, q, c and d. From this follows

$$z \cdot (q \cdot z + d) = p \cdot z + c$$

$$q \cdot z^2 + (d - p) \cdot z = c$$

$$(d - p) \cdot z = c - q \cdot n$$

---

[37] Oskar Perron: *Die Lehre von den Kettenbrüchen*, Bd.1, Darmstadt 1977, recommended replacement in English: C. D. Olds, Continued Fractions, Random House, New York, 1963
Harald Scheid: *Zahlentheorie*, 2. Aufl. Mannheim 1994

Since z is not rational, it follows that $d - p = 0$ and $c - q \cdot n = 0$. Thus

$$z = \frac{p \cdot z + n \cdot q}{q \cdot z + p}. \tag{14}$$

This equation is satisfied by all number pairs $(p|q) \neq (0|0)$. Rewriting the continued fraction in 11 as ordinary fractions leads to the unique solution $p = p_{k-1}$, $q = q_{k-1}$ where k is the period of the continued fraction. Then according to the recursive formulas 12 and 13 one has, by substituting $a_n = a_0 + z$:

$$p_k = (a_0 + z) p_{k-1} + p_{k-2} \qquad\qquad q_k = (a_0 + z) q_{k-1} + q_{k-2}$$
$$p_k = p_{k-1} \cdot z + a_0 \cdot p_{k-1} + p_{k-2} \qquad q_k = q_{k-1} \cdot z + a_0 \cdot q_{k-1} + q_{k-2}$$

and hence $z = \frac{p_{k-1} \cdot z + a_0 \cdot p_{k-1} + p_{k-2}}{q_{k-1} \cdot z + a_0 \cdot q_{k-1} + q_{k-2}}$ with $\frac{p}{q} = \frac{p_{k-1}}{q_{k-1}} = [a_0, a_1, \ldots, a_{k-1}]$.

According to a theorem of Lagrange (1752-1833) the numerator and denominator of this fraction are solutions of Pell's Equation; in fact,

$$p^2 - n \cdot q^2 = 1 \qquad \text{when } k \text{ is even}$$
$$p^2 - n \cdot q^2 = -1 \qquad \text{when } k \text{ is odd.}$$

From this it follows that $\left(\frac{p}{q}\right)^2 = n + \frac{1}{q^2}$ (in case k is even), resp., $\left(\frac{p}{q}\right)^2 = n - \frac{1}{q^2}$ (when k is odd). Pell's Equation has infinitely many solutions, and each solution represents an approximating fraction of an infinite continued fraction; in fact

$$p_{mk-1}^2 - n \cdot q_{mk-1}^2 = 1 \qquad \text{with } m = 1, 2, 3, \ldots \text{ when } k \text{ is even and}$$
$$\qquad\qquad\qquad\qquad\qquad\qquad m = 2, 4, 6, \ldots \text{ when } k \text{ is odd}$$
$$p_{mk-1}^2 - n \cdot q_{mk-1}^2 = -1 \qquad \text{with } m = 1, 3, 5, \ldots \text{ when } k \text{ is odd.}$$

The numerator p_{mk-1} and the denominator q_{mk-1} of the approximating fractions for $\sqrt{n}$ can be calculated using the recursive formulas 12 and 13. The following formulas for the calculation of solutions of Pell's Equation from the minimal solution p_{k-1} and q_{k-1}, are simpler:

$$p_{mk-1} = \frac{1}{2}\left[(p_{k-1} + \sqrt{n}q_{k-1})^m + (p_{k-1} - \sqrt{n}q_{k-1})^m\right]$$
$$q_{mk-1} = \frac{1}{2\sqrt{n}}\left[(p_{k-1} + \sqrt{n}q_{k-1})^m - (p_{k-1} - \sqrt{n}q_{k-1})^m\right].$$

When one substitutes on the RHS of 14 the approximation $\frac{p}{q}$ for z, one obtains:

$$z \approx \frac{p \cdot \frac{p}{q} + n \cdot q}{q \cdot \frac{p}{q} + p} = \frac{\frac{p^2}{q} + n \cdot q}{2p} = \frac{1}{2} \cdot \frac{p}{q} + \frac{n}{2} \cdot \frac{q}{p}.$$

If we substitute here $n = z^2$ and $\frac{p}{q} = z_n$, we obtain the formula 5 from Bombelli:

$$z_{n+1} = \frac{z_n}{2} + \frac{z^2}{2z_n}.$$

The new approximating fraction $z_{n+1} = \frac{p'}{q'} = \frac{p^2+nq^2}{2pq}$ also satisfies, as a matter of fact, Pell's Equation. Namely

$$p'^2 - n \cdot q'^2 = (p^2 + nq^2)^2 - n \cdot (2pq)^2$$
$$p'^2 - n \cdot q'^2 = (p^2 - n \cdot q^2)^2$$
$$p'^2 - n \cdot q'^2 = 1$$

The following table contains, for the roots $\sqrt{n}$ of the first 55 integers, the period k of the continued fraction and the minimal solution $p = p_{k-1}$, $q = q_{k-1}$ of Pell's Equation.

n	k	p	q
2	1	1	1
3	2	2	1
5	1	2	1
6	2	5	2
7	4	8	3
8	2	3	1
10	1	3	1
11	2	10	3
12	2	7	2
13	5	18	5
14	4	15	4
15	2	4	1
17	1	4	1
18	2	17	4
19	6	170	39
20	2	9	2
21	6	55	12
22	6	197	42
23	4	24	5
24	2	5	1
26	1	5	1
27	2	26	5
28	4	127	24
29	5	70	13

n	k	p	q
30	2	11	2
31	8	1520	273
32	4	17	3
33	4	23	4
34	4	35	6
35	2	6	1
37	1	6	1
38	2	37	6
39	2	25	4
40	2	19	3
41	3	32	5
42	2	13	2
43	10	3482	531
44	8	199	30
45	6	161	24
46	12	24335	3588
47	4	48	7
48	2	7	1
50	1	7	1
51	2	50	7
52	6	649	90
53	5	182	25
54	6	485	66
55	4	89	12

On Arithmetic and Algebra for the 9th Grade

An instructional example

F.J. HARTMANN

1 Preliminary remarks

The following article presents the framework of a main lesson of about 3 weeks in length, as it might unfold – and as it actually has unfolded – in a 9th grade. Exactly how the discussions are set in motion, how it's fitted out with exercises and experiences for the pupils, how it's brought to a point in questions, how solutions are introduced, how one leads over to new questions – all that depends very much on the character of the class itself. A general presentation of these details, so decisive for the concrete classroom experience, doesn't seem to me to make much sense. Whoever has an urge to take hold of the themes presented here, can't get around having to pay attention to the abilities of the class, to engage these abilities, to encourage them, and to support them in all directions – and that with fantasy and quick-wittedness, out of his/her own initiative.

The first step is for the students and the teacher to write out the odd numbers beginning with 1, in columns of 10 numbers, as follows:

1	21	41	61	...
3	23	43	...	...
5	25	.	...	...
.	.	.	...	...
.	.	.	...	...
.	.	.	...	...

The table ends, provisionally, at 199. Next, one adds these numbers to each other cumulatively. Start with 0, add 1, 0+1=1, add to this number the next odd number, that is, 3, 1+3=4, and continue so until the end of the table. The results are entered in the "'gaps'".

	0		100		400		...
1		21		41		...	
	1		121		441		...
3		23		43		...	
	4		144		484		...
5		25		45		...	
	9		169		...		
7	.	27	.	...			
.	.	.	.				
.	.	.	.				
.	.	.	.				

The table ends with 10 000, if no mistakes were made in the calculations. One should make sure to detect such errors as soon as possible; a further recommendation is to use different colors for the odd numbers and the sums. A pocket calculator is out-of-place here; one doesn't want the weaker students to have the relentless reminder that their abilities don't extend beyond pushing buttons.

One finds numerous patterns in the table: the final digits of the sums repeat themselves, each column is mirror-symmetric around a 5, which is always preceded by a 2 (that is, a 5 in the ones place is always accompanied by a 2 in the tens place); not all digits appear as final digits; there are other "mirror points" in the table; all the sums are square numbers... The phase of observation and collection shouldn't be shortened: in this process, *everyone* can participate. Previous knowledge is really not required.

What is observed and what is surmised should then be more exactly analyzed and proved, and here there are a wide variety of ways that can happen. At this point one can very easily kill off a student's interest by statements like, "but this or that you really *must* know."

The pupils have *done* something, which has apparently *produced* something that "obeys a law". But that means, it must be possible, out of the activity itself, to *draw conclusions* regarding the particularities of the obtained results: so, one now *describes* what one has done. Here again, everyone can do that: Here the teacher has the task, to make sure that also students, about whom other students say "they can't do that anyway", get a fair hearing. In this way a discussion can come about in the class, in which arguments are presented, tested, rejected, revised; the detailed course of the discussion can't be planned. What at the end is extracted, should not simply be plopped down in the classroom and announced by the teacher; it should arise in a some kind of orderly, moderated sequence out of the classroom discussion itself.

1. Structure of the first column. How can you generate the list of odd numbers, what is really going on? – always added 2. You can even predict which odd number belongs at a particular place, even when the previous one isn't known, as long as one knows where one is in the table; this leads to numbering the calculated numbers, starting with 0. (Important to have left space for this in the table).

	0	0		10	100	20	400 ...
1			21			41	
	1	1		11	121	21	441 ...
3			23			43	
	2	4		12	144	.	.
5			25				
	3	9	.	13	169	.	.
7							
	4	16	.		.		
9							
.	.						
.	.						

We denote an arbitrary number with n, the next odd number then is given by doubling the number and adding 1, $2n+1$. A reason (yet another) that it's an *odd* number.

2. Cumulative addition of the odd numbers produces the square numbers. The first sums are obviously square numbers, by the others one can check it. So what has to be proved? Well, something like this: that one always gets a square number, no matter how far one calculates the table – which means, one can no longer check by multiplying a concrete result. The proof has to be so constructed, that it takes into account the recursive construction of the table. We have to convince ourselves that at each step we must obtain the next square number. Let's take a look at what we calculated, and how we might modify it; we choose some examples as paradigms. Suppose we've confirmed our suspicion up to $25^2 = 625$; from the table we can read off that we have to add 51 now:

$$25^2 + 51 = 676$$

This doesn't yield anything that could function as a proof, also the calculation of 26^2 provides only the correct answer in this case, but no insight. It has to become clearer, what happens when we take a further step. The 51 that we added can be further analyzed:

$$26^2 = 25^2 + 51 = 25^2 + 50 + 1 = 25^2 + 2 \cdot 25 + 1^2$$

Now it's clear, *how* the next odd number leads to the following square number – and also, that this is always going to be the case. The formula

$$(n+1)^2 = n^2 + 2n + 1$$

however becomes effective only *after* the discussion of the examples, since it's only this that is accessible to the direct experience of the active pupil. To formalize this process of complete induction would here be naturally out-of-place: the pupils lack the mathematical experience.

3. Examples like 226^2, 234^2 (that essentially can be immediately calculated, taking 230^2 as the starting point), larger numbers, decimal numbers, fractions: they can all be squared, in doing so, one gets good practice with the binomial formula.[38] At this point one can also prove the patterns noted earlier in the table, for example, why does every square number that ends with a 5, end also with 25? why are such numbers "mirror points" in the table for the last digit, while other numbers, for example 50^2, are mirror points for the final 2 digits? Here, the teacher should pursue the discoveries of the pupils patiently and thoroughly, check them, organize them, and prove them.

4. Now the process can be reversed: One is given a square number, and looks for its square root. First from the table, then beyond the table. At this point, one solicits approximations,

---

[38] See also the article by R. Rosbigalle in this volume.

conjectures, checks from the students, for example:

$$\sqrt{149769} = ?$$

To start with we consider *not* the given number, but one that's simpler for the process of extracting the square root, for example, 1/100, 1/10000, etc., of the radicand. Of course we aren't going to find 1497,69 in the table, but we do find two neighbors of this number:

$$
\begin{array}{ll}
38 & 1444 \\
& 1497,69 \\
39 & 1521
\end{array}
$$

These roots have to be multiplied by 10, then we obtain

$$
\begin{array}{l}
380^2 = 144400 \\
149769 \\
390^2 = 152100
\end{array}
$$

The last digit, that was at first ignored, now becomes important: 9 can only appear as the last digit of a square number when the number being squared ends with a 3 or a 7, now one checks to see whether one is closer to the smaller or to the larger neighbor and carries out a check – with the appropriate version of the binomial formula, not by multiplying out, and definitely not with a calculator. Further examples can be chosen, also by students, and provide an initial experience of certainty.

5. It's now time to turn to roots that don't come to an end, for example

$$\sqrt{2} = ?$$

If the method of 4 has been successfully learned, one quickly arrives at the approximation $\sqrt{200} \approx 14$, hence $\sqrt{2} \approx 1,4$ – but what now? Here one needs to come up with a conceptual explanation: what kind of number is $\sqrt{2}$? Since we're not able to begin with to give an exact answer, we give it a name for the sake of convenience:

$$\sqrt{2} = x$$

uand then we express what we know about x:

$$x^2 = 2.$$

Is there some other way to write this equation? Once more: remember to let the pupils seek an answer, give some hints, be patient! At some point it will come up, that

$$x = \frac{2}{x}$$

that is, dividing 2 by $\sqrt{2}$ gives exactly $\sqrt{2}$. Substituting our approximation from above on the RHS gives

$$2 : 1,4 = 1,428...$$

The result is too large, that first approximation was clearly too small. Let's try again with the average of the two numbers

$$\sqrt{2} \approx 1,414... \quad (2^{\text{nd}} \text{ approximation})$$

$$2 : 1,414 =$$

The result of the division shows how precise the current approximation is; the number of digits can be doubled from step to step (and usually one can also obtains an additional digit also). After 4 or 5 steps one has reached the limit of what an ordinary pocket calculator at the present time can calculate.[39]

The class can now be divided into groups, each of which is set to work calculating $\sqrt{3}$, $\sqrt{5}$, $\sqrt{7}$, $\sqrt{11}$ ... to 20 or 30 decimal places.[40]

6. How does one *calculate* with such roots? For example, can you evaluate $1/\sqrt{2}$, $(\sqrt{3}+1)/(\sqrt{3}-1)$ and similar expressions? Is this possible without making an exhausting effort? Yes, one can use fractions for this task! And one ought at this point to review how to do that. Not only examples of "rationalizing the denominator", but also simple expressions like:

$$\frac{1}{\frac{1}{\sqrt{5}}} = \sqrt{5}$$

have to be made transparent.

For $\sqrt{2}-1$ one can write, for example,

$$\sqrt{2}-1 = \frac{1}{\frac{\sqrt{2}-1}{(\sqrt{2}-1)(\sqrt{2}+1)}} = \frac{1}{\frac{\sqrt{2}+1}{2-1}} = \frac{1}{\sqrt{2}+1}$$

since it's reasonable to assume that we are concerned here with a fraction (since its value is less than 1). Other, similar, examples should be handled here, too.

---

[39] This algorithm is due to Heron (75 A. D.) and was generalized by Newton using the differential calculus. If one considers the function $y = x^2 - 2$, then the task reduces to the approximate, recursive determination of its positive zeroes. The process *converges quadratically*, that is, the error becomes quadratically smaller at each step. That's the basis of the rule of thumb given above for the number of correct decimal places. It is also *self-correcting*. To obtain the count of correct decimals at a given step, one should count only the number of digits of the approximation that repeat in the result of the division, and then double this possibly smaller number.

[40] One can't expect every pupil to be up to such a task. But in groups, such a task always meets with a positive reaction.

7. What just made its appearance as a kind of game, can actually be applied with startling consequences: we start all over again to calculate square roots, and restrict ourselves to the crudest sort of approximation, that of whole numbers, while preserving the remainder in exact form. As an example:

$$\sqrt{3} = 1 + (\sqrt{3}-1) \quad \text{(absurd, typical mathematics...)}$$

We take the remainder and make clear that it's *not* a whole number:

$$\sqrt{3} - 1 = \frac{1}{\frac{1}{\sqrt{3}-1}}$$

Since $\sqrt{3}-1$ is less than one, the denominator of this fraction is greater than 1. We can calculate the integer part of this denominator, which has to be at least 1, by rationalizing the fraction in the denominator by multiplying with $\sqrt{3}+1$:

$$\sqrt{3} - 1 = \frac{1}{\frac{\sqrt{3}+1}{3-1}} = \frac{1}{\frac{\sqrt{3}+1}{2}}$$

Since $\sqrt{3} \approx 1,,$ we can extract 1 as the greatest integer part of the fraction in the denominator and the remainder can then be expressed as follows:

$$\sqrt{3} - 1 = \frac{1}{1 + \frac{\sqrt{3}-1}{2}}$$

The new remainder can then be handled in the same way:

$$\frac{\sqrt{3}-1}{2} = \frac{1}{\frac{2}{\sqrt{3}-1}} \quad \text{(Have you made sure that the calculations with fractions are clear and transparent?)}$$

Once more, the fraction in the denominator is rationalized:

$$\frac{\sqrt{3}-1}{2} = \frac{1}{\frac{2(\sqrt{3}+1)}{2}} = \frac{1}{\sqrt{3}+1}$$

We extract, once more, the greatest integer out of the fraction in the denominator:

$$\frac{\sqrt{3}-1}{2} = \frac{1}{2 + (\sqrt{3}-1)}$$

Here something has happened that, based on the experience with the original approximation method, is completely unexpected: a remainder appears that has already shown up, the process becomes periodic. The square root can be expressed as an infinite, repeating continuing fraction:

$$\sqrt{3} = 1 + \cfrac{1}{1 + \cfrac{1}{2 + \cfrac{1}{1 + \cfrac{1}{2 + \ldots}}}}$$

$\sqrt{2}$, $\sqrt{5}$, $\sqrt{6}$, etc., can be computed using this procedure. It becomes clear, that none of these roots can be ordinary fractions, they are all irrational. For practical calculation, the continued fractions are not appropriate – for this we need ordinary, approximating fractions. Calculating these ordinary fractions is the next stage:

8. One obtains such approximating fractions by truncating the infinite continued fraction at some point. These calculations provide further good practice in evaluating fractions. The approximations can be squared using the method introduced at the beginning of the main lesson.

Approximation #	Approximation value	Squared
1	$\sqrt{3} \approx 1$	1
2	$\sqrt{3} \approx 1 + \frac{1}{1} = 2$	4
3	$\sqrt{3} \approx 1 + \cfrac{1}{1+\frac{1}{2}} = 1 + \frac{1}{\frac{3}{2}}$ $= 1 + \frac{2}{3}$ $= \frac{5}{3}$	$\frac{25}{9}$
4	$\sqrt{3} \approx 1 + \cfrac{1}{1+\frac{1}{2+\frac{1}{1}}} = \frac{7}{4}$	$\frac{49}{16}$

The approximating values alternate between being too small and too big. The obtained precision is easy to evaluate.

9. The exact value of a given periodic (and symmetric) continued fraction can be found:

$$x = 3 + \cfrac{1}{1 + \cfrac{1}{1 + \cfrac{1}{1 + \cfrac{1}{1 + \cfrac{1}{6 + \ldots}}}}}$$

Six can be split into 3+3, so that we obtain

$$x = 3 + \cfrac{1}{1 + \cfrac{1}{1 + \cfrac{1}{1 + \cfrac{1}{1 + \cfrac{1}{3+x}}}}}$$

The infinite continued fraction is, due to its periodicity, reduced to a finite form. What has been practiced with the approximating fractions in 8. can now be applied to evaluate the above expression. Deliberate calculation leads most quickly, and hence also most reliably, to the goal.

Step 1: $\quad 1 + \dfrac{1}{3+x} = \dfrac{(3+x)+1}{3+x}$

Step 2: $\quad 1 + \dfrac{1}{\frac{(3+x)+1}{3+x}} = 1 + \dfrac{3+x}{(3+x)+1}$

$$= \dfrac{1((3+x)+1) + (3+x)}{(3+x)+1}$$

$$= \dfrac{2(3+x)+1}{(3+x)+1}$$

Step 3: $\quad 1 + \dfrac{1}{\frac{2(3+x)+1}{(3+x)+1}} = \dfrac{3(3+x)+2}{2(3+x)+1}$

Step 4: $\quad 1 + \dfrac{1}{\frac{3(3+x)+2}{2(3+x)+1}} = \dfrac{5(3+x)+3}{3(3+x)+2}$

Step 5: $\quad 3 + \dfrac{1}{\frac{5(3+x)+3}{3(3+x)+2}} = \dfrac{18(3+x)+11}{5(3+x)+3}$

Step 6: $\quad x = \dfrac{18(3+x)+11}{5(3+x)+3} = \dfrac{65+18x}{18+5x}$

$$18x + 5x^2 = 65 + 18x$$
$$x^2 = 13$$

Since the continued fraction is, positive

$$x = \sqrt{13}$$

10. It's natural at this point, possibly after working out some further examples of this sort, to consider the simplest possible infinite continued fraction that one can have, namely,

$$g = \cfrac{1}{1 + \cfrac{1}{1 + \cfrac{1}{1+\ldots}}}$$

It converges very poorly, the approximate values stabilize to a value very slowly. On the other hand, it's clearly even easier to find a finite form for it than for the previous example:

$$g = \frac{1}{1+g}$$

which yields

$$g^2 + g - 1 = 0:$$

which provides a beautiful opportunity to recall the quadratic equation. g represents the golden section.

11. We return now, at the end, to the beginning and consider a method for extracting square roots that is remarkably stable and quite fast, ideally designed for a computer (and is also in fact implemented there): Calculation of a square root by counting minus signs (shared by Walter Motte). Here is an example with hints regarding *what* is done:

$\sqrt{28879876} =$ Splitting the radicand into 2-digit blocks, beginning on the
$\sqrt{28|87|98|76} =$ *right*, so one might end up with a 1-digit block on the left).

$\sqrt{28|87|98|76} =$
$\quad \underline{-1}$
$\quad 27$
$\quad \underline{-3}$
$\quad 24$
$\quad \underline{-5}$ We begin to remove the consecutive odd numbers from the left
$\quad 19$ block, until the odd number is too big.
$\quad \underline{-7}$
$\quad 12$
$\quad \underline{\underline{-9}}$
$\quad 3$

$\sqrt{28|87|98|76} = 5*$

$\quad .$
$\quad .$
$\quad .$ The number of minus signs in the preceding calculation is the
$\quad .$ first digit of the answer; write it out and pull down the second
$\quad \overline{\overline{387}}$ block next to the remainder of the first block. The previous
                             result is doubled, and shifted one digit to the left; in the free
                             space a 1 is placed, so: :
                             $5 \rightarrow 10 \rightarrow 101$

$\sqrt{28|87|98|76} = 5$

$\cdot$

$\cdot$

$\cdot$

$\overline{\overline{387}}$
-101
$\overline{286}$
-103
$\overline{183}$
-105
$\overline{\overline{3}}$

The number calculated in this way is first subtracted: then it continues with the following odd numbers (replacing the 1 on the right), as long as one can keep subtracting.

From here, repeat exactly as in *

$\sqrt{28|87|98|76} = 53$

$\cdot$

$\cdot$

$\overline{\overline{7898}}$
-1061
$\overline{6837}$
-1063
$\overline{5774}$
-1065
$\overline{4709}$
-1067
$\overline{3642}$
-1069
$\overline{2573}$
-1071
$\overline{1502}$
-1073
$\overline{\overline{429}}$

One more repetition:

$$\sqrt{28|87|98|76} = 537$$

$$\overset{\cdot}{\underset{\cdot}{}}$$

$$\overset{\doteq}{42976}$$
$$-10741$$
$$\overline{32235}$$
$$-10743$$
$$\overline{21492}$$
$$-10745$$
$$\overline{10747}$$
$$-10747$$
$$\overline{0}$$

All that's left is to write out the answer.

$$\sqrt{28|87|98|76} = 5374$$

Check that the answer is correct, and show why the procedure works! *How* you might do so, can be found under point 2, but of course not yet in the appropriate formulation!

Literature

Louis Locher-Ernst: Arithmetik und Algebra, Dornach 1984

C. D. Olds, Continued Fractions, Random House, New York, 1963 (available online)

Division by 9 and "Casting Out Nines"

ARNOLD BERNHARD

Introduction (KLAUS LABUDDE)

The theme of the following article is quite different from the theme "Combinatorics", which is widely-taught in the 9th grade in Waldorf schools. In my view, it's as valuable a theme as combinatorics is, and therefore can be recommended for being studied in the 9th grade.

In both domains one must learn to rely on thinking focused on how numbers are connected with one another. For exactly this reason, it is worthwhile to take them up as objects of study at this time. One faces the task, especially for pupils of this age group, to establish order in their thinking, as a counter-weight to the psychological turbulence, in which many young people get caught up.

We will also refer to "casting out nines" as the "9-check" in this article. The next article in this collection concerns itself with a similar check, the 11-check. In contrast to the 9-check, I find the 11-check to be an appropriate theme for group-work or as a theme for a class report by a particularly gifted student.

Some class teachers already introduce "casting out nines" in the 7th or 8th grade, usually however just as a practical recipe to check whether whole numbers are divisible by 9. In such cases, it makes particular sense, to take it up again in the 9th grade – this time, however, in order to penetrate it clearly in thinking. In this regard, it is then an example of the recommendation, which as far as I know was made by Rudolf Steiner, that what's been learned in the 8th grade ought to be taken up, from new points of view, in the 9th.

The 9-Check

Dividing by 9 yields some interesting experiences. For best results, we carry out the division partly as we would in writing it out, partly as we would verbally:[41]

$$573 : 9 = (540 + 33) : 9 = 60 + 3 \quad R=6$$

We split the dividend into two parts so that the division of the first part yields the number of tens in the answer. Now we exchange two digits of the dividend and represent this division in the same way. We switch for example the tens place with the ones place:

$$537 : 9 = (450 + 87) : 9 = 50 + 9 \quad R=6$$

---

[41] We retain from the German original the symbolism '$a:b$' for the operation 'a divided by b' rather than replacing it by the more common 'a/b'. '$a:b$' is already known in the English-speaking world as an expression for ratio or proportion, and is hence logically indistinguishable from division.

Further swaps:

$$357 : 9 = (270 + 87) : 9 = 30 + 9 \quad R=6$$
$$375 : 9 = (360 + 15) : 9 = 40 + 1 \quad R=6$$
$$735 : 9 = (720 + 15) : 9 = 80 + 1 \quad R=6$$
$$753 : 9 = (720 + 33) : 9 = 80 + 3 \quad R=6$$

The switches produce 6 different dividends; there are no further possibilities with these digits. Two things jump out: the remainder is always 6, and as second summand only 3 numbers appear, each occurring twice. Does this always happen, when a 3-digits number is divided by 9? We carry out a further example:

$$239 : 9 = (180 + 59) : 9 = 20 + 6 \quad R=5$$
$$293 : 9 = (270 + 23) : 9 = 30 + 2 \quad R=5$$
$$923 : 9 = (900 + 23) : 9 = 100 + 2 \quad R=5$$
$$932 : 9 = (900 + 32) : 9 = 100 + 3 \quad R=5$$
$$392 : 9 = (360 + 32) : 9 = 40 + 3 \quad R=5$$
$$329 : 9 = (270 + 59) : 9 = 30 + 6 \quad R=5$$

The same results! A third example:

$$234 : 9 = (180 + 54) : 9 = 20 + 6 \quad R=0$$
$$243 : 9 = (180 + 63) : 9 = 20 + 7 \quad R=0$$
$$423 : 9 = (360 + 63) : 9 = 40 + 7 \quad R=0$$
$$432 : 9 = (360 + 72) : 9 = 40 + 8 \quad R=0$$
$$342 : 9 = (270 + 72) : 9 = 30 + 8 \quad R=0$$
$$324 : 9 = (270 + 54) : 9 = 30 + 6 \quad R=0$$

Based on these experiences, we can presume that there is a general law at work. In order to arrive at it, we work with smaller dividends. We work with 2-digit dividends; then there is only one possible exchange of digits.

$$52 : 9 = 5 \quad R=7 \qquad 24 : 9 = 2 \quad R=6 \qquad 31 : 9 = 3 \quad R=4$$
$$25 : 9 = 2 \quad R=7 \qquad 42 : 9 = 4 \quad R=6 \qquad 13 : 9 = 1 \quad R=4$$

$$35 : 9 = 3 \quad R=8 \qquad 12 : 9 = 1 \quad R=3 \qquad 41 : 9 = 4 \quad R=5$$
$$53 : 9 = 5 \quad R=8 \qquad 21 : 9 = 2 \quad R=3 \qquad 14 : 9 = 1 \quad R=5$$

In these examples, one can't avoid noticing that the sum of the digits equals the remainder:

$$5 + 2 = 7 \qquad 2 + 4 = 6 \qquad 3 + 1 = 4$$
$$2 + 5 = 7 \qquad 4 + 2 = 6 \qquad 1 + 3 = 4$$
$$3 + 5 = 8 \qquad 1 + 2 = 3 \qquad 4 + 1 = 5$$
$$5 + 3 = 8 \qquad 2 + 1 = 3 \qquad 1 + 4 = 5$$

The sum of the digits we call the *digit sum* (or DS for short). In case the remainder always equals the digit sum, then it would be clear, that switching the digits can't change the remainder. We consider further examples:

$$28 : 9 = 3 \quad R=1 \; (QS=10) \qquad 75 : 9 = 8 \quad R=3 \; (QS=12)$$
$$82 : 9 = 9 \quad R=1 \; (QS=10) \qquad 57 : 9 = 6 \quad R=3 \; (QS=12)$$
$$68 : 9 = 7 \quad R=5 \; (QS=14) \qquad 78 : 9 = 8 \quad R=6 \; (QS=15)$$
$$86 : 9 = 9 \quad R=5 \; (QS=14) \qquad 87 : 9 = 9 \quad R=6 \; (QS=15)$$

In these examples, the remainder isn't equal to the DS; but rather to the remainder obtained by dividing the DG by 9.

$$10 : 9 = 1 \quad R=1 \qquad 12 : 9 = 1 \quad R=3$$
$$14 : 9 = 1 \quad R=5 \qquad 15 : 9 = 1 \quad R=6$$

We also obtain the remainder when we build the DS of the DS, the second digit sum DS_2.

$$QS = 10 \quad QS_2 = 1 \qquad QS = 12 \quad QS_2 = 3$$
$$QS = 14 \quad QS_2 = 5 \qquad QS = 15 \quad QS_2 = 6$$

What about the numbers that leave no remainder when divided by 9? Consider the series formed by the multiples of 9:

$$9, 18, 27, 36, 45, 54, 63, 72, 81, 90, \ldots$$

The DS of these numbers is always 9. Continuing with the series...

$$99, 108, 117, 126, 135, 144, 153, 162, 171, 180, \ldots$$

Except for 99, all these numbers also have DS 9. 99 has the DS 18, the QS_2 however is once more 9. Consider the next stretch of the series of multiples of 9:

$$189, 198, 207, 216, 225, 234, 243, 252, 261, 270, \ldots$$

For the first two numbers, $DS_2 = 9$, while for the rest, already $DS = 9$. Up until now, we have found for members of the 9's times table, DS equal to 9 or to 18, that is, numbers that themselves are divisible by 9. Is that a law for the whole series of multiples of 9? Let's check it on the three groups of digit exchanges:

$573 : 9 = 63 \quad R = 6$ $\qquad$ $239 : 9 = 26 \quad R = 5$ $\qquad$ $234 : 9 = 26 \quad R = 0$

$537 : 9 = 59 \quad R = 6$ $\qquad$ $293 : 9 = 32 \quad R = 5$ $\qquad$ $243 : 9 = 27 \quad R = 0$

$357 : 9 = 39 \quad R = 6$ $\qquad$ $923 : 9 = 102 \quad R = 5$ $\qquad$ $423 : 9 = 47 \quad R = 0$

$\cdot$ $\qquad\qquad\qquad\qquad$ $\cdot$ $\qquad\qquad\qquad\qquad$ $\cdot$

$\cdot$ $\qquad\qquad\qquad\qquad$ $\cdot$ $\qquad\qquad\qquad\qquad$ $\cdot$

$\cdot$ $\qquad\qquad\qquad\qquad$ $\cdot$ $\qquad\qquad\qquad\qquad$ $\cdot$

$DS = 5 + 7 + 3 = 15$ $\qquad$ $DS = 2 + 3 + 9 = 14$ $\qquad$ $DS = 2 + 3 + 4 = 9$

$DS_2 = 1 + 5 + 6 = R$ $\qquad$ $DS_2 = 1 + 4 + 5 = R$ $\qquad$ DS is divisible by 9

The suspicion grows: the remainder by division by 9 is the DS, when this is smaller than 9. The remainder is 0 when the DS is 9, or a multiple of 9; the DS is then divisible by 9. The remainder equals the DS_2, when the DS is greater than 9. In case the DS_2 is also greater than 9, then the remainder equals the DS_3, etc.

Before we prove our conjectured rules, we test them out on some bigger examples. $58734 : 9 = ?$ $DS = 5 + 8 + 7 + 3 + 4 = 27$ The DS is divisible by 9; is the number itself also?

$58734 : 9 = 6526 \qquad R=0$
47
23 $\qquad$ The rule has passed the test!
54

$347028 : 9 = ?$ $\quad DS = 3 + 4 + 7 + 0 + 2 + 8 = 24$ $\quad DS_2 = 2 + 4 = 6$

$347028 : 9 = 38558 \qquad R=6$
77
50
52
78
6

Also this rule has passed the test!

Division by 9 and Casting Out Nines
Arnold Bernhard

In order to understand the conjectured rules, we have first to observe that we write the numbers in the *decimal* system, that is, the individual digits represent the number of ones, tens, hundreds, thousands, etc.

$$5834 : 9 = (5000 + 800 + 30 + 4) : 9$$

We divide each of the terms in the sum separately:

```
5000 : 9 = 555 R=5        800 : 9 = 88 R=8        30 : 9 = 3 R=3
  50                       80
  50                        8                      4 : 9 = 0 R=4
   5
```

The sum of the individual remainders is $5+8+3+4 = 20$. This is, however, exactly the DS. Because it is bigger than 9, it also has to be divided by 9, and yields the final remainder 2; this is the same as $DS_2 = 2+0 = 2$. That the calculation has to proceed in this way, can be made particularly clear, if one expresses it algebraically. Suppose a number has a ones, b tens, c hundreds, d thousands, etc; $a,b,c,d,...$ are digits from 0 to 9. The calculation looks like:

$$(...d \cdot 1000 + c \cdot 100 + b \cdot 10 + a \cdot 1) : 9$$

We rewrite the individual terms in such a way that the result of the division is particularly clear to see:

$$[...(d \cdot 999 + d) + (c \cdot 99 + c) + (b \cdot 9 + b) + a \cdot 1] : 9$$
$$= ...d \cdot 111 + c \cdot 11 + b \cdot 1 + \frac{...d+c+b+a}{9}$$
$$= ...d \cdot 111 + c \cdot 11 + b \cdot 1 + \frac{DS}{9}$$

When $\frac{DS}{9}$ is a whole number, then $DS = 9$ or equal to a multiple of 9, and we obtain:

Rule 1 (Divisibility Law): *A number is divisible by 9, if the digit sum is divisible by 9.*

If the digit sum is not divisible by 9, then it (when $DS < 9$), or the second, third, ...digit sum (when $DS > 9$), is equal to the remainder of the division of the original number by 9, and we have:

Rule 2 (Rule of the remainder): *If the digit sum is not divisible by 9, then it (or the second, third, etc. digit sum) is equal to the remainder when the original number is divided by 9.*

What does the "nine rule" (also known as "casting out nines") bring for the pupils? Well, they can easily check, after any division by 9, whether an error has been made. If the remainder doesn't agree with the DS, they can be sure to have made a mistake, and they can then repeat the calculation. If the two agree, they can be pretty sure that his answer is correct; that gives them a feeling of certainty and strengthens their self-confidence.

The check is, however, not completely fool-proof, for the remainder and the DS can agree with each other, even when the answer is wrong; the following error occurs frequently:

$$4863 : 9 = 54 \text{ R}=5 \qquad QS = 4+8+6+3 = 21$$
$$36$$
$$3 \qquad QS_2 = 3$$

DS_2 agrees with the remainder; but the pupil has forgotten, that the last remainder 3 in the calculation has to be divided by 9 (it goes in 0 times), the answer should then be 540 R=3. This error is not detected by casting out nines. In the following, we'll see that casting out nines can be applied to every arithmetic operation. As part of this, one can develop facility in determining the final remainder. Every 9 that occurs in the DS, contributes nothing to the final remainder, since it yields a remainder of 0; for the same reason, pairs of numbers that add together to give 9. Such numbers can be left out when computing the DS.

DS of $49263 = 4+2 = 6$ (since 9 and $6+3$ contribute nothing to the remainder). After some practice pupils can even recognize the remainder of large numbers at a glance.

$$427\ 935\ 436 \qquad \text{R}=7 \qquad (2+7 = 9,\ 5+4 = 9,\ 3+6 = 9)$$
$$5\ 391\ 684 \qquad \text{R}=0 \qquad (5+4 = 9,\ 3+6 = 9,\ 1+8 = 9)$$

The 9-check for multiplication

One can apply the principle of casting out nines not only to division by 9, but to every arithmetic operation: the so-called 9-check. The best-known example is the 9-check for multiplication; an example:

$$83 \cdot 421$$
$$1263$$
$$3368$$
$$\overline{34943}$$

(The number on the right is multiplied by the number on the left; those used to doing it in the opposite order can of course do so.)

After each step we ask the question: does the result make sense? We want to have a confirmation of our progress. In case of uncertainty, we'll repeat the calculation. But it's not necessary, to repeat the whole calculation; it's enough, to carry out the check with the 9-remainders (the remainders arising by division by nine). So, we first determine the 9-remainders with the help of the DS of both factors:

$$83 \quad \text{R}=2 \qquad 421 \quad \text{R}=7$$

Division by 9 and Casting Out Nines — Arnold Bernhard

Now we multiply these 9-remainders together:

$$2 \cdot 7 = 14$$

We next find the 9-remainder of 14: 5. In case this remainder doesn't agree with the 9-remainder of the product, we can be sure we've made a mistake, and we have to repeat the calculation.

$$34943 \quad R=5$$

Since the two remainders agree, we can be pretty sure that the result is correct. We want to next explain, why we can't be completely sure.

We often arrange the calculation with the 9-remainders in a cross format next to the actual multiplication.

```
  83 · 421
    1263
    3368
   34943
```

$$\begin{array}{c} 5 \\ 2 \times 7 \\ 5 \end{array}$$

In the left field of the cross we write the 9-remainder of 83 (2), in the right, the 9-remainder of 421 (7); we multiply these two remainders together: $2 \cdot 7 = 14$; the 9-remainder of 14 (5) we write in the upper field. In the lower field we write the 9-remainder of 34943 (5). If the two numbers in the upper and lower fields don't agree, then there is certainly an error somewhere: either in the actual multiplication or in the 9-check. In recognizing the 9-remainders (the smallest DS) the pupils quickly attain certainty and agility; they can carry out the test with really small numbers, where they commit many fewer errors than with large numbers. Each time that the upper and lower numbers agree, the pupil experiences a subtle strengthening of their ego, and confirmation of their own activity. It's therefore a good habit, if the students get used to carrying out a quick 9-check after each larger multiplication; it can be done in the twinkling of an eye.

If we find that the smallest DS for a number is 9, then we may set the 9-remainder to 0, since DS=9 means that the number is evenly divisible by 9. Further examples:

```
  328 · 473              214 · 536
     3784                   2144
      946                    536
     1419                   1072
   155144                 114704
```

$$\begin{array}{c} 2 \\ 4 \times 5 \\ 2 \end{array} \qquad \begin{array}{c} 8 \\ 7 \times 5 \\ 8 \end{array}$$

```
  369 · 517              579 · 4863
     4653                  43767
     3102                  34041
     1551                  24315
   190773                2815677
```

$$\begin{array}{c} 0 \\ 0 \times 4 \\ 0 \end{array} \qquad \begin{array}{c} 0 \\ 3 \times 3 \\ 0 \end{array}$$

Why is it, that the 9-check doesn't always guarantee a correct multiplication? It can happen, that we make errors that cancel each other out, so that the DS isn't effected; such errors cannot be detected by the 9-check. Example:

$$56 \cdot 573$$
$$3438$$
$$\underline{2875}$$
$$31188$$

The 9-check is satisfied; but there are two mistakes in the calculation. We write it correctly:

$$56 \cdot 573$$
$$3438$$
$$\underline{2865}$$
$$32088$$

Where is the first error in the calculation? In the second line we have multiplied by 5 incorrectly and written down 7 hundreds instead of only 6. Then, in adding we have forgotten the carry digit from the hundreds to the thousands, and so we've written down only 1 thousand. One hundred too many, one thousand too few, such an error naturally can't be detected by DS. But such errors occur seldom.

We introduce a relevant notation and terminology: to express that the 9-remainder of 5873 is 5, we write in short-form as $5873 \equiv 5$; the symbol "$\equiv$" is read as "congruent", to be precise "congruent modulo 9"; that is, both numbers give the same remainder upon division by 9. It's also valid to write: $5873 \equiv 14 \equiv 32$ etc.

The 9-check for addition

5873	5
462	3
512	8
18743	5
31	4
25621	$\equiv$ 7

To the right of each of the summands we write the 9-remainder and add them together also. From the sum (25) we write down the 9-remainder (7). If this doesn't agree with the 9-remainder of the sum on the left, there's a mistake somewhere. The remainders here agree with each other.

The pupils' reckoning becomes very smooth and confident, when they consistently replace the given numbers with their 9-remainders and carry out the 9-check. It can also be carried out with decimal numbers:

77,46	6
121,39	7
17,03	2
4863,57	6
5079,45 ≡ 3	

Actually, the 9-remainder of 77,46 is 0,06. But we can leave the comma out (as long as we do so consistently for all numbers); then it has no influence on the outcome of the 9-check.

The 9-check for subtraction

Also by subtraction, the 9-check consists of subtracting the 9-remainders instead of the given numbers.

58732	7	14573	2
-43284	-3	-9635	-5
15448 ≡ 4		4938 ≡ 6 ≡ -3	?

In the second example, the 9-remainder of the answer is 6; the subtraction of the second 9-remainder (5) from the first (2) yields however -3. Is $6 \equiv -3$? We can avoid the negative remainder by the 9-check if we assign to the minuend 14573 not the 9-remainder 2 but rather the 9-remainder 11, which is allowed since $2 \equiv 11$. The the 9-check produces $11 - 5 = 6$ and the 9-remainders of the subtraction and the test then agree. On the basis of such examples, the pupils learn to deal with remainders in a particularly flexible and mobile way. The negative remainder has, however, also its own logic; for example, calculate:

$$24 : 9 = 3 \quad R = -3 \quad \text{since} \quad 24 = 3 \cdot 9 - 3$$
$$15 : 9 = 2 \quad R = -3 \quad \text{since} \quad 15 = 2 \cdot 9 - 3$$
$$6 : 9 = 1 \quad R = -3 \quad \text{since} \quad 6 = 1 \cdot 9 - 3$$

If we picture the remainder to be a correction, then the correction is smaller, if we subtract 3 at the end, than when we add 6 ($24 = 2 \cdot 9 + 6$). In this regard, then, the remainder -3 is actually to be preferred. This becomes particularly conspicuous in quotients such as 17 : 9; 9 goes into 17 much closer to 2 times than 1 time; the remainder is accordingly. If the pupils have already learned to work with negative numbers, then working with negative remainders leads to particularly flexible thinking. And we can find the smallest positive remainders which correspond to the smallest negative remainders, simply by adding 9 to the latter. Examples:

$$-1 : 8 \equiv 3 \quad \text{since} \quad 44 : 9 = 5 \quad R = -1 \quad \text{or} \quad 44 : 9 \cdot = 4 \quad R = 8$$
$$-2 : 7 \equiv 2 \quad \text{since} \quad 34 : 9 = 4 \quad R = -2 \quad \text{or} \quad 34 : 9 \cdot = 3 \quad R = 7$$
$$-3 : 6 \equiv 1 \quad \text{since} \quad 24 : 9 = 3 \quad R = -3 \quad \text{or} \quad 24 : 9 \cdot = 2 \quad R = 6$$

The 9-check for division

The 9-check for division is quite distinctive. It can't simply be carried out as the previous checks by carrying out a parallel calculation using 9-remainders. Example:

$$523 : 15 = 34 \quad R = 13$$
$$\underline{-45}$$
$$73$$
$$\underline{-60}$$
$$13$$

If we simply replace the dividend and divisor with their 9-remainders, we obtain the result $1 : 6 = 0$ $R = 1$; there isn't much of a connection left with the original calculation. In order to discover a result with a meaningful connection, we have to call to mind, what the division actually means, namely:

$$523 = 34 \cdot 15 + 13$$

We replace these numbers with their 9-remainders, and ask, whether this yields a congruence.

$$\overset{?}{1 \equiv 7 \cdot 6 + 4}$$
$$1 \equiv 42 + 4$$
$$1 \equiv 46$$
$$\checkmark$$

Yes, since 46 is congruent to 1. Further examples:

$$476 : 12 = 39 \quad R = 8 \qquad\qquad 476 = 39 \cdot 12 + 8$$
$$\underline{-36} \qquad\qquad\qquad\qquad\qquad\qquad\qquad ?$$
$$116 \qquad\qquad\qquad\qquad\qquad 8 \equiv 3 \cdot 3 + 8$$
$$\underline{-108} \qquad\qquad\qquad\qquad\qquad 8 \equiv 17$$
$$8 \qquad\qquad\qquad\qquad\qquad\qquad 8 \equiv 8$$
$$\qquad\qquad\qquad\qquad\qquad\qquad\qquad \checkmark$$

$$837 : 11 = 76 \quad R = 1 \qquad\qquad 837 = 76 \cdot 11 + 1$$
$$\underline{-77} \qquad\qquad\qquad\qquad\qquad\qquad\qquad ?$$
$$67 \qquad\qquad\qquad\qquad\qquad 0 \equiv 4 \cdot 2 + 1$$
$$\underline{-66} \qquad\qquad\qquad\qquad\qquad 0 \equiv 9$$
$$1 \qquad\qquad\qquad\qquad\qquad\qquad 0 \equiv 0$$
$$\qquad\qquad\qquad\qquad\qquad\qquad\qquad \checkmark$$

It's good, if the students are conscious of the meaning of division and can turn it back into a multiplication. You can start practicing on small numbers:

$$37 : 8 = 4 \quad R = 5 \quad \text{d.h.} \quad 37 = 4 \cdot 8 + 5$$

It's immediately clear that these results agree with each other. For larger numbers, it's no longer immediately clear, but the 9-check is. One further example:

$$8327 : 23 = 362 \quad R = 1$$
$$-69$$
$$142$$
$$-138$$
$$47$$
$$-46$$
$$1$$

$$8327 = 362 \cdot 23 + 1$$
$$? $$
$$2 \equiv 2 \cdot 5 + 1$$
$$2 \equiv 11$$
$$\checkmark$$

After some practice, pupils find that applying the 9-check to division is uncomplicated.

I've often begun the first main lesson of a ninth grade with the 9-check. In general, the students weren't yet acquainted with it, or only vaguely. The topic quickly found a resonance within the students. They learned something new in the familiar environment of the four basic arithmetic operations. It was a repetition of something well-known from a new point of view. And, furthermore, the 9-check strengthened their self-confidence; to experience with the 9-check "Yes, I have calculated correctly", or when they discovered a mistake and had to re-calculate a result, but then it checked out: "Now I've done it correctly": such an experience each time represents a subtle strengthening of self-confidence. And thereby arises a bridge of trust between the student and the teacher: "He was able to show me, how I can become confident in calculation, confident to stand on my own feet." This experience is a blessing for the ninth-grader, who inwardly often experiences a lack of confidence.

Of course, students can also learn the 9-check in the middle school. It would also give them confidence there, and perhaps some of the lack of confidence, which the students sometimes bring into the high school, would never arise in the first place. The students would then bring with them a sound basis for further development, and also for the step from *knowing* to *understanding* (a step which Rudolf Steiner pointed out as characteristic for this grade), since the basic question must still arise in the students: Why does the 9-check work?

Beginning with the 9th grade, this question can be answered. Let's look once more at the 9-check for a multiplication:

$$75 \cdot 62$$
$$310$$
$$434$$
$$4650$$

$$3 \times 8 \quad \begin{matrix} 6 \\ 6 \end{matrix}$$

In order to recognize, on what foundation the 9-check stands, we have to see how the factors 75 and 62 are imbedded in the 9-series:

$$75 : 9 = 8 \quad R=3 \quad \text{d. h.} \quad 75 = 8 \cdot 9 + 3$$
$$62 : 9 = 6 \quad R=8 \quad \text{d. h.} \quad 62 = 6 \cdot 9 + 8$$

$$75 \cdot 62 = (8 \cdot 9 + 3) \cdot (6 \cdot 9 + 8)$$

$$75 \cdot 62 = 48 \cdot 9^2 + 64 \cdot 9 + 18 \cdot 9 + 3 \cdot 8$$

We multiply these parentheses out, applying the Parenthesis Rule; the arcs show, how we multiply. The first three partial products all contain the factor 9; this common factor can be factored out:

$$75 \cdot 62 = (48 \cdot 9 + 64 + 18) \cdot 9 + 3 \cdot 8$$

$3 \cdot 8 = 24$ can also be taken into the 9-series: $24 = 2 \cdot 9 + 6$. Hence:

$$75 \cdot 62 = (48 \cdot 9 + 64 + 18 + 2) \cdot 9 + 6$$

Thus, 6 is the 9-remainder of $75 \cdot 62$; where does it come from? From

$$3 \cdot 8 = 24 \equiv 6$$

We read off: *The 9-remainder of the product $75 \cdot 62$ is congruent to the product $3 \cdot 8$ of the 9-remainders of the factors.*

That's the basis of the 9-check for multiplication. Already on this concrete numerical examples we can read off, that the rule is generally valid: **The 9-remainder of a product is the product of the 9-remainders.**

The general truth becomes clearer, if we carry out the calculation algebraically. Two numbers A and B are to be multiplied together. We embed them into the 9-series:

$$A = a \cdot 9 + \alpha \qquad\qquad B = b \cdot 9 + \beta$$
$$\alpha = \text{9-remainder of } A \qquad \beta = \text{9-remainder of B}$$

$$A \cdot B = (a \cdot 9 + \alpha) \cdot (b \cdot 9 + \beta)$$
$$A \cdot B = a \cdot b \cdot 9^2 + a \cdot \beta \cdot 9 + \alpha \cdot b \cdot 9 + \alpha \cdot \beta$$
$$A \cdot B = (a \cdot b \cdot 9 + a \cdot \beta + \alpha \cdot b) \cdot 9 + \alpha \cdot \beta$$

Thus: *The 9-remainder of $A \cdot B$ is congruent to the product $\alpha \cdot \beta$ of the 9-remainders.*

For the other arithmetic operations one can recognize the validity of the 9-check in the same way: by embedding the numbers in the 9-series.

Division by 11 and the 11-check

ARNOLD BERNHARD

The remainder of division by 11 can also be read off of the digits of the dividend; we find it by *alternatively adding and subtracting* the digits. Te be exact, the ones are added, the tens are subtracted, the hundreds added, the thousands subtracted, ... etc. The number calculated in this way is called the *alternating digit sum*, or aDS for short. It is congruent (modulo 11) to the 11-remainder.

$$\text{Example: } 5\overset{+}{2}4\overset{+}{6}3\overset{+}{5} : 11 =? \text{ aDS} = 5-3+6-4+2-5 = 1 \text{ Remainder}$$

One can place, alternating, a plus sign above and a minus sign below the digit, beginning with a plus sign above the ones digit. Let's check whether the division really yields the remainder 1.

```
524635 : 11 = 47694
 84
  76
   103
     45
      1 Remainder
```

It can happen, that the aDS is bigger than 10; then the remainder of the division is equal to the remainder obtained by dividing the aDS by 11.

$$\text{Example: } 9\overset{+}{1}8\overset{+}{2}\overset{+}{7} : 11 =?$$

aDS = 7−2+8−1+9   = 21
21 : 11 = 1   Remainder = 10

Does the division really yield a remainder of 10?

```
91827 : 11 = 8347
 38
  52
   87
   10 Remainder
```

In case the aDS is divisible by 11, then the number is also divisible by 11.

$$\text{Example: } 3\overset{+}{8}2\overset{+}{7}3\overset{+}{4} : 11 =? \qquad \text{aDS} = 4 \cdot 3 + 7 \cdot 2 + 8 \cdot 3$$

Does the division yield no remainder?

$$382734 : 11 = 34794$$
$$52$$
$$87$$
$$103$$
$$44$$
$$0 \text{ Remainder}$$

$$\overset{++}{87\underset{--}{4}5} : 11 = ? \qquad dQS = 5 - 4 + 7 - 8 = 0$$
$$8745 : 11 = 795$$
$$104$$
$$55$$
$$0 \quad \text{Remainder}$$

$$\overset{+\;+\;+}{91\underset{-\;\;\;-}{7}18} : 11 = ? \qquad dQS = 8 - 1 + 7 - 1 + 9 = 22$$
$$891718 : 11 = 8338$$
$$37$$
$$41$$
$$88$$
$$0 \quad \text{Remainder}$$

It can also happen, that the aDS is negative. Do negative remainders make sense? Yes! We see that most clearly using small dividends. When we divide 32 by 11, then it makes more sense to say it goes 3 times with a remainder of -1, than to say it goes only 2 times with a remainder of 10.

$$33 : 11 = 3 \quad \text{Remainder} = -1 \quad \text{means} \quad 32 = 3 \cdot 11 - 1$$
$$33 : 11 = 2 \quad \text{Remainder} = 10 \quad \text{means} \quad 32 = 2 \cdot 11 + 10$$

The remainder -1 is much smaller in absolute value than the remainder 10.
Further examples:

$$42 : 11 = 4 \quad R = -2 \qquad aDS = 2-4 = -2$$
$$52 : 11 = 5 \quad R = -3 \qquad aDS = 2-5 = -3$$
$$120 : 11 = 11 \quad R = -1 \qquad aDS = 0-2+1 = -1$$

The remainders -2 and 9, -3 and 8, and -1 and 10, are all pair-wise congruent modulo 11. When we add 11 to the negative remainders, we arrive at the kongruent positive remainder. It's easy to see that this is generally true.

Division by 11 and 11-check — Arnold Bernhard

Examples with bigger dividends:

$$1\overset{+}{8}\overset{+}{5}\overset{+}{3}2 : 11 = ? \qquad dQS = 2-3+5-8+1 = -3$$

If we are working with positive remainders, we have to arrive at the remainder $-3+11=8$.

```
18532 : 11 = 1684
   75
   93
   52
    8  Remainder
```

$$8\overset{+}{3}\overset{+}{9}\overset{+}{2}63 : 11 = ? \qquad dQS = 3-6+2-9+3-8 = -15$$

In order to arrive at congruent positive remainders, we have to add 11 twice: $-15+22=7$

```
839263 : 11 = 76296
    69
    32
   106
    73
     7  Remainder
```

If the aDS is negative that is divisible by 11, then the original number is also divisible by 11.

Example: $1\overset{+}{9}\overset{+}{2}\overset{+}{8}3 : 11 = ? \qquad dQS = 3-8+2-9+1 = -11$

```
19283 : 11 = 1753
   82
   58
   33
    0  Remainder
```

Reckoning with negative remainders and the corresponding positive remainders can provide a strong support for mobility in thinking.

What's the basis of the 11-rule? Just like 9, 11 is a neighbor of 10, the base number of the decimal system. And all powers of 10, the all further base numbers of the decimal system, give a remainder upon division by 11 of either +1 or -1. Division of the base numbers of the decimal system by 11:

$$
\begin{array}{llll}
10^0 = 1 & 1:11 = 0 & \text{Remainder} = +1 \\
10^1 = 10 & 10:11 = 1 & \text{Remainder} = -1 \\
10^2 = 100 & 100:11 = 9 & \text{Remainder} = +1 \\
10^3 = 1000 & 1000:11 = 91 & \text{Remainder} = -1 \\
& \quad\ \ 10 \\
& \quad -1 \\
& 10000:11 = 909 & \text{Remainder} = +1 \\
& \quad 100 \\
& \quad\ \ \ 1
\end{array}
$$

It's clear to see, that from here on the remainders -1 and +1 alternate; since by the division the next-to-last remainder is alternately 10 and 100.

$$
\begin{array}{lll}
10^5 = 10000 & 10000:11 = 9091 & \text{Remainder} = -1 \\
& \quad 100 \\
& \quad\ \ 10 \quad \text{next-to-last Remainder} \\
& \quad -1 \\
10^6 = 1000000 & 1000000:11 = 90909 & \text{Remainder} = +1 \\
& \quad 100 \\
& \quad 100 \quad \text{next-to-last Remainder} \\
& \quad\ \ \ 1
\end{array}
$$

In general: $10^n:11$ yields the remainder +1, when n is *even*, and the remainder -1, when n is *odd*. Let's check the last division by reverse-multiplication:

$$
\begin{array}{r}
11 \cdot 90909 \\
90909 \\
\underline{90909\ \ } \\
999999
\end{array}
$$

The remainder +1 is all that is need to produce 1 000 000. And the next-to-last division in multiplicative form:

Division by 11 and 11-check — Arnold Bernhard

$$\begin{array}{r} 11 \cdot 9091 \\ 9091 \\ \underline{9091} \\ 100001 \end{array}$$

The result of the multiplication is 1 too big; therefore the remainder is -1.

Let's now divide the general number with a ones, b tens, c hundreds, d thousands etc. by 11.

$$\ldots gfedcba : 11$$
$$=$$
$$(\ldots g \cdot 1000000 + f \cdot 100000 + e \cdot 10000 + d \cdot 1000 + c \cdot 100 + b \cdot 10 + a \cdot 1) : 11$$

If we divide the base numbers of the decimal system, that is, the powers of 10, by 11, then the remainders +1 and -1 appear alternately, the +1 by the even powers of 10 and the -1 by the odd powers. Since the base numbers are multiplied by a, b, c, etc., so are the remainders +1 and -1. Hence the remainder is congruent modulo 11 to: $+a - b + c - d + e - f + g\ldots$ But that is exactly the alternating digit sum.

In conclusion, we formulate this as a rule: *When a number is divided by 11, it yields a remainder that is congruent to the alternating digit sum of the number.* Alternating digit sum = ones - tens + hundreds - thousands, etc. Congruent remainders differ by 11 or a multiple of 11: *If the aDS is congruent to 0 modulo 11 (that is, is divisible by 11) then the number itself is divisible by 11, and that doesn't depend on whether the aDS is negative or positive.*

By dividends with an *odd* number of digits, one can assign a positive sign to the most significant digit (left-most digit); if one then alternating assigns + and - to the digits to the right, one ends by assigning + to the ones digit. If, on the other hand, the dividend has an even number of digits, one must either begin with a plus sign in the ones place and proceed alternating to the left, or a minus sign in the left-most digit and proceed, alternating, to the right. If you do it backwards, then the calculated "aDS" is not congruent to the 11-remainder (but to its negative). Example:

$$\overset{+\ +\ +}{\underset{-\ -\ -}{538246}} : 11 = ? \qquad \text{dQS} = 5 - 4 + 7 - 8 = 0$$

```
538246 : 11 = 48931
 98
 102
  34
  16
   5    actual remainder
```

The right aDS is $6 - 4 + 2 - 8 + 3 - 5 = -6$. Is -6 congruent to 5? Yes, since $-6 + 11 = 5$.

The 11-check

Exactly as with the 9-remainders (and for the same reasons) one can test every arithmetic operation with the 11-remainders. Since the aDS can also take on negative values, this requires confidence in calculating with positive and negative numbers; this can of course be practiced by applying the 11-check.

Examples of the 11-check applied to multiplication

$$\begin{array}{r} \overset{+\,+\,+\,+}{568\cdot 732} \\ \overline{--} \\ 5856 \\ 4392 \\ 3660 \\ \overset{+\,+\,+}{\underline{}} \\ 415776 \\ \overline{\overline{}} \end{array}$$

$$\begin{array}{c} 4\;2 \\ -2 \\ 7 \diagup\!\!\!\!\diagdown 6 \\ -2 \end{array}$$

$$\begin{array}{r} \overset{+\,+\,+\,+}{527\cdot 283} \\ \overline{--} \\ 1981 \\ 566 \\ 1415 \\ \overset{+\,+\,+}{\underline{}} \\ 149141 \\ \overline{\overline{}} \end{array}$$

$$\begin{array}{c} -3\;0 \\ -8 \\ 10 \diagup\!\!\!\!\diagdown -3 \\ -8 \end{array}$$

$$\begin{array}{r} \overset{+\,+\,+\,+}{382\cdot 273} \\ \overline{--} \\ 546 \\ 2184 \\ 819 \\ \overset{+\,+\,+}{\underline{}} \\ 104286 \\ \overline{\overline{}} \end{array}$$

$$\begin{array}{c} +6 \\ -3 \diagup\!\!\!\!\diagdown -2 \\ -5 \\ +6 \end{array}$$

Examples of the 11-check applied to division

$$\begin{array}{r} 328 : 17 = 19 \\ -\underline{17} \\ 158 \\ -\underline{153} \\ 5\ \text{Remainder} \end{array}$$

 = 19·17+5

$9 \overset{?}{\equiv} 8·6+5$

$9 \overset{?}{\equiv} 48+5 = 53$

$9 \equiv -2$

Division by 11 and 11-check

$$5713 : 24 = 238$$
$$\underline{-48}$$
$$91$$
$$\underline{-72}$$
$$193$$
$$\underline{-192}$$
$$1 \text{ Remainder}$$

$$\overset{++}{5\underset{-}{7}1\underset{-}{3}} = \overset{++}{2\underset{-}{3}8} \cdot 24 + 1$$

$$4 \overset{?}{\equiv} 7 \cdot 2 + 1 = 15$$

$$9 \equiv 4$$

$$\checkmark$$

$$958172 : 29 = 33040$$
$$\underline{-87}$$
$$88$$
$$\underline{-87}$$
$$117$$
$$\underline{-116}$$
$$12 \text{ Remainder}$$

$$\overset{+++}{9\underset{-}{5}8\underset{-}{1}7\underset{-}{2}} = \overset{+++}{3\underset{-}{3}0\underset{-}{4}0} \cdot 29 + 12$$

$$-16 \overset{?}{\equiv} (-4) \cdot 7 + 1 = -27$$

$$-16 \equiv -16$$

$$\checkmark$$

Theory of equations

KLAUS LABUDDE

Some preliminary remarks

1. It's possible to assign a purely "service" role to the theory of equations, a role that it has earned in the context of activity in the most varied mathematical domains. Under this assumption, the teacher's primary role is to explain the various solution techniques and to guide the student in working out concrete examples. The current article is based on a wider point-of-view, which holds that the theory of equations should itself be considered as an object of mathematical thinking and used pedagogically, in as fundamental a way as is possible.

2. The style of presentation is intentionally not purely mathematical. The article is in fact concerned with mathematical themes that one can assume are generally known (by the high school teacher). Furthermore, in the process of writing I always had, before my mind's eye, concrete situations with my students; and I wanted to incorporate these in the writing. After all, my goal here is to offer perspectives for designing lesson plans, particularly oriented to the differing treatment of the subject in the 9th and 10th grade.

3. Experience has shown, that one doesn't need to use the main lesson for this material. With a thoughtful differentiation into smaller units, accompanied by sufficient practice, I believe it can also be carried through in the skills classes.

4. The reader will find in the presentation almost no numerical examples, and really no detailed calculations. That is intentional. I want in this way to stimulate readers themselves to seek out appropriate examples.

5. How can one understand the pedagogical significance of working with the theory of equations? There are first some remarks to be made, that have a more general validity. I'd like to emphasize an educational task that is characteristic for Waldorf pedagogy. In the context of the training of thinking, we should take care that the concepts that we introduce can be recognized by the students as meaningful, and are, moreover, flexible. The latter means that new concepts should be open to further development. They shouldn't serve to fix or rigidify our thinking. This aspect is of great significance, beyond the purely mathematical context. Just imagine how important it is for human relationships or for work on solutions of social problems, whether the participating partners can think only with fixed, unmoving concepts, or whether they are capable of mobility in their thinking. With regard to the conceptual content needed for such work, the mathematical concepts have in general little or nothing to offer. But one can within mathematics particularly clearly experience, what it means to develop concepts so that they are open for further development. The theory of equations

accompanies the students from the 7th grade to the end of high school. My position is that it's possible to fulfill the pedagogical task mentioned above, in that one doesn't just teach the students how to solve equations, but also works with the students on the *concept of equation* itself. This article is an attempt to show how that can take place. At the same time, I hope it will stimulate the search for further concepts in mathematics, that are appropriate candidates for this pedagogical task.

Introduction

The following treatment assumes that the important branch of algebra has already received an introductory treatment in the middle grades (5 through 8) and that this study is to be continued in the high school (grades 9 to 13) – if for no other reason, than that without it, essential prerequisites for the high school curriculum will be missing.

The mathematical content can be assumed to be known. The purpose of this presentation is to give new impulses for *how* the theory of equations is handled in the school. In the process, we want to show how a high school teacher can set new accents in the 9th grade, and then how she can take up the same material quite differently in the 10th grade, at the same time deepening the content treated.

The content meant here, for the middle school and the lower high school, shouldn't be categorically assigned to specific grades. The high school teacher has no influence on what the class teacher undertakes up until the end of the 8th grade. The class teacher knows his students best and knows what they need. And anyway, if he needs advice, he will come to the high school teacher and ask for it. My experience has been, that the majority of class teachers only get as far as linear equations with one unknown, including word problems. So, as a general rule, the treatment of systems of linear equations and quadratic equations, that come next in the curriculum, are reserved for the 9th grade. The high school teacher generally has a more comprehensive background knowledge of mathematics than the class teacher can. So he's better equipped to impress on the students that a new era is beginning, both with respect to content and to method of working, not just that the homework problems become harder. There are certainly possibilities in the domain of linear equations with one unknown, to "feed" gifted and/or interested students with difficult exercises. Therefore I don't see any necessity to introduce quadratic equations or systems of linear equations in the 8th grade.

I consider it important from a mathematical standpoint that it becomes ever more clear to students, in the course of high school, that algebra consists of more than solving equations. In the introduction of algebra in the 6th grade they in fact experience the truth of this[42], but then it recedes usually into the background. That one can use equations to vanquish concrete word problems and that then one has to be able to solve these equations, that's what appears to be essential in

---

[42] Relevant literature: A. Bernhard "Algebra für die 7. und 8. Klasse an Waldorfschulen" and E. Schuberth "Der Mathematikunterricht in der sechsten Klasse an Waldorfschulen, Teil 1"; Verlag Freies Geistesleben – E. Schuberth "Mathematics Lessons for the sixth grade", Awsna Publications.

algebra. The relation of most ninth-graders to mathematics is, to begin with, characterized by this practical orientation – and that's as it should be.

As the mathematical point-of-view is subservient in the current context to the pedagogical, the question arises now, what is is possible to achieve through a focus on algebra in the 9th and 10th grade, in an educational (not strictly mathematical) sense. The following discussion is intended to yield hints in this direction.

The situation at the beginning of high school

When a Waldorf student arrives at the end of the 8th grade, it's pretty sure that he knows how to solve linear equations with one unknown. One doesn't need particular mathematical gifts, in order to be able to solve such equations. What is more important, is to have solid reckoning skills. Experience shows, that the necessary skills are present in very diverse levels in different students.

Almost all students have in common, that they grasp an equation exclusively as a computational task, that consists of determining the unknown. Just as they essentially identify the subject "mathematics" with "solving problems" (some students have not yet added "mathematics" to their vocabulary and still call this subject "reckoning"). They are not aware yet of any other aspects of an equation than the practical ones mentioned above. If they are capable of calculating in the realm of the rational numbers and have acquired a meaningful picture of the required transformation steps, then they will be able to move with confidence in the field of equations. Hereby the image of the balance accompanies the student as an aid to understanding, that despite all apparent changes has always to remain in equilibrium.

Separate from their individual ability, many students bring with them from the middle school a certain "imprint" due to the class teacher, that influences their relationship to mathematics, and judging from my experience, particularly to algebra. Since the high school teacher has to take up and develop further what has been laid down by the class teacher, he is well-advised to put together an accurate picture of the class, as soon as he can, at least through conversation, and preferably through visiting the class and observing (in the 8th grade). He ought to be aware how the class has worked in this realm up until now. Independent of this, it is also useful to be acquainted with the individual students, before you start teaching them.

From the understanding of an equation that the students until now possess, it is self-evident that they treat x exclusively as an unknown, that is, as a number that they unconsciously and unquestionably assume to exist, but which they do not yet know. The question, whether a given equation has a solution at all, hardly arises in the middle school at all. At least, as long as the class teacher limits the study to equations with well-defined unique solutions. The same goes for word problems. Indeed, a word problem takes its departure from a concrete situation and describes a problem in such a way that the existence of a solution is not questioned. What's essential is the path to the solution, which, as is well-known, is paved with significant obstacles.

On the entry to high school, the student to begin with experiences his mathematics teacher as the new element. In so far as the teacher leads the class into new algebraic territory, he has to be particularly careful at the beginning that his students, and particularly the weaker ones, don't experience a sudden break with what they are familiar with. The following exposition devotes itself to showing, how one can also introduce a new method of working along with the new content. It can only be presented as a "snapshot", that shows what has arisen up until now, from many years of experimenting, always changing as it develops. After several more years, it would possibly appear differently.

Theory of equations for the 9th grade

To the question, whether the quadratic equation or systems of linear equations should be first introduced, I usually have decided for the latter. Based on my experiences, they convey more strongly the impression that something really new is underway.

We restrict ourselves in this school year to systems in which the number of unknowns is equal to the number of equations. Whatever new results appear, ought to arise from out of practical work (homework, exercises, problems, etc.). To begin with, we review in a very concentrated way, on the basis of some examples, arranged in increasing order of difficulty, the linear equation with one unknown. In this way we get to know how the class works together. At the same time, we can gauge the difficulty level at which all students – or at least the majority – can still work independently on the exercises. When we get to the point, at which something new may be introduced in the lesson, we bring in without warning an equation which in addition to an x also has a y; to be precise:

$$ax + by = c.$$

It's intentional that there is only *one* equation. In this way we link up to what is familiar and then guide the students to the insight, that one needs a further equation, in order to arrive at a *single* solution. Most of the students are not aware that one equation can have several, or even arbitrarily many, solutions.

Now we ask the question, which values of x, resp., y, satisfy the equation. How the answers come: quickly or after long deliberation, confident or uncertain, all this can be very revealing for the teacher. He writes the suggested values for x and y, whether right or wrong, on the board, in such a way that one does not yet recognize a pattern. The first task is to check whether the given answers are also correct. It's time to practice substituting and then, to calculate – as far as possible mentally (not on paper)!

The next question for the students is a deeper one: how did they arrive at their x- and y-values? Here one can distinguish between those who simply somehow made a guess, and those who can work systematically. Above all, it becomes clear, who can formulate clearly, what he wants to say; whether he limits himself to his single example, or can already express what the essential idea is. In such conversations one comes to know the students better and then knows, how to speak to the individual student in a way that takes into account his possibilities and what one can expect from him. Talents are usually widely scattered in the class, and we have to exert ourselves, to differentiate in an appropriate way.

Usually, a student discovers during this conversation, that the equation possesses not just several sollutions, but arbitrarily many, and how to economically find them. Now one can bring the attention to the fact that the y-value changes in identical steps, when the x-value does. It's not necessary to introduce the general concept of a function, as it will later be used in analysis, in this context. It's not a matter of concealing the concept from the students, but rather only allowing it to be present, to the extent it plays a role here. It's not important that the word "function" should be held back from the conversation, just that the associated general concept has no place in the discussion. The full significance of the concept cannot in this context be realized. What is essential here, is to develop in the class a secure feeling for the linearity of the relationship between x and y, and the underlying reasons.

On various examples, one can discover that there are two essentially different possibilities: either y gets larger when x does, or it gets smaller. The next theme for discussion is how to tell from an equation, which of the two cases occurs. In such classroom situations, the main thing is that the teacher holds himself back and, via short remarks or questions, encourages the students to speak up. Experience shows that this speaking up is much harder in mathematics than it is, for example, in the humanities.

After the investigation of specific equations it is then time to approach the kernel of our theme. Next to one equation, that we have perhaps already gotten to know, we place a second one and compare the two with one another. This can take place, in that we set the same x-values in both equations and let it then grow in equal-sized steps. Now we see whether both y-values also grow, or both get smaller, or whether one gets larger while the other gets smaller. Assuming we have chosen the two equations so that the y-step of the two equations is different (here the teacher must be careful), than sooner or later the y-values will come together, either at a "crossing" or the one will "pass" the other. If a particularly alert student points out that the step-sizes of the y-values could be equal to each other, he/she should be given vigorous praise; and also promised, that this special case will be looked into at a later point. From the above considerations one realizes that in general there is a unique number pair (x,y), which satisfies both equations. We call it *the* solution of both equations.

In connection with these observations that we have carried out until now, it also happens almost automatically, that the word "variable" shows up in discussion. Now it's a good time to introduce the concept that this word represents. It's a basic principle that one introduces new concepts only once they are "in the air" and the meaning of the concept can also be recognized by the students. It's also not intended, that one should thereby banish the word "unknown" from the vocabulary. Depending on which aspect is actually in play, one uses the one or the other word.

The foregoing work has prepared the ground to ask the question, how one finds the solution (x, y) for two given equations. Perhaps one has already gotten to know some examples in which the solution appears in a table of values. But other examples show that this isn't always so. Then one can try – either randomly or with some guiding thought – to get closer to the solution. But this approach isn't really satisfying. Mainly because for each example there are very specific features which play a role, making it almost impossible to extract a general applicable procedure in this way. Ninth-graders in particular often insist on recipes, that one presses into their hand, so they can solve problems. For some, that's the real goal of mathematical activity.

We shouldn't make it too easy for our students! Of the three popular methods, the "setting-equal" method is, in my opinion, the best candidate to be discovered by the students themselves[43]. By the production of tables of values for individual equations, it's already usually been noticed that the computation is considerably simplified, if one solves the given equation first for x or y, so that by substitution one can quickly find solutions. From here, it's just a short way to the "'setting-equal'" method. It's important to point out, to begin with, that the same letter denotes the same numerical values. This also repeatedly plays a role later on. Especially in this regard: when one doesn't know for sure if two variable numbers are identical, then one should use two different letters to represent them. The "setting-equal" method will also be used often in the higher grades and should on this account be thoroughly practiced. That's much less the case for the "substitution" method, in my experience. I have accordingly spent less time on it.

In view of the later extension of the problem to three or even more unknowns, experience teaches that one should also handle the addition procedure thoroughly. Here, some hints in this regard that I find important. There are some colleagues, that insist on *adding* only – if they want to *subtract* they add after multiplying by -1. Some do both and refer then, more precisely and long-windedly, to the addition *and* the subtraction method. I consider it a waste of time to argue about which is preferable. Much more important is that as many students as possible can confidently apply *one* solution procedure, while a few will in any case soon master both. The less inwardly active students, not seldom a quite numerous group, are grateful when the teacher provides a clear guideline in such matters. Another such useful rule, especially helpful in this procedure, is that one indicates, to the right of a vertical stroke, which transformation is being currently applied. For two unknowns that not so important, but becomes so for three or more. It aids in getting an overview of the path to the solution, helpful for both student and teacher, especially for the latter in light of the many homework assignments, etc., that he has to read through.

The attempt to tease out what is characteristic for each of the three solution methods, in a conceptual or pictorial form, yields a more conceptual form for the setting-equal and substitution methods. For the setting-equal method it is a single, simple step in thinking: y is equal to the right hand sides of both equations, so these two can be set equal to each other. – By the substitution method one discovers a kind of nesting. It assumes that one equation (1) has been solved for y, while the other equation (2) remains in the original form. Then one has to convince oneself, that

---

[43] There are three traditional methods for solving systems of linear equations. The "'setting-equal'" method, where one solves each equation for y and then sets the results equal to each other; the "'substitution'" method, where one solves one equation for y (or x) and the substitutes the found expression into the other equation for y (resp., x); and the "'addition'" method, where one multiplies one or both equations by suitable non-zero constants so that when the resulting equations are added, the result is an equation of one variable only. All three of these methods are mentioned here.

the unknown y in equation (2) is identical to the expression in equation (1) that has been found for y. Hence, the latter may be substituted in (1). (Note that it's more trouble to formulate the thought process here than for the simpler process involved in the setting-equal method.)

One gains access to the addition method more easily through the image of the balance, which the students have generally met in the middle school. It needs only to be extended a bit. What's on the pans of the first balance can have another weight than what's on the pans of the second balance. The addition then corresponds to combining the contents of the two left pans, and also the contents of the two right pans. The new, heavier configuration is also in equilibrium. In the same way, one can represent subtraction by taking away equal amounts from the pans on each side; one can also form a picture of the multiplication of an equation with a number, should one want to push the analogy so far.

Here, a further hint regarding the concept of *equivalent transformation*. This will make clear, why it's so important to be careful when handling concepts. For the middle school it's the case, that all the transformations that one makes to solve a linear equation with one unknown are equivalent transformations[44] In other words: one can guarantee that the x-value that one obtains at the end, really is a solution of the original equation. The same remains true in the 9th grade, as long as we handle linear systems of equations that have a unique solution. In this regard, it becomes interesting only when the question of the equivalence properties of the transformation becomes an issue, when the students are confronted with a problem. That is, for example, the case when after some transformations of a system of linear equations suddenly all the unknowns have vanished and we find ourselves having to ask, what is meant by equations like "$4 = 0$" or "$0 = 0$". Now we have to think about the solution sets. In other words: we have to look more closely at the applied transformation. Could it have brought about a change in the solution? Could the solution even have "disappeared"? What's going on here?

One guiding principle here is that concept formation should be brought into consciousness only when the practical work has reached a particular point. That is similar to a ripening process. This "raising up into consciousness" in this case can occur by coining a new mathematical expression: *equivalent transformation*.

For the continuation of the work, one now faces the question of whether one should remain with systems of equations with unique solutions, or whether one should now investigate equations with two unknowns that have no solution, or infinitely many. This decision should be made based on the class being taught. The uniquely solvable linear systems with three and more unknowns present barely any new intellectual challenges. They require more calculational effort, and one needs to be even more careful in presenting the path to the solution, if it is to be understandable. Precisely for this reason, the addition method is to be recommended here. How one can advantageously apply one of the other methods, or a mixed method, to a favorably-configured single case can be left to the more ambitious students to discover, possibly on their own. In any case, such systems

---

[44] By this is meant that the equation is rewritten in a such a way that the solution set is not changed thereby, for example, multiplying an equation by a non-zero constant doesn't change the solution set.

of equations are to be recommended as long as the class is a genuine ninth grade is, that is, the school year is not far advanced and the students are still more impressed by the practical side of mathematics than the conceptual. The latter aspect is what's called for, if one really wants to penetrate what's going one, when after some transformations "$4 = 0$" or "$0 = 0$" suddenly appears. Such equations are *due* to particular circumstances, but are not at all an *explanation* of them.

If one tries to get to the bottom of the matter, it's well-known that one can, in the case of an unsolvable system, arrive at the conclusion that the two equations are not *compatible*. One may not see it immediately but after some transformations, one observes that the left-hand sides $(ax+by)$ are identical, that is, they take the same value for every choice of x and y, although the right-hand sides are different concrete numbers. Then it's clear that at most one of the equations can be satisfied (for a given *(x, y)* pair), so that the combined system of equations can have no solution. A particularly alert student can now discover that exactly here one meets the case previously mentioned (and excluded): the step-sizes of both *y*-values are equal.[45]

The system of equations behaves differently when it has infinitely many solutions. In this case, after suitable transformations, not only the left-hand sides but also constants on the right-hand sides are identical. Then any solution of the one equation is also a solution of the other. But since one equation with two unknowns has infinitely many solutions, that's also true for the whole system. It's now no wonder that by subtraction of the equations, "$0 = 0$" appears. It would be a false simplification to say: "Since $0 = 0$ appeared, there are infinitely many solutions. x und y can be chosen arbitrarily, and you get a possible solution." Here one must be very careful to think logically.

With this discussion of both special cases, we also want to point out that the quality of the thinking here is different from the previous. It's in fact quite different, whether one is occupied with problems that, while posing certain calculational challenges, have nevertheless a unique solution; or whether one is occupied with questions such as the foregoing. What in the 10th grade will become fully developed music, sounds here for the first time via this faint melody.

Before we leave the domain of linear systems of equations in the 9th grade, we want to address questions that perhaps are beginning to appear. – What about word problems, that still represent an important learning instrument? That we've only referred to them fleetingly, doesn't mean that they don't play an important roll. Just the opposite! They are, in my opinion, to be thoroughly practiced, particularlly in the 9th grade. As we have moved on to new types of equations, we could also have extended the class of word problems correspondingly. On the specific requirements, namely, to represent concrete situations in the form of equations, nothing essential has changed in the transition from 8th to 9th grade. Hence, the sparseness of the comments included here.

Another question arises when one asks: How "up-to-date" are the word problems that one can find in printed exercise collections or textbooks? The so-called "number riddles" serve as a sort of bridge between pure equations and genuine word problems. Their value lies, in my opinion,

---

[45] See p.162

precisely in this bridge function. Also the exercises that have come down in the form of riddles from the far or farthest reaches of the past, are certainly appropriate. But they don't provide enough practice material. So the bulk of the exercises that we have at our disposal, or that we create, come "from practical life". They are really – and now without quotation marks – from practical life. And, in fact, from the practical life of our time! I assume, that most teachers have not practiced another profession sufficiently, that they can contribute something contemporary here from their own experience. Furthermore, the contemporary has to be brought into such a form, that systems of equations for ninth graders can be produced from it. This opens a wide field of activity for colleagues who can contribute something here, based on their own experiences in other professions. There are more than a few thoroughly well-disposed students, who only develop an interest in mathematics when they are convinced, that one can thereby solve problems that arise in practical life. This attitude, which appears particularly strongly in ninth graders, ought to be taken seriously! When I have used exercises, of whose practical significance I wasn't completely convinced, then I made a habit to react honestly to skeptical questions from students, along with the observation, that one could perhaps nevertheless learn something from the exercise. A discussion about this can, depending on the circumstances, awaken new insights in a student into the value of practicing mathematics. In any case one should take the students' questions seriously and not attempt to persuade, where no persuasion is possible, or desirable.

It's known that the various solution possibilities for two equations in two unknowns can be made visible, in that one interprets them, using a cartesian coordinate system, as positions of two lines in a plane. The general case corresponds to lines that intersect. If there is no solution, this corresponds to two parallel but different lines. Finally, the lines are identical when there are infinitely many solutions. One reason to bring this visualization into the instruction, is that many students simply feel more secure, when they have such an overview on a problem. There are certainly classes for which it is advisable to take advantage of this teaching aid. But I also advise, not to do so in every case. Under some circumstances I would in fact avoid it. Algebraic equations and system of equations are essentially based on arithmetic, not geometric, principles. Geometry provides an interpretation of algebra, but not an objective explanation. This subtle but essential difference is lost on the typical ninth grader.

A further reason to omit the geometrical in this context, is that the essentials of analytic geometry are anticipated by including it. Of course, visualizing linear equations in a coordinate system and applying that to examine the relative positions of two lines, hardly qualifies as an introduction to analytic geometry. But one nonetheless approaches the subject in a way, but not the way it should later happen, that is, as geometry that has been expressed by algebra. In our connection, we are dealing with algebra that has been expressed as geometry. And ninth graders cannot yet distinguish these intellectually. If one has the wish, to introduce analytic geometry in the 11th grade so that it connects geometry and algebra in a completely new way (that is, by showing how one can solve geometric problems with algebraic means), then he will avoid coming in the vicinity of this realm beforehand. In the end, the teacher has to decide, whether he accommodates his ninth graders by providing the algebraic facts with a geometric image.

The quadratic equations represent for the ninth graders something less fundamentally new, than linear systems of equations, compared to what they have learned in their years with their class teacher. The binomial formulas are generally known to them, but are not necessarily "on hand" without a review. But thereby a preparatory piece is achieved, that helps them to understand the solution path for the quadratic equation. What is important for the beginning, is not to move too quickly to one of the known solution formulas. On the one hand, it's important for the higher grades, that one masters the theme "completing the square", while on the other, we ought to prevent our students from solving the quadratic equation too soon in such a mechanical way. This remains valid as long as these equations remains the actual theme. Later, when such formulas are used as a tool to solve problems in higher mathematics, the situation is different. In any case, I can advise on the basis of my experience, to postpone the derivation and application of any of the solution formulas until towards the end of the 9th grade. When the time is then ripe, one should try to convey a distinct impression, how one profits from such a formula. It's so: one has determined the solution, once and for all, for a particular type of problem, and now when it's applied to concrete examples, one can skip the individual steps of the path to solution. The students have, it is true, already encountered formulas. But it is entirely possible, that until now this practical aspect was not really consciously grasped. That's entirely as it should be, in my opinion, since that's not the purpose of the first introduction of formulas in algebra.

If the theme quadratic equations is now to be taken up, then one can, as already done with equations of two unknowns, just immediately assign examples as problems. These examples should chosen so the class has a chance to find the solution by guessing. Some students remain by this method. Others attempt, basing on what they've learned, to reach the goal by transformations. As a general rule, among all the students' suggested solutions, there are some that provide workable approaches. I don't recall any student arriving, all by himself, at a complete solution. But the classroom discussions usually provide sufficient ideas, so that the teacher has to give only minor hints, in order that the students find the complete solution.

Before the beginning of the actual work on the quadratic equation, one can naturally practice how one completes expressions of the form

$$x^2 + px$$

to a "square" expression. One gets an impression of the problem, by working through various examples, not only of the form

$$x^2 + px + \ldots = (x + \ldots)^2.$$

Here are some other examples, chosen to stimulate the imagination:

$$x^2 - \ldots + 36 = (\ldots\ldots)^2$$
$$\ldots 16x \ldots = (2x\ldots)^2$$
$$(\ldots \frac{1}{2}x)^2 = 9x^2 \ldots\ldots$$

Such examples offer abundant opportunity for mental reckoning. Furthermore, one can set up the exercises in such a way, that the possibility of two different but correct solutions exists, which also serves the task at hand.

Here we want to bring attention to a sensitive point in the solution of a quadratic equation. Suppose, for example, that an equation appears takes the following form after a first transformation:

$$(x-5)^2 = 49,$$

One can be tempted, to take the root now. Usually there is no problem with the fact that to obtain the two solutions one uses two different signs ($\pm$) before the root symbol. In this case, however, there are root symbols on both side of the equation, which leads to the following result:

$$\pm(x-5) = \pm 7$$

The equation that is shown isn't wrong, but is more complicated than it needs to be. It appears to involve $2 \times 2 = 4$ possibilites but, upon inspection, it is clear that there are in reality only two distinct possibilities, since choosing both minus signs or both plus signs yields the same solution, as does one minus and one plus. In this way one can demonstrate that in such a case, one needs only to apply the doubled sign on *one* side of the equation. If a student objects, "But we have learned that if you do something to one side of the equation you have to do it also to the other!", then point out that one hasn't done anything to one or the other side of the equation; each root symbol comes with a doubled sign, and in this special case, one of these can be omitted.

Of course one should choose examples which yield integer (and later, rational) solutions. Since the irrational numbers are a special theme for the 9th grade, one should also provide examples with irrational solutions. I would only mention equations having no real solutions in response to a corresponding question from a student. How one reacts, depends on the concrete circumstances. The simplest, and also not incorrect, answer is to say, "In fact there is no solution". But I find it preferable that the answer hints at the existence of a new theme, that at the present is too difficult. It's a matter of finding the balance between what the students can understand and giving an indication of one of the most significant discoveries of modern mathematics. In principle, one meets here the idea of extending the concept of number itself, a theme which should unquestionably be pursued in the higher grades. That can mean that later the complex numbers will be handled in detail. But in any case, a first encounter with this new world of numbers, in connection with any remaining open questions, is due before the end of high school.

It's my experience that any deepening of the treatment of quadratic equations, and also any extension to equations of higher degree, can wait until the 10th grade. The goal of the foregoing exposition has been to open up new territory to the students, so that they can now solve problems that previously were too difficult. That corresponds in the 9th grade roughly to their picture of mathematics and hence to one of our tasks in instruction in this subject. Another task consists of introducing our students in the high school in an appropriate way to mathematical thinking, challenging and at the same time quite elementary. Questions that arise in a 9th grade and which they accept as meaningful, should lead at first into practice, through exercises, problems, and homework. From these activities arise then the impulses for the conceptual work. The same goal is also followed in combinatorics, with the difference that in this domain the questions are quite different and the teacher can work virtually without prerequisites, while in the theory of equations she has to rely on, what the class has already achieved in this realm.

The theory of equations in the 10th grade

With the transition to the 10th grade, it's time once again for a new impulse in the theory of equations. If you want to lead a ninth-grader to think mathematically, then you should choose as your point of departure the most concrete questions possible. What in regards to general lawfulness should appear in consciousnes, is developed based on examples. These should be handled in such a way, that what points beyond them, shines through them. This type of approach by no means has to suddenly come to an end. But, beginning around the 10th grade, one should also begin to introduce considerations whose point of departure is the "general case", and therefore pose greater demands on the capacity for abstraction, as has previously been the case. The exact timing of this transition to such challenges has to be decided by the teacher based on his knowledge of the class. The development of the class as well as the distribution of individual gifts should be taken into account. In this sense, what follows should be seen as something that might also be introduced already in the 9th grade. Indeed, it's not primarily a matter of the specific content, with which we are concerned, but rather *how* we work upon it.

Beginning from quadratic equations, there are several possible paths for further exploration. One such path leads to root equations. One restricts the attention thereby in general to equations involving square roots. As is well-known, one extends the allowable equation transformations with the operation of squaring both sides. And that can have consequences! Students with reliable reckoning skills in high school tend to neglect checking the solutions they obtain to an equation. But now a new experience arises. It can happen, that with a root equation one obtains a value which is actually not a solution. That becomes clear when one checks it. Here it turns out that the check is necessary; and not because one doesn't trust one's own ability to calculate. The question arises: how can one obtain an answer, that isn't really an answer? This new has to be explored. Here it is necessary, to think more deeply than previously about the quality of the individual transformation steps. If one tries, beginning with the equation that has been solved for x, to step backwards, reversing the individual transformation steps, one arrives at a "branch in the path". The one branch leads to the original equation, the other, to another equation. The two equations resemble each other closely, but, with regard to their roots, are quite different. One obtains thereby the opportunity, to discover the concept of equivalent transformation anew.

Here we have a characteristic example of how one can recognize the meaning of a mathematical concept formation. Namely, one becomes aware that the logical negation also exists. If there were only equivalent transformations, we could attach a label on something which we take to be self-evident and therefore always raise *it* into consciousness. But concept formation is not limited here.

Quite a few students have a feeling for the meaning of a phenomenon and also want to grasp what this meaning is. If they aren't able to do so, they give vent to their ueasiness with phrases such as, "What's that for?" "That's obvious!". – What they are seeking, they generally can't express in words. What's unmistakable is that they miss something. And, in my opinion, what they are missing is the meaning of the new phenomenon.

Another path leads from the quadratic equations to equations of higher degree. Since one sometimes needs these later for analysis, it's appropriate that one handles them at a beginning level. The representation of a quadratic equation in the linear factor form (LFF) provides a bridge to these equations. It's known how one can obtain the LFF of the quadratic equation by reversing the path to the solution, that is, that one constructs the linear factors $(x-x_1)$ and $(x-x_2)$ from the solutions x_1 und x_2, and from these the equation

$$(x-x_1)\cdot(x-x_2)=0.$$

This reveals itself, after multiplying out the factors, as the original equation, naturally in the normalized polynomial form

$$x^2+px+q=0$$

The known relations $x_1+x_2=-p$ and $x_1\cdot x_2=q$ are however not the only thing that one can obtain here. The LFF prepares the way also for equations of higher degree, along with approaches for their solution, at least in favorable special cases. For this we only need to increase the number of factors, and we get already an equation of higher degree – along with its solutions. Unfortunately, such equations don't usually do us the favor, of appearing in LFF form. The polynomial form is more familiar. But it doesn't reveal the solutions. It can nonetheless provide us with hints. For example, when the solutions are whole numbers, then each one has to be a divisor of the constant term of the polynomial. That follows from multiplying all the constant terms of the linear factors out and identifying the resulting constant with the constant of the polynomial form. The signs of the coefficients of the polynomial and the degree of the equation also give information about the solutions. In this way, involvement with equations of higher degree leads away from the schematic approach, which almost inevitably arises with respect to the quadratic equation, once one has begun to apply one of the formulas for its solution. One immerses oneself in a network of numbers, given through the equation, and, sets off on the search for solutions, observing various aspects and combining them with each other. If one is successful or if one solution is already given in the posing of the problem, then by removing the corresponding linear factors one can, in some circumstances, arrive at all the solutions of the equation. In this context, polynomial division reveals its significance, and so this is also a good time to introduce it.

For many years, vectorial analytic geometry has been a fixed component of the curriculum of the high school in many Waldorf schools. Many colleagues consider the treatment of this form of analytic geometry as more important than the classical coordinate geometry. The revised requirements for the high school diploma[46] have since the 1980's also played a role. In any case, this situation makes it necessary to handle systems of linear equations with more than two unknowns. When already in the 9th grade, one has dealt thoroughly with the simplest system of equations with two equations and two variables, then one can deal with the more complicated systems in an abbreviated fashion, at least as far as solution techniques go. This goes primarily for systems in which the number of equations equals the number of variables, and for which a unique solution exists. This case won't be further discussed here, since in comparison with the simpler systems, nothing really new occurs. I just want to point out, that with increasing number of equations and variables it becomes more ever more important, to represent the solution path in an organized, readable way. That means also, that each transformation step is to be clearly labeled, just as in the times of the class teacher. My experience has been that using the addition (or subtraction) method gives the best results here.

How can one now set new accents in the work on linear systems of equations that are consistent with the nature of 10th graders? One possibility that I see is to handle the determinant method (only for systems with two equations and two unknowns). Not with the goal, of adjoining a fourth solution method to the previous three, but rather to get to know a new type of question. If one has found for the system

$$\begin{cases} a_1 x + b_1 y = c_1 \\ a_2 x + b_2 y = c_2 \end{cases}$$

the solution $x = \frac{b_2 c_1 - b_1 c_2}{a_1 b_2 - a_2 b_1}$, $y = \frac{a_1 c_2 - a_2 c_1}{a_1 b_2 - a_2 b_1}$, then the question of what happens when the denominator is zero (and the numerators are non-zero) is perplexing. The next step is to go back to the beginning, to see how this peculiarity expresses itself there. There one finds, that the left side of the two equations (in their original form) are either identical or can be made identical through multiplication of one of the equations by a suitable number. But the right sides are different. So it's not possible that a solution of the one equation is also a solution of the other. The system is therefore insoluble. If however the right sides are equal, then things are entirely different. Every solution of the one equation – of which there are known to be infinitely many – is also a solution of the other. The system therefore has infinitely many solutions. Does this express itself also in the

---

[46] This is obtained in Germany by passing an exam called the *abitur*, which has become increasingly centralized in the past few decasdes.

general solution, that we already calculated? And if so, how? Here the circle closes on itself, since we now return to what we in the previous section said in connection with "4 = 0" und "0 = 0".

The students can however now understand, that the question whether a system of equations has any solution, has priority over the question of the (potential) solution. If in the discussion of such a theme, the recognition grows, that the point is to learn to pose questions properly, and to be able to arrange different points of view of the same problem in an objective fashion, then one has achieved something for the education of the whole person that goes beyond the strictly mathematical.

One can wrestle with similar questions when one investigates systems of equations with three equations, in which the number of equations differs from the number of variables. Such systems of equations, as far as I know, don't play a role in the 10th grade. This happens first in the treatment of certain questions in vector geometry (three-dimensional), hence not before the 11th grade. Consequently, I haven't taken up this theme in the 10th grade. But not only for this reason. It provides an opportunity to return later to equations and systems of equations with a fundamentally new approach.

A further domain, that one can handle already in the 10th grade, has to do with the exponential equation. Although there are reasons which speak for reserving this for the 11th grade, it has a direct connection to the logarithm main lesson, that takes place in the 10th grade. Since one probably sets different accents in this main lesson compared to earlier ones, one could conceivably handle exponential equations here, as they are based on a conceptual confrontation with the general concepts of "raising to a power" and "finding the logarithm".

All the previously-handled equations and systems of equations can be easily classified (degree of the equation, number of unknowns and equations). This simplifies the systematic treatment of seeking solutions, right down to the application of formulas. With the exponential equation that is almost totally different. A systematic overview is in principle no longer possible. Be that as it may, one can systematically solve certain simple types of equations, such as, for example, $a^x = b$ or $a^{y(x)} = b$. There are other equations of quite simple form, which are, in fact, *not* solvable by means of a finite number of transformations. Nevertheless, through purely numerical considerations, one can convince oneself that there has to be this or that solution. One considers, for example, the equation $2^x = x + 1$.

Through such considerations it can become clear, that one has to distinguish between the question of the existence of a solution (at all) and the question of the path to this solution (if it exists). In other words: One arrives at the insight, that one can be absolutely certain of the existence of a thing, but still see no possibility, to "grab it by the hair", i. e., actually encounter it. Purely from the point of view of the mathematics curriculum, one can argue that such considerations don't belong in the school. But isn't this a question, that one continually meets in life, in striving for knowledge outside of mathematics? In this sense, the involvement with such issues does fit within the school. But perhaps more in the 11th than the 10th grade.

Practically speaking, in the classroom instruction, the first goal will be to find methods with which one can come step-by-step closer to a solution. The graphical method has the advantages that it is simple and that it satisfies the need of many students to have an overview that aids their mathematical activities. It assumes however familiarity with the coordinate system and the foundations of analytic geometry. That speaks for treating the exponential equation first in the 11th grade. The procedure that is brought to light by the graphical method is primarily a matter of the will. Careful drawing and perseverence in calculating (with the use of the pocket calculator) – since each step (for example, by an iterative procedure) comes only somewhat nearer to the solution – that stands over against the relatively simple conceptual foundation in the foreground. If, on the other hand, one decides to follow the more tedious and, at least at the beginning, not very promising path of finding one's way into the number relations of the given equation, then one is much more challenged to *think*. Both activities have their particular value. And both offer good possibilities, to stimulate the student to inner activity. And, pedagogically, this topic prepares the students, more at the feeling than thinking level, for the concept of function, as it is later applied in analysis.

Regardless of whether one handles the exponential equation in the 10th or 11th grade, the world of equations is revealed thereby to be much more comprehensive, than previous experience had shown. That the concept of equation can be still further developed, will then be shown in the 12th grade treatment of analysis.

Theory of equations

UWE HANSEN

Also in the theory of equations the student can be shown how his own ideas and his immediate understanding can be led to a comprehensive theory. For example, a student can immediately solve a simple system of two equations in two unknowns without any directions:

Example 1: One seeks two numbers whose sum is 20 and whose difference is 6. The student thinks: if the numbers were equal, one would have 10 and 10. If one increases by 1, then the other shrinks by 1, so the difference grows twice as fast as the increase. Since the difference is 6, the numbers have to be $10+3=13$ and $10-3=7$

For the student it is satisfying to understand this problem better by separating it from the concrete numbers: Let the sum of the two numbers be a, and the difference be b. The foregoing thought process arrives at the result that

$$\text{the one number is } \frac{a}{2}+\frac{b}{2}, \text{ and the other is } \frac{a}{2}-\frac{b}{2}$$

The formulation of the solution using letters lends itself to the recognition: Add half the sum with half the difference, etc. If finally one writes the equations as

$$x+y=a$$
$$x-y=b$$

then addition (resp., subtraction) of the two equations yields $2x=a+b$, $2y=a-b$ and thus to the first of the discovered solutions. The equation $2x=a+b$ follows immediately from a conceptual consideration. If one adds the sum of two numbers to their difference, one gets twice the larger number (assuming x is the larger number). If one on the other hand subtracts the difference from the sum, then the larger summand disappears and one obtains twice the smaller number.

This example can be generalized in the following way: the second equation is changed, while the first remains the same; this strengthens the inner mobility of the student.

Example 2: The sum of two numbers is 30. What are they, if

   a) the numbers are equal??

   b) one is 8 bigger than the other?

   c) one is twice the other?

   d) one is 4 times the other?

   e) one is 2 more then 3 times the other?

f) twice the bigger plus the smaller equals 46?

Regarding:

b) If one takes the 8 from the 30, one obtains twice the smaller number, this must be 11. Or (compare to example 1), one decreases, resp., increases, 15 by 4.

c) The sum has to be three times the smaller. Generalization: The bigger number is n times the smaller number. This example is a preparation for the substitution method.

d) 30 must then be 5 times the smaller number. Answer: 6 and 24.

e) Take the 2 away from 30, one obtains four times the smaller number; this is 7.

f) The difference of 46 and 30 has to be the larger number, since the sum 46 contains the larger number twice but it contains the smaller number just once.

There are many possibilities, to practice on simple examples the transition from intuitive insight to formal calculation with equations. These remarks are intended to serve as inspiration. The examples should above all show that active investigation and and hammering out a formalism are complementary, mutually fructifying activities. Hence it's very important, after the unmediated discovery of a solution, to determine the solution using equations. Just writing down the equations leads to a clarification, since the experienced thought process comes thereby into focus. Here are some more examples:

Example 3: If one increases one number by three times a second number, one gets 18. Twice the second plus 3 yields the first.

If you decrease 18 by 3, you get 5 times the second number; this has to be 3 and the first is 9. This exercise, too, prepares the way for the substitution procedure. A similar problem:

Example 4: If one increases twice the larger of two numbers by the smaller, one gets 24. The larger is 9 more than the smaller.

The sum of 24 and 9, 33, is three times the larger, since adding 9 to the smaller yields the larger. The solution is thus 11 and 2.

The need to have a clear overview of the connections that have been found is satisfied auch by graphical representations. Students are not surprised by the idea of placing two number axes next to each other.

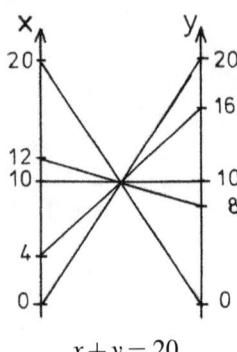

The first example from Example 1 $x+y=20$ can be represented by a line pencil. x- und y-values which sum to 20 are connected with a line.

$x+y=20$

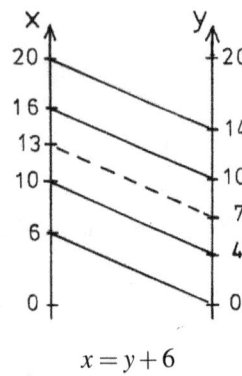

The equation $x=y+6$ appears as a pencil of parallel lines. The dotted line represents the solution of example 1. It belongs to both "pencils".

$x=y+6$

This representation of the separate equations shows quite well the relationship between the variables. It's makes a stronger impact than the usual graphical representation of lines. In general, every linear equation with 2 unknowns is represented by a line pencil, whose center can also lie at infinity. The solution of a system of equations with two such equations means then to find the common line, which will be the joining line of the centers of the two pencils. One more example in closing:

Example 5: If one increases a number by twice a second number, you get 60. What are the two numbers, if
    a) they are equal?
    b) the one number is twice the other?
    c) the one number is 12 more than the other?
    d) the one number is 20 more than twice the other?

Regarding:
    b) either the proportion 1 : 2 becomes equal (2 : 2), then 60 is twice cut in half – solution is (30, 15); or it is intensified to 1 : 4 – solution is (12, 24).
    c) beginning with the equal solution (20,20), a third of 12, that is, 4, must either added or taken away from 20. First solution is (12, 24), second is (28,16).
    d) Here the solutions are (40,10) and (4, 28). In this case it appears difficult to get by without using equations.

Combinatorics Main Lesson 9th Grade

KARL-FRIEDRICH GEORG

According to the view of the human being put forth by Rudolf Steiner, the developing human being in all phases of his development re-enacts the previous epochs in the history of western civilization. The content and methods of school lessons has to take this into account.

The 9th grade corresponds to the time of the Renaissance, when the human being came to know the outer world as objective fact. Just as in that time, the student is now in a phase of discovery and invention, in which newly awoken forces for thinking and making combinations are coming to life. Hence, at the beginning of the 9th grade, a main lesson finds its place, that when carried further can be brought into connection with the underlying ideas of classical probability theory. In getting to know the various possibilities of arranging things, the student can make different experiences: he notices that his consequent thinking leads him into a realm that extends beyond the limits of the experienced world, he enters into a what-if world. There he can reflect on everything, he can move playfully around in this what-if world, and yet all the while he remains within the orbit of the logically known. He can think about everything, but he must still find his way back to reality.

Combinatorics offers the student the possibility, with almost no algebraic prerequisites from the middle school, to immerse himself fully at the beginning of high school.

The following remarks reproduce in essence the text of the main lesson book of my last combinatorics main lesson, suppplemented by exercises, designed to help students engage with the new content, to be worked on either together or alone.

1 Permutations

The main lesson begins with the question: there are 38 students in your class. The classroom has exactly 38 stairs. What do you think, how many different seating arrangements are there?

Depending on the make-up of the class, the most varied answers are given: $2 \cdot 38$; 38^2; 38^3; 38^4; more than 1 million; 38^{38} (which provokes laughter), etc.

In order to obtain an orderly overview, we simplify the question and investigate the number of seating arrangements for 2, 3, and 4 people (with the same number of seats). For 2 and 3 people, the students generally find the answer quickly. For 4 people there are usually different answers. It's clear, one has to find a systemic approach!

We imagine 4 people: <u>B</u>arb, <u>E</u>dgar, <u>I</u>rene und <u>L</u>ou. We begin with 2 of them, and investigate where a third person can sit: there are 6 cases. In each of these cases, a fourth person has four different places to sit. All this we make clear in a tree diagram:

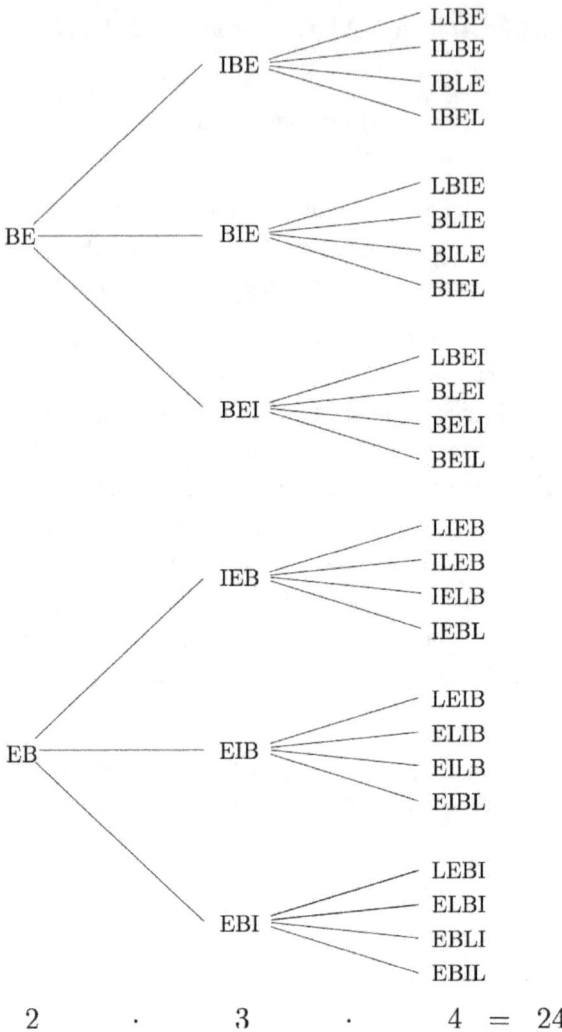

2 · 3 · 4 = 24

Exercise: The four elements B, E, I, L are given. Write out the 24 possible *"Permutations"*, without first writing out the permutations for 2 and 3 elements.

Solution:

BEIL	EBIL	IBEL	LBEI
BELI	EBLI	IBLE	LBIE
BIEL	EIBL	IEBL	LEBI
BILE	EILB	IELB	LEIB
BLEI	ELBI	ILBE	LIBE
BLIE	ELIB	ILEB	LIEB

Remark: In tree diagrams the permutations are ordered by "insertion"; in this exercise they are ordered "lexicographically".

A further possibility to arrive at the total number 24 of arrangements is the following: we imagine four seats before us, all empty. Person A comes, he has four possibilities to choose a seat. Now person B arrives, for him only 3 of the 4 possibilities are still available. When A and B exhaust all the different ways to choose their seats, there are $4 \cdot 3 = 12$ possibilities. There still however remain two empty seats. Now person C arrives. He can choose from 2 seats, but this in 12 different ways. Hence, A, B, and C can take their places in 24 different ways, and when D comes, there is only one empty seat, which he naturally takes. So, seating D causes no increase in the number of seating arrangements.

In this way we find the number of the seating arrangements in our classroom: For the 1st student there are 38 places available. For each of these possibilities, there are then 37 places for the 2nd student, together they have therefore $38 \cdot 37$ possibilities, for the 3rd student there are always 36 free places, the first three have then $38 \cdot 37 \cdot 36$ possibilities, the first four $38 \cdot 37 \cdot 36 \cdot 35$ possibilities, etc. The last, that is, the 38th students has always only one possibility. The number of seating arrangements is accordingly given by: $38 \cdot 37 \cdot 36 \cdot 35 \cdot \ldots \cdot 4 \cdot 3 \cdot 2 \cdot 1$. Multiplied out, one obtains the unusually large number:

$$523\ 022\ 617\ 466\ 601\ 111\ 760\ 007\ 224\ 100\ 074\ 291\ 200\ 000\ 000$$

(Writing this number on the board never fails to impress! And now we attempt to read it.)

Definition: *n* different things can be arranged in a row in different ways. Such an ordering is called a *"Permutation of n different elements"*.

Theorem: The number $P(n)$ of possible permutations of *n* different elements is equal to the product of the natural numbers from 1 to *n*:

$$P(n) = 1 \cdot 2 \cdot 3 \cdot 4 \cdot \ldots \cdot (n-2) \cdot (n-1) \cdot n$$

The product $1 \cdot 2 \cdot 3 \cdot \ldots \cdot n$ is abbreviated by the symbol "$n!$" (read: "*n* factorial")

Some factorial numbers

$1! = 1$ $\hspace{4cm} = 1$
$2! = 1 \cdot 2$ $\hspace{4cm} = 2$
$3! = 1 \cdot 2 \cdot 3$ $\hspace{4cm} = 6$
$4! = 1 \cdot 2 \cdot 3 \cdot 4$ $\hspace{4cm} = 24$
$5! = 1 \cdot 2 \cdot 3 \cdot 4 \cdot 5$ $\hspace{4cm} = 120$
$6! = 1 \cdot 2 \cdot 3 \cdot 4 \cdot 5 \cdot 6$ $\hspace{4cm} = 720$
$7! = 1 \cdot 2 \cdot 3 \cdot 4 \cdot 5 \cdot 6 \cdot 7$ $\hspace{4cm} = 5040$
$8! = 1 \cdot 2 \cdot 3 \cdot 4 \cdot 5 \cdot 6 \cdot 7 \cdot 8$ $\hspace{4cm} = 40320$
$9! = 1 \cdot 2 \cdot 3 \cdot 4 \cdot 5 \cdot 6 \cdot 7 \cdot 8 \cdot 9$ $\hspace{4cm} = 362880$
$10! =$ $\hspace{4cm} = 3628800$
$11! =$ $\hspace{4cm} = 39916800$
$12! =$ $\hspace{4cm} = 479001600$
$13! =$ $\hspace{4cm} = 6227020800$
$14! =$ $\hspace{4cm} = 87178291200$
$15! =$ $\hspace{4cm} = 1307674368000$
$16! =$ $\hspace{4cm} = 20922789888000$
$17! =$ $\hspace{4cm} = 355687428096000$
$18! =$ $\hspace{4cm} = 6402373705728000$
$19! =$ $\hspace{4cm} = 121645100408832000$
$20! =$ $\hspace{4cm} = 2432902008176640000$

Exercise: At what position in the lexicographical ordering of the permutations of the letters C, I, K, S, T does the word STICK occur?

Solution:	With	C	begin exactly 4!	= 24 words
	with	I	begin exactly4!	= 24 words
	with	K	begin exactly4!	= 24 words
	with	SC	begin exactly3!	= 6 words
	with	SI	begin exactly3!	= 6 words
	with	SK	begin exactly3!	= 6 words
	with	STC	begin exactly2!	= 2 words
		STICK		1 word
			Summe:	93 words

Solution: STICK is the 93rd word in the sequence of lexicographically ordered permutations of its letters.

Exercise: What is the 639th permutation of the six elements a,h,m,o,s,t?

Solution		Sum	Remainder
With a	begin 5! = 120 words	120	519
with h	begin 5! = 120 words	240	399
with m	begin 5! = 120 words	360	279
with o	begin 5! = 120 words	480	159
with s	begin 5! = 120 words	600	39
with ta	begin 4! = 24 words	624	15
with tha	begin 3! = 6 words	630	9
with thm	begin 3! = 6 words	636	3
with thoa	begin 2! = 2 words	638	1
with thomas	begins 2! = 1 word	639	0

Exercise: thomas is the 639th word in the lexicographical ordering of its letters.

Practice problems

1. How many permutations of the elements 1,2,3,4,5,6,7,8 begin
   a) with 5,   b) with 123,   c) with 8642?
   Answer:

   a) Since there are 7 other elements besides 5, there are 7! = 5040 permutations that begin with 5.

   b) Since 1,2,3, are fixed at the beginning, there are 5 elements remaining that can be freely placed. So there are 5!=120 permutations that begin with 123.

   c) In the same way, there are 4!=24 permutations beginning with 8642.

2. In how many permutations of the 8 elements 1,2,3,4,5,6,7,8 are the elements 2,4,5,6 next to each other,
   a) in the given ordering? b) in some (arbitrary) ordering?
   Answer:

   a) Permute the five elements 1,3,7,8,2456: $P(5) = 5! = 120$

   b) In each of the foregoing 120 permutations one can then permute the elements of the 4-block containing 2,4,5,6: this produces 4!=24 for each permutation for a total of 120·24 = 2880 permutations.

3. How many permutations of the 26 letters of the alphabet start
   a) with f   b) with sch,   c) with aber?
   Answer: a) $P(25)$,   b) $P(23)$,   c) $P(22)$.

4. How many 8-digit numbers are there, in which the 2-digit blocks 16, 26, 36 und 46 appear?
   Answer: $P(4) = 4! = 24$

5. In which positions in the lexicographic ordering do the words "devil" and "lived" appear in the lexicographical ordering of the letters d,e,i,l,v?
   Answer: devil is the 5th, lived is in the 90th place.[47]

6. Which permutation of the letters "deeilx" is the word "exiled"?

Solution:

with d	begin	$P(5) : 2 = 60$	permutations,	
with ed	begin	$P(4) = 24$	perm., sum is	84
with ee	begin	$P(4) = 24$	perm., sum is	108
with ei	begin	$P(4) = 24$	perm., sum is	132
with el	begin	$P(4) = 24$	perm., sum is	156
with exd	begin	$P(3) = 6$	perm., sum is	162
with exe	begin	$P(3) = 6$	perm., sum is	168
with exid	begin	$P(2) = 2$	perm., sum is	170
with exie	begin	$P(2) = 2$	perm., sum is	172
with exild	begin	$P(1) = 1$	perm., sum is	173
exiled			1 perm., sum is	174

Exiled is the 174th word in the lexicographical ordering of its letters.

---

[47] One can ask similar questions for the word pairs "crime" and "merci", "large" and "regal" (and "lager" and "glare"!), "spire" and "piers", "dream" and "armed", "aspen" and "panes", "raged" and "grade", ... etc.

2 Permutations with repetition

It can happen, as in the final exercise above, that not all the elements are distinct, that is, some of the elements are repeated.

Exercise: Write out the permutations of the elements 1, 1, 1, 2, 3 in lexicographical order

Solution:

11123	21113	31112
11132	21131	31121
11213	21311	31211
11231	23111	32111
11312		
11321		
12113		
12131		
12311		
13112		
13121		
13211		

The number of permutations of 5 elements, which include a group of 3 identical elements, is written P(5). Apparently $P_3(5) = 20$.

If 3 of 5 elements are the same, for example, c = d = e, then all permutations of 5 elements that only differ by a permutation of the triple c,d,e collapse down to one permutation. For example:

$$\left.\begin{array}{cccccc} a & b & c & d & e \\ a & b & c & e & d \\ a & b & d & c & e \\ a & b & d & e & c \\ a & b & e & c & d \\ a & b & e & d & c \end{array}\right\} \text{ leads to ab}\underline{ccc}$$

$$\left.\begin{array}{cccccc} a & c & b & d & e \\ a & c & b & e & d \\ a & d & b & c & e \\ a & d & b & e & c \\ a & e & b & c & d \\ a & e & b & d & c \end{array}\right\} \text{ leads to a}\underline{c}b\underline{cc}$$

$6 = 3!$ permutation collapse down to one permutation. And there remain only $\frac{5!}{3!} = 5 \cdot 4 = 20$ (instead of 120) permutations.

In general: If among n elements, α elements are the same, then their $\alpha!$ permutations collapse down to *one*. To arrive at the number of distinct permutations (with α equal ones) $P_\alpha(n)$ one has to divide the total number $P(n) = n!$ by $\alpha!$:

Karl-Friedrich Georg Combinatorics Main Lesson 9th Grade

Theorem: If among n elements there are α identical ones of one type, β identical ones of another type, and γ identical ones of a third type, then the number of distin:

$$P_{\alpha,\beta,\gamma}(n) = \frac{n!}{\alpha!\beta!\gamma!}$$

(The students should choose 2 problems from the exercises and enter them into their notebooks.)

Example 1: In front of the entrance to a swimming pool there are 12 people standing in line: 6 children, 2 women, and 4 men. How many different lines are there, if one only pays attention to the properies "child", "woman" and "man"?

Solution $\quad P_{6,2,4}(12) = \dfrac{12!}{6! \cdot 2! \cdot 4!} = \dfrac{12 \cdot 11 \cdot 10 \cdot 9 \cdot 8 \cdot 7 \cdot 6!}{6! \cdot 2 \cdot 4 \cdot 3 \cdot 2} = 13860$

13860 different queues are possible.

Example 2: In an right-angled street network in a big city one wants to get from point A to point B along a shortest path. How many different routes are there?

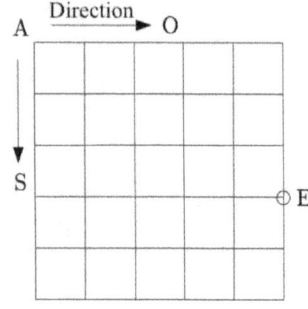

Every shortest path consists of 8 street segments, 5 going east and 3 going south. Whichever route one chooses, one alwas has 5 segments labeled O and 3 labeled S; these can be arranged in every possible sequence and one obtains a possible shortest path from A to B. The total number of such paths is then the number of permutations of 8 elements, with the condition that one group of 5 elements are all the same (O) and another group of 3 is identical (S). The above formula yields:

$$P_{5,3}(8) = \frac{8!}{5! \cdot 3!} = \frac{8 \cdot 7 \cdot 6 \cdot 5!}{5! \cdot 3 \cdot 2} = 56$$

So there are 56 different paths from A to B fulfilling the condition of shortest path.

Tip: From this exercise one can derive the Pascal Triangle. (See: Bengt Ulin, "Finding the Path", 1991, AWSNA)

Practice problems

1. How many 5-digit numbers can you write with the digits 1,1,1,3,4?
   Answer: $P_{3,1,1}(5) = \frac{5!}{3! \cdot 1! \cdot 1!} = 20$

2. How many even 6-digit numbers can you write with the digits 1,1,1,2,2,4?
   Answer: $P_{3,2}(5) + P_{3,1,1}(5) = 10 + 20 = 30$

3. How many 7-digit numbers can you write with the digits 1,2,3,3,0,0,0? (Numbers beginning with '0' are not allowed.)
   Answer: $P_{2,3}(7) - P_{2,2}(6) = 420 - 180 = 240$

Combinatorics Main Lesson 9th Grade   Karl-Friedrich Georg

4. How many permutations of a^5b^2c begin with a, with b, and with c?

   Answer: If the element a is fixed in the first position, any distinct permutation of the elements a^4b^2c can fill the remaining places:

   $$P_{4,2}(7) = \frac{7!}{4! \cdot 2!} = 7 \cdot 3 \cdot 5 = 105 \text{ mal.}$$

   Similarly for b: $P_5(7) = \frac{7!}{5!} = 42$

   And for c: $P_{5,2}(7) = \frac{7!}{5! \cdot 2!} = 21$

   Answer: 105 permutations start with a, 42 start with b, and 21 start with c.

5. How many permutations of the elements a,b,b,b,c,c,c,c,d,d,d begin with bb, wih cac and with abcd?

   Solution: If bb is at the beginning, the the elements abccccddd are left to permute. And similarly for the other cases.

   With bb: $P_{4,3}(9) = \frac{9!}{4! \cdot 3!} = 9 \cdot 8 \cdot 7 \cdot 5 = 2520$

   With cac: $P_{3,2,3}(8) = \frac{8!}{3! \cdot 2! \cdot 3!} = 8 \cdot 7 \cdot 5 \cdot 2 = 560$

   With abcd: $P_{2,3,2}(7) = \frac{7!}{2! \cdot 3! \cdot 2!} = 7 \cdot 3 \cdot 5 \cdot 2 = 210$

   That is, 2520 permutations start with bb, 560 with cac, and 210 with abcd.

6. What is the 116th permutation of the letters AAABBRR?

   Solution

					Sum	Remaining
With A	begin	$P_{2,2,2}(6) = 90$	words		90	26
With B	begin	$P_{3,2}(6) = 60$	words	too many!		
With BA	begin	$P_{2,2}(5) = 30$	words	too many!		
With BAA	begin	$P_2(4) = 12$	words		102	14
With BAB	begin	$P_{2,2}(4) = 6$	words		108	8
With BAR	begin	$P_2(4) = 12$	words	too many!		
With BARA	begin	$P(3) = 6$	words		114	2
BARBAAR	ist		1	word	115	1
BARBARA	ist		1	word	116	0

185

3 k-Permutations

Exercise: How many different two-color flags can be produced using four colors?

Let the colors be a, b, c, d.   Then:

ab ba ca da
ac bc cb db
ad bd cd dc

Answer: $4 \cdot 3 = 12$ different two-color flags.

We have combined two colors at a time into a block. We call that a *2-permutation of 4 elements*, written: $P_2(4)$.

Exercise: Make 3-colored flags from the four colors a,b,c,d!

abc bac cab dab
abd bad cad dac
acb bca cba dba
acd bcd cbd dbc
adb bda cda dca
adc bdc cdb dcb

This 3-permutation of 4 elements gives:
$P_3(4) = 4 \cdot 3 \cdot 2 = 24$ arrangements.

General: If one has n different elements and chooses k different ones to form a block, one calls this a *variation of the kth class of n elements*. Symbol: $P_k(n)$.

Exercise: With 9 blocks, each labeled with a different digit 1, 2, 3, 4, 5, 6, 7, 8, 9, one can construct:

9   1-digit numbers (1-perms. of 9 el. = $P_1(9)$)
$9 \cdot 8$ 2-digit numbers (2-perms. of 9 el. = $P_2(9)$)
$9 \cdot 8 \cdot 7$ 3-digit numbers (3-perms of 9 el. = $P_3(9)$)
$9 \cdot 8 \cdot 7 \cdot 6$ 4-digit numbers (4-perms of 9 el. = $P_4(9)$)
$9 \cdot 8 \cdot 7 \cdot 6 \cdot 5$ 5-digit numbers (5-perms of 9 el. = $P_5(9)$)
$9 \cdot 8 \cdot 7 \cdot 6 \cdot 5 \cdot 4$ 6-digit numbers (6-perms of 9 el. = $P_6(9)$)
$9 \cdot 8 \cdot 7 \cdot 6 \cdot 5 \cdot 4 \cdot 3$ 7-digit numbers (7-perms. of 9 el. = $P_7(9)$)
$9 \cdot 8 \cdot 7 \cdot 6 \cdot 5 \cdot 4 \cdot 3 \cdot 2$ 8-digit numbers (8-perms. of 9 el. = $P_8(9)$)
$9 \cdot 8 \cdot 7 \cdot 6 \cdot 5 \cdot 4 \cdot 3 \cdot 2 \cdot 1$ 9-digit numbers (9-perms. of 9 el. = $P_9(9)$)

On the basis of this exercise we recognize the construction principle of k-permutations:

From, for example,.: $P_4(9) = \underbrace{9 \cdot 8 \cdot 7 \cdot 6}_{4\ factors} = \dfrac{9!}{5!} = \dfrac{9!}{(9-4)!}$

$P_6(9) = \underbrace{9 \cdot 8 \cdot 7 \cdot 6 \cdot 5 \cdot 4}_{6\ factors} = \dfrac{9!}{3!} = \dfrac{9!}{(9-6)!}$

it follows in general:

$$P_k(n) = \underbrace{n \cdot (n-1) \cdot (n-2) \cdot \ldots \cdot (n-(k-1))}_{k \text{ factors}} = \frac{n!}{(n-k)!}$$

Theorem: The number of k-permutations of n different elements is:

$$P_k(n) = \frac{n!}{(n-k)!}$$

Note: The final product (after cancelling common terms) has k factors. When $k = n$, one obtains $P(n)$, the number of permutations of n elements.

Practice exercises

1. In how many ways can you build a 6-pointed star in eurythmy from a group of 18 students?

   $n = 18$ and $k = 6$, hence

   $$P_6(18) = \frac{18!}{(18-6)!}$$
   $$= \frac{18 \cdot 17 \cdot 16 \cdot 15 \cdot 14 \cdot 13 \cdot 12 \cdot 11 \cdot 10 \cdot 9 \cdot 8 \cdot 7 \cdot 6 \cdot 5 \cdot 4 \cdot 3 \cdot 2 \cdot 1}{12 \cdot 11 \cdot 10 \cdot 9 \cdot 8 \cdot 7 \cdot 6 \cdot 5 \cdot 4 \cdot 3 \cdot 2 \cdot 1}$$
   $$P_6(18) = 18 \cdot 17 \cdot 16 \cdot 15 \cdot 14 \cdot 13 = 13.366.080$$

2. 36 students in the 9th grade write to each other, that is, each one writes to every other student a New Year's greeting. How many cards are written in all?

   Solution: $P_2(36) = 36 \cdot 35 = 1260$

3. A company parking lot has places for 10 cars. In how many ways can the parking lot be occupied, if 6 customers park their cars there?

   Lösung: $P_6(10) = 151.200$

4. There are 6 different flower pots. In how many ways can one arrange 3 at a time on a window sill?

   Solution: $P_3(6) = 120$

5. Five streets come together at a plaza. How many ways are there to cross the plaza, assuming all streets are two-way streets?

   Solution: $P_2(5) = 20$

6. A new state wants to design a national flag consisting of three horizontal stripes of different colors with a circle in the middle of a fourth color. How many different designs are possible when one has 10 colors to choose from?

Solution: $P_4(10) = 5040$.

7. How many 3-digit numbers are there with distinct digits?
   a) without 0,   b) with 0

   Solution: a) $P_3(9) = 504$ b) $P_3(10) - V_2(9) = 648$.

8. Show that one can construct just as many "words" using each of the letters of the word PEARS as one can construct 3-letter "words" using the letters of the word ORANGE!

   PEARS: $P(5) = 5! = 120$
   ORANGE: $P_3(6) = 120$

9. Which position does the word NUMBER occupy in the lexicographical ordering of the permutations of its letters?

B, E, M, N, R, U		
With each of B, E, and M begin	5! words =	360 words
With each of NB, NE, NM, and NR begin	4! words =	96 words
With each of NUB and NUE begin	3! words =	12 words
NUMBER	=	1 word
	Total =	469 words

   NUMBER is the 469th word in the lexicographical ordering of the permutations of its letters.

4 The product rule

Exercise: Karen has 2 coats, 4 pairs of pants, 7 T-shirts, and 5 pairs of shoes. How many different ways can she dress?

Answer: There are $A = 2 \cdot 4 \cdot 7 \cdot 5 = 280$ different arrangements. That is, Karen can dress in 280 different ways.

Exercise: In how many different ways can 6 ladies and 5 gentlemen arrange themselves for a photo, if all the ladies stand on the first row and all the gentlemen on the second?

Solution: For each of the $P(5) = 5!$ permutations of the gentlemen there are $P(6) = 6!$ permutations of the ladies. The total is then

$$A = 5! \cdot 6! = 120 \cdot 720 = 86400$$

possible arrangements..

Product Theorem: The total number of possibilities for choosing one element each from different groups, where the individual groups have the possibilities $A_1, A_2, A_3, \ldots$, is given by the product of the possibilities of the individual groups:

$$A = A_1 \cdot A_2 \cdot A_3 \cdot \ldots$$

Example: A car dealer wants to keep on his lot one examplar for each possible choice of options available for each model. There are 8 different choices of paint, 6 choices of upholstery, 3 different motors and also optional sun-roof, automatic transmission, built-in navigation, and parking assist. – How many cars must he have on his lot?

Solution: $A = 8 \cdot 6 \cdot 3 \cdot 2 \cdot 2 \cdot 2 \cdot 2 = 2304$ different cars.

Practice problems:

1. A car has the license plate EZS 123. How many cars can have license plates with the same letters and digits?
   Solution: $P(3) \cdot P(3) = 36$.

2. From the ninth grade 13 girls and 8 boys take a dance course. How many different (heterosexual) couples are possible? To practice, boys dance with boys and girls with girls. How many practice pairs are possible?
   Solution: $13 \cdot 8 = 104$ pairs; $P_3(10) + \{P_2(9) = 78 + 28 = 106$ pairs.

3. A small airline has 5 pilots, 7 co-pilots, 6 flight engineers, and 18 stewardesses. In how many different ways can one put together a crew (1 pilot, 1 co-pilot, 1 flight engineer, 2 sterwardesses) ?
   Solution: $5 \cdot 7 \cdot 6 \cdot \frac{1}{2} P_2(18) = 34020$ Crews.

5 Combinations

Exercise: There are 6 people available to work, but only 3 are required. How many different work teams of 3 people can be chosen from the 6 available people?

Solution: Let the six people be A, B, C, D, E und F. A lexicographical ordering helps to list all the possibilities (Note: The order of the members of the team is irrelevant!)

ABC	BCD	CDE	DEF
ABD	BCE	CDF	
ABE	BCF	CEF	
ABF	BDE		
ACD	BDF		
ACE	BEF		
ACF			
ADE			
ADF			
AEF			

There are 20 possibilities.

Exercise: From a bag containing 7 numbered balls, one is to pull out 5 (without looking). How many different outcomes are there?

Solutions: Here, too, a lexicographical ordering helped to find the number of possible outcomes.

12345	23456	34567
12346	23457	
12347	23467	
12356	23567	
12357	24567	
12367		
12456		
12457		
12467		
12567		
13456		
13457		
13467		
13567		
14567		

There are 21 possibilities. We can generalize what is com-. mon to both of these exercises:

If one chooses from a set of n Elemente a sub-set of k elements, and considers these k elements without regard to their ordering, one calls such a collection of elements a k-combination of n elements and writes the number of possible k-combinations as $C_k(n)$.

For the first exercise one obtains: The number of 3-combinations of 6 elements $C_3(6) = 20$.
For the second exercise we found: The number of 5-combinations of 7 elements $C_5(7) = 21$.

The number of k-combinations in in most cases much smaller than the corresponding k-permutations, for example, the 6 arrangements 123, 132, 213, 231, 312 und 321, all contain the same set of elements 1,2,3. But since combinations don't distinguish between different orderings, all the 6 arrangements are equivalent. All arrangements which consist of the same elements correspond to a *single* combination. Since the number of permutations of k different elements is k!, one obtains the number of k-combinations by dividing the number of k-permutations by k!:

$$C_k(n) = \frac{V_k(n)}{k!} = \frac{n \cdot (n-1) \cdot (n-2) \cdot \ldots \cdot (n-(k-1))}{1 \cdot 2 \cdot 3 \cdot \ldots \cdot k}$$

The short form for this quotient is $\binom{n}{k}$, (read "n choose k"), and called the EULER symbol.

Theorem: The number of k-*combinations of n elements* is:

$$C_k(n) = \binom{n}{k}$$

Note: In numerator and denominator there are the same number of factors. After cancellation: in the numerator they begin with n and count down; in the denominator they begin with 1 and count up.

Examples of EULER symbol:

$$\binom{12}{3} = \frac{12 \cdot 11 \cdot 10}{1 \cdot 2 \cdot 3} = 220$$

$$\binom{12}{9} = \frac{12 \cdot 11 \cdot 10 \cdot 9 \cdot 8 \cdot 7 \cdot 6 \cdot 5 \cdot 4}{1 \cdot 2 \cdot 3 \cdot 4 \cdot 5 \cdot 6 \cdot 7 \cdot 8 \cdot 9} = 220$$

$$\left. \begin{array}{c} \\ \\ \end{array} \right\} \binom{12}{9} = \binom{12}{3} = \binom{12}{12-9}$$

$$\binom{8}{2} = \frac{8 \cdot 7}{1 \cdot 2} = 28$$

$$\binom{8}{6} = \frac{8 \cdot 7 \cdot 6 \cdot 5 \cdot 4 \cdot 3}{1 \cdot 2 \cdot 3 \cdot 4 \cdot 5 \cdot 6} = 28$$

$$\left. \begin{array}{c} \\ \\ \end{array} \right\} \binom{8}{6} = \binom{8}{2} = \binom{8}{8-6}$$

We recognize the pattern

$$\binom{n}{k} = \binom{n}{n-k}$$

If k is bigger than n (k > n), for example, k = 7, n = 3, then

$$\binom{3}{7} = \frac{3 \cdot 2 \cdot 1 \cdot 0 \cdot (-1) \cdot (-2) \cdot (-3)}{1 \cdot 2 \cdot 3 \cdot 4 \cdot 5 \cdot 6 \cdot 7} = 0$$

and we see, whenever $k > n$, it must be that $\binom{n}{k} = 0$.

Using the pattern $\binom{n}{k} = \binom{n}{n-k}$ we can determine special cases of the Euler symbols, i. e.: $\binom{4}{0}$. Then it has to be true that

$$\binom{4}{0} = \binom{4}{4-0} = \binom{4}{4} = \frac{4 \cdot 3 \cdot 2 \cdot 1}{1 \cdot 2 \cdot 3 \cdot 4} = 1$$

From this follows in general: $\binom{n}{0} = 1$

One can also define the following: $\binom{0}{0} = 1$ und $0! = 1$.

Braille (writing for blind people)

A B C D E F G H I J K

For a long time, one could share literature with blind people could only by reading out loud. This changed when the Frenchman *Louis Braille* (1809 – 52), who was blinded at the age of 3, developed a script that the blind could "read" (by touching) and also could write. The individual letters and symbls consist of points (of two different sizes) that are impressed into thick paper. Braille found this script after a long search, beginning with the 6 "eyes" on the face of a dice. By making some of these eyes large and others small, he created the different "'letters"'. This system was able to represent 63 symbols, since with $n = 6$ one has $C_1(6) = 6$ (one big eye) ,$C_2(6) = 15$ (two eyes, etc.), $C_3(6) = 20$, $C_4(6) = 15$, $C_5(6) = 6$, $C_6(6) = 1$ (all small eyes is not allowed).

Practice problems:

1. If 5 points form a pentagon, one can join two of them at a time. How many connecting lines are there?
   Solution: We concerned here with a 2-combination of 5 elements, hence $C_2(5) = 10$

2. How many 3-combinations of the elements 1, 2, 3, 4, 5, 6, 7, 8 don't contain 2, 4, or 6?
   Solution: $C_3(5) = 10$

3. How many 3-combinations of the elements 1, 2, 3, 4, 5, 6, 7, 8, 9 contain at least one even digit?
   Solution: $C_3(9) - C_3(5) = 74$

4. In a regular decagon (10-sided polygon) one can connect vertices to create triangles, quadrilaterals, etc. How many different a) triangles, b)quadrilaterals, c) heptagons (7-sided) can be created in this decagon?
   Solution: a) $C_3(10) = 120$, b) $C_4(10) = 210$, c) $C_7(10) = 120$.

5. a) How many lines joining vertices of a 12-gon are there?

   b) How many diagonals (i. e., lines joining non-adjacent vertices) are there in the 12-gon?

   Solution. a) 66;   b) 54.

6. A farmer buys 2 cows, 3 pigs, and 4 hens from an animal dealer, that is offering 7 cows, 5 pigs, and 10 hens. In how many different ways can the farmers choose his animals?

7. In a village there are 201 mobile phone users. How many difference connections between these phones can be made?

8. In a class of 13 girls and 16 boys, 2 students are chosen each week to clean the board, and 2 are chosen to clean the floor.

   a) How many possible teams of 4 are possible, if only boys perform the floor duty, and only girls perform the board duty?

   b) How many teams of 4 are there, when only boys are allowed to participate?
   Solution: a) $C_2(16) \cdot C_2(13)$;   b) $C_2(16) \cdot C_2(14)$

9. On a tennis court appear one afternoon 5 gentlemen and 7 ladies. How many combinations are there, in which 2 gentlemen play against 2 ladies? Solution: $C_2(5) \cdot C_2(7) = 210$.

6   The general binomial theorem

We are acquainted with the binomial formula $(a+b)^2 = a^2 + 2ab + b^2$ (Latin: bi = twice, nomen = expression).

Exercise: Calculate out the powers of the binomial $(a+b)^n$ for $n = 1, 2, 3, \ldots, 6$.

Answer:

$$(a+b)^1 = 1a + 1b$$
$$(a+b)^2 = 1a^2 + 2ab + 1b^2$$
$$(a+b)^3 = 1a^3 + 3a^2b + 3ab^2 + 1b^3$$
$$(a+b)^4 = 1a^4 + 4a^3b + 6a^2b^2 + 4ab^3 + 1b^4$$
$$(a+b)^5 = 1a^5 + 5a^4b + 10a^3b^2 + 10a^2b^3 + 5ab^4 + 1b^5$$
$$(a+b)^6 = 1a^6 + 6a^5b + 15a^4b^2 + 20a^3b^3 + 15a^2b^4 + 6ab^5 + 1b^6$$

The terms which appear on the first and last place are always powers of a (resp., b). The terms which appear in between are, ignoring the number appearing in front, products of powers. The number appearing in front are called *coefficients*. How they are connected with one another becomes clear, when one arranges the coefficients by themselves in the form of an isosceles triangle.

1. Row					1	1		
2. Row				1	2	1		
3. Row			1	3	3	1		
4. Row		1	4	6	4	1		
5. Row	1	5	10	10	5	1		
6. Row	1	6	15	20	15	6	1	

This triangle is named PASCAL'S Triangle after its inventor (BLAISE PASCAL, 1623 – 62, French philosopher, mathematician, and physicist). One obtains the numbers in the interior of the triangle by adding adjacent numbers in the preceding row. These numbers can be written as EULER symbols, for example, the last row looks like:

$$6 = \binom{6}{1}; \quad 15 = \binom{6}{2}; \quad 20 = \binom{6}{3}; \quad 15 = \binom{6}{4}; \quad 6 = \binom{6}{5}$$

And for the 1's on the border we have $1 = \binom{6}{0}$, resp., $1 = \binom{6}{6}$. This is what PASCAL's Triangle looks like when it is completed at its tip with $1 = \binom{0}{0}$:

$$\begin{array}{c}
\binom{0}{0} \\
\binom{1}{0} \quad \binom{1}{1} \\
\binom{2}{0} \quad \binom{2}{1} \quad \binom{2}{2} \\
\binom{3}{0} \quad \binom{3}{1} \quad \binom{3}{2} \quad \binom{3}{3} \\
\binom{4}{0} \quad \binom{4}{1} \quad \binom{4}{2} \quad \binom{4}{3} \quad \binom{4}{4} \\
\binom{5}{0} \quad \binom{5}{1} \quad \binom{5}{2} \quad \binom{5}{3} \quad \binom{5}{4} \quad \binom{5}{5} \\
\binom{6}{0} \quad \binom{6}{1} \quad \binom{6}{2} \quad \binom{6}{3} \quad \binom{6}{4} \quad \binom{6}{5} \quad \binom{6}{6}
\end{array}$$

Hence, we can write the powers of a binomial with the help of Euler symbols:

$$(a+b)^0 = \binom{0}{0}$$
$$(a+b)^1 = \binom{1}{0}a + \binom{1}{1}b$$
$$(a+b)^2 = \binom{2}{0}a^2 + \binom{2}{1}ab + \binom{2}{2}b^2$$
$$(a+b)^3 = \binom{3}{0}a^3 + \binom{3}{1}a^2b + \binom{3}{2}ab^2 + \binom{3}{3}b^3$$
$$(a+b)^4 = \binom{4}{0}a^4 + \binom{4}{1}a^3b + \binom{4}{2}a^2b^2 + \binom{4}{3}ab^3 + \binom{4}{4}b^4$$
$$(a+b)^5 = \binom{5}{0}a^5 + \binom{5}{1}a^4b + \binom{5}{2}a^3b^2 + \binom{5}{3}a^2b^3 + \binom{5}{4}ab^4 + \binom{5}{5}b^5$$
$$(a+b)^6 = \binom{6}{0}a^6 + \binom{6}{1}a^5b + \binom{6}{2}a^4b^2 + \binom{6}{3}a^3b^3 + \binom{6}{4}a^2b^4 + \binom{6}{5}ab^5 + \binom{6}{6}b^6$$

We can recognize that in every row, for each of its summands, the sum of the powers of a and b is constant, for example
in the fourth row, $(a+b)^4 \quad a^4$, then a^3b^1, then a^2b^2, then a^1b^3, then b^4: the constant sum is 4. Everything that we have up until now discovered, can be expressed in the so-called power series for the n-th power of a binomial:

$$(a+b)^n =$$
$$\binom{n}{0}a^n + \binom{n}{1}a^{n-1}b^1 + \binom{n}{2}a^{n-2}b^2 + \binom{n}{3}a^{n-3}b^3 + \cdots + \binom{n}{k}a^{n-k}b^k + \cdots$$
$$\cdots + \binom{n}{n-2}a^2b^{n-2} + \binom{n}{n-1}a^1b^{n-1} + \binom{n}{n}b^n; \quad n = 1, 2, 3, \ldots$$

That is the general binomial theorem.

Exercise: Write the expansion of $(a + b)^8$ out:

$$(a+b)^8 = \binom{8}{0}a^8 + \binom{8}{1}a^7b + \binom{8}{2}a^6b^2 + \binom{8}{3}a^5b^3 + \binom{8}{4}a^4b^4 + \binom{8}{5}a^3b^5$$
$$+ \binom{8}{6}a^2b^6 + \binom{8}{7}ab^7 + \binom{8}{8}b^8$$
$$= 1a^8 + 8a^7b + 28a^6b^2 + 56a^5b^3 + 70a^4b^4 + 56a^3b^5$$
$$+ 28a^2b^6 + 8ab^7 + 1b^8$$

Exercise: What is the fourth element of the expansion of $(2x - \frac{y}{2})^9$?

Solution: $\binom{9}{3}(2x)^6(-\frac{y}{2})^3 = \frac{9 \cdot 8 \cdot 7}{1 \cdot 2 \cdot 3} 2^6 x^6 (-\frac{y^3}{2^3}) = -672x^6y^3$

Exercise: A solid iron cube has edge length $l = 5.00$ cm at $0°$C. It is warmed up to $\vartheta = 40°$C and expands in volume, so that each edge now has the edge length 5 cm $+ h$, whereby h according to the theory of heat has the value $h = l \cdot \vartheta \cdot 0,000012/°$C. The constant is the so-called "linear expansion coefficient". We calculate $h = 5 \cdot 40 \cdot 0,000012$ cm $= 0,0024$ cm. What is the new volume?

Solution: The volume of the cube is given by $V = a^3$. In this case, $V = (5+h)^3$. We have to expand $(5+h)^3$ and obtain:

$$(5+h)^3 = 5^3 + 3 \cdot 5^2 \cdot h + 3 \cdot 5 \cdot h^2 + h^3$$
$$= 125 + 75h + 15h^2 + h^3$$
$$= 125 + 75 \cdot 0,0024 + 15 \cdot (0,0024)^2 + (0,0024)^3$$

Auxilliary calculations:

$$75 \cdot 0,0024 = 0,18$$

$$15 \cdot (0,0024)^2 = 15 \cdot \left(\frac{24}{10000}\right)^2 = 15 \cdot \frac{576}{100000000} = \frac{8640}{100000000}$$
$$= 0,0000864.$$

This value is so small, that we can ignore it.
$(0,0024)^3$ is even smaller, we can ignore it even more:-).

The new volume of the heated-up cube by $40°$C is with good precision:
$V = (125 + 0,18) \text{ cm}^3 = 125,18 \text{ cm}^3$

As **shorter alternative** for this main lesson one could immediately proceed to "III. Combinations" after "II. Permutation with repetition"', using a somewhat modified version, since the observed patterns have to be derived using other paths:

Exercise 1: In how many different ways can you choose 5 students from a group of 7? Here, too, a lexicographical ordering can be helpful to find the possible combinations.

12345   23456   34567
12346   23457
12347   23467
12356   23567
12357   24567
12367
12456
12457   There are 21 ways to choose 5 students from 7 stu-
12467   dents. We call this the *k-combination of 7 elements*
12567   and write it:
13456
13457 $C_5(7) = 21$.
13467
13567
14567

Exercise 2: From 5 policemen, groups of 3 are to be chosen for duty on a patrol. How many different groups of 3 can be created and how often does each policeman come on duty?

Solution: We write at first the ways to choose 3 out of from 5 elements. Then, next to each group, we write a string of 5 letters consisting of an 'c' if the policeman is chosen, and 'n' if not.

123 ⟷ cccnn
124 ⟷ ccncn
125 ⟷ ccnnc
134 ⟷ cnccn   Apparently there are so many 3-combinations of 5 ele-
135 ⟷ cncnc   ments as there are permutations of 5 elements, where 3
145 ⟷ cnncc   of the 5 elements are identical of one type, and 2 of the 5
234 ⟷ ncccn   are identical of a second type. We can compute with our
235 ⟷ nccnc   symbols:
245 ⟷ ncncn
345 ⟷ nnccc $C_3(5) = P_{3,2}(5) = \dfrac{5!}{3! \cdot 2!} = 10$
$C_3(5)$ $P_{3,2}(5)$

For the general case of *k-combinations of n elements* the following formula holds:

$$C_k(n) = \frac{n!}{k!(n-k)!}$$

The quotient $\frac{n!}{k!(n-k)!}$ is shortened to the symbol $\binom{n}{k}$, introduced by LEONHARD EULER (1707 - 1783) and read as "n choose k". Hence:

$$Ck(n) = \frac{n!}{k!(n-k)!} = \binom{n}{k}$$

Answer to exercise 2: There are $C_3(5) = 10$ 3-groups of policemen. Each policeman comes on dutry as many times as there are 2-combinations of the group of the 4 other policemen, that is: $C_2(4) = \frac{4!}{2! \cdot 2!} = 6$.

Example of EULER symbols:

$$\binom{12}{3} = \frac{12!}{3! \cdot (12-3)!} = \frac{12!}{3! \cdot 9!} = \frac{12 \cdot 11 \cdot 10 \cdot 9!}{1 \cdot 2 \cdot 3 \cdot 9!} = \frac{12 \cdot 11 \cdot 10}{1 \cdot 2 \cdot 3} = 220$$

$$\binom{12}{9} = \frac{12!}{9! \cdot (12-9)!} = \frac{12!}{9! \cdot 3!} = \frac{12 \cdot 11 \cdot 10 \cdot 9 \cdot 8 \cdot 7 \cdot 6 \cdot 5 \cdot 4 \cdot 3!}{1 \cdot 2 \cdot 3 \cdot 4 \cdot 5 \cdot 6 \cdot 7 \cdot 8 \cdot 9 \cdot 3!} = 220$$

We recognize a pattern: $\binom{n}{k} = \binom{n}{n-k}$

Furthermore we can see that for practical calculation, one can quickly compute an EULER symbol, since both the numerator and in the denominator has k factors.

The Braille Script (As above)

Practice exercises (As in the complete version)

Finally, **"IV. The general binomial theorem"** (as above)

A contribution regarding the combinatoricsmain lesson in the ninth grade

KLAUS LABUDDE

With emphasis on combinations and Pascal's triangle

One of the important problems of combinatorics is the following: in how many ways can you choose k elements from a set of n elements ($k \leq n$)? Each possible choice is called a k-combination. The number of k-combinations is well-known to be

$$\binom{n}{k} = \frac{n!}{k! \cdot (n-k)!}$$

In the first geometry lessons in the 6th grade, many class teachers have the students draw a figure based on 24 points, regularly distributed on a circle. Each of these points is joined with every other one. A wonderful figure arises, featuring circles appearing as the envelopes of their tangents, and regular polygons and star-polygons. The ninth grade can recognize an example of combinatorics here, namely, the totality of all 2-combinations of 24 elements, each combination represented by the joining line of two of the 24 points, hence

$$\binom{24}{2} = \frac{24!}{2! \cdot 22!} = 276 \text{ segments}$$

Systematic counting and adding leads to the same result:
1st point, joined with the 23 others .... 23 segments
2nd point, joined with the remaining 22 others .... 22 segments
3rd point, joined with the remaining 21 others .... 21 segments

.   .

.   .

.   .

.   .

22nd point, joined with the remaining 2 others .... 2 segments
23rd point, joined with the remaining one other .... **1 segment**
276 segments

One can apply this in the framework of the combinatorics main lesson and proceed on to other examples. But if one spends some time looking more deeply, the figure proves itself to be the source of a multitude of discoveries and activities for the students, with only a minimal amount of stimulation required from the teacher's side. A first level of deepening occurs when the searching gaze recognizes how certain lines combine to form regular polygons:

8 triangles,
6 squares,
4 hexagons,
3 octagons,
2 dodecagons

and the single 24-sided polygon, that contains the whole figure. [48] The class teacher might bring

---

[48] In this early stage of investigation we forego consideration of "2-gons" (which arise from diagonals, or chords of the circle) und "1-gons" (which arise from single corners), even though this – considered mathematically – is possible.

his class to this point, as they reflect on the result of their drawing, without of course establishing any connection to combinatorics.

For the mathematics teacher, this offers the opportunity to lay hold of what was begun in the middle school, and to lead it bear fruit for the treatment of combinatorical questions.

In what follows, the aim is not to discover regular quadrilaterals, but rather irregular ones. Even someone who is practiced in the realm of pictorial geometry meets signficant difficulties, to recognize in the regular 24-gon, with its multitude of diagonals, the various forms of irregular polygons even approximately in their totality.

It's therefore advisable to choose a regular polygon with significantly fewer vertices. We'll call it from now on the *frame polygon*. The search for all inscribed polygons should require some effort, but it shouldn't be so difficult, that the forces are thereby lamed. From there, one can proceed either to more difficult polygons with more vertices or to a simpler one with fewer.

Let's start with the regular *hexagon*! It contains three different forms for triangles:

2 equilateral,

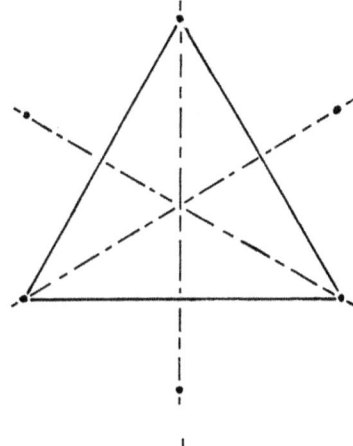

6 isosceles,

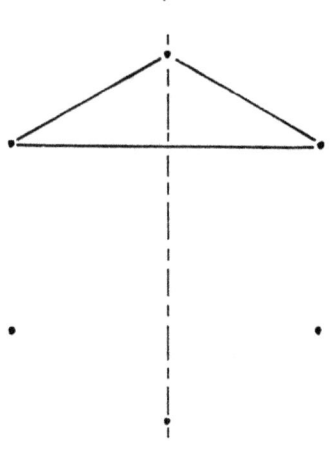

12 irregular,

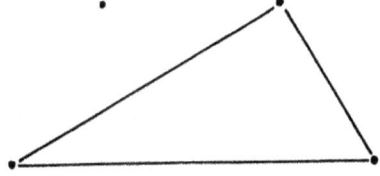

so 20 triangles in all.

Now the quadrilaterals:

3 rectangles,

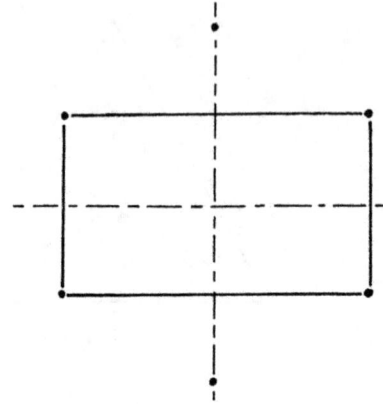

6 trapezoids,

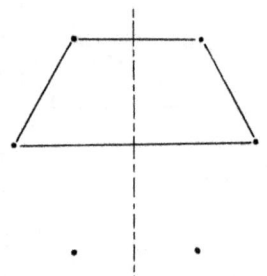

6 kites,

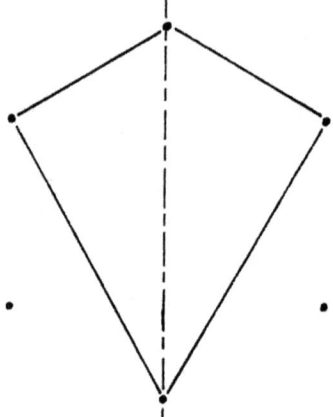

for a total of 15 quadrilaterals.

There is only one type of pentagon. One obtains it, by omitting one of the vertices of the hexagon, and this is possible in 6 different ways.
Hence a total of 6 pentagons. The hexagon itself is also there. Once!

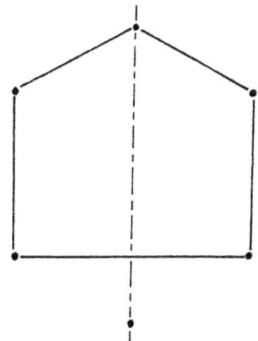

It doesn't make much sense, to mention the question of chords ("2-gons") und single vertices ("1-gons"); and the same goes even more so for the "0-gon". The complete comprehension of all possible special cases in, in view of the overarching mathematical goal – Pascal's triangle in its combinatorical significance – is certainly important. But first, there are further discoveries to make.

We next look at the regular *heptagon* (7-gon)!

Among the inscribed triangles are to be found 3 types of isosceles triangles, each occurring 7 times.

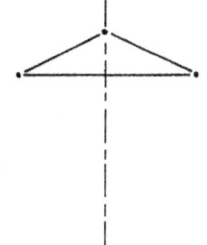 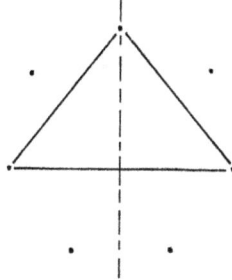 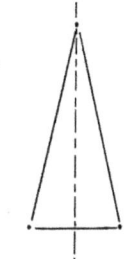

Additionally there are 14 irregular triangles, 7 directly congruent to each other, and the other seven congruent and mirror-reversed to the first.
This yields a total of 35 triangles.

It's really not so easy to be sure that thereby one has gotten all of the triangles. It's quite possible that one misses one or counts another one twice, without noticing. This difficulty intensifies naturally, the more vertices the frame polygon has.

Now the inscribed quadrilaterals! Among these are 3 groups of 7 isosceles trapezoids.

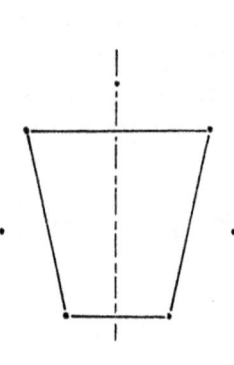

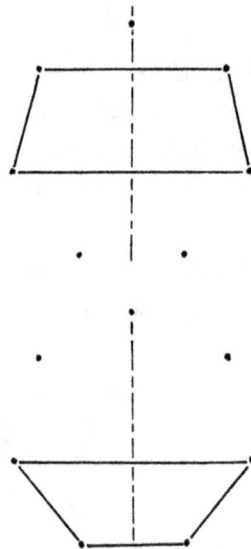

Furthermore there are 14 irregular quadrilatersl, 7 congruent to each other, and the other 7 congruent to each other, and mirror-reversed to the first. This yields a total of 35 quadrilaterals. Exactly as many as the number of triangles!

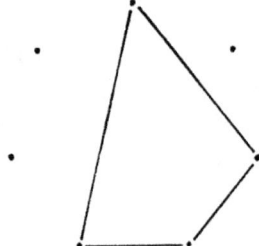

There are 3 types of axially-symmetric pentagons, each occurring 7 times, and no other pentagons, for a total of 21.

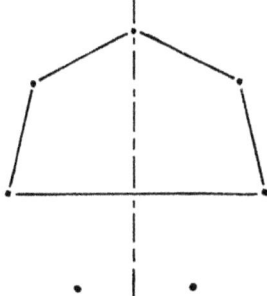

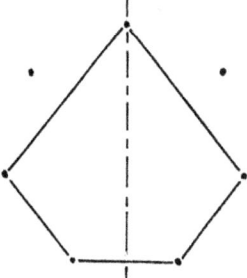

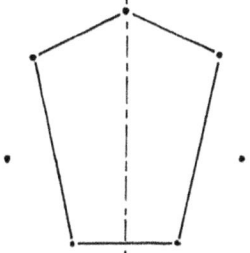

There is only one type of hexagon in the heptagon (just like pentagons in the hexagon), for a total of 7 hexagons.

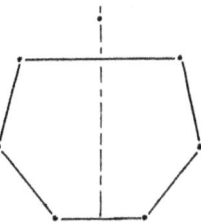

The heptagon itself has to be counted, once.

Whether one now proceeds onto the octagon or the pentagon, is a question of available time and the teacher's abilities: to bring the theme to life, to divide the work among the students, to split off parts to be done at home, etc. In any case, there are abundant opportunities here to let the students apply their individual gifts to the investigation: fast or slow, concrete "hands-on" explorers or more overview-seeking organizers, etc.

Let's continue to expand our horizons on more polygons!!

The octagon

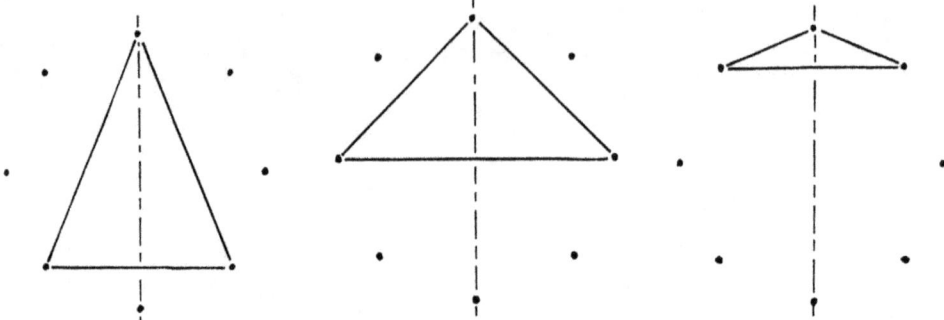

It contains 3 types of isosceles triangle, in groups of 8.

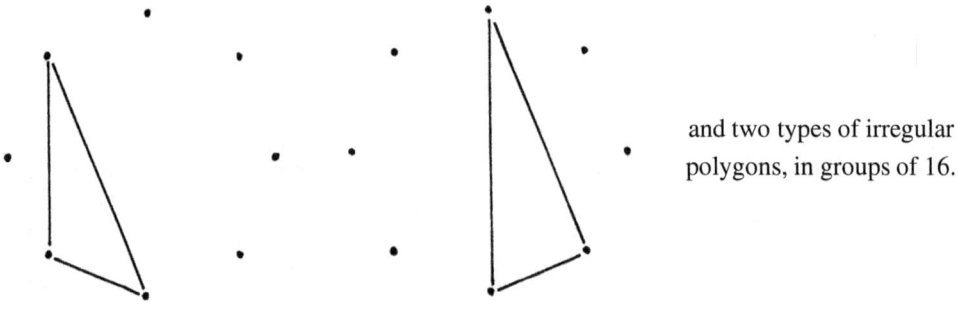

and two types of irregular polygons, in groups of 16.

For a total of 56 triangles..

There are many quadrilaterals, in many different forms.

Among these are two squares, with 4 axes of symmetry.

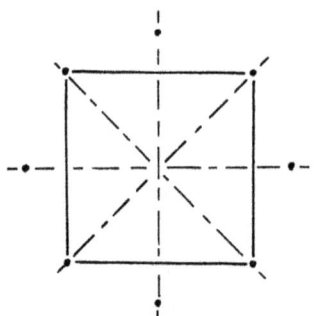

4 rectangles
with two axes of symmetry

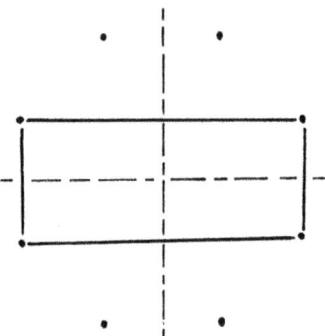

four types of trapezoid (resp., kite)
with a single axis of symmetr

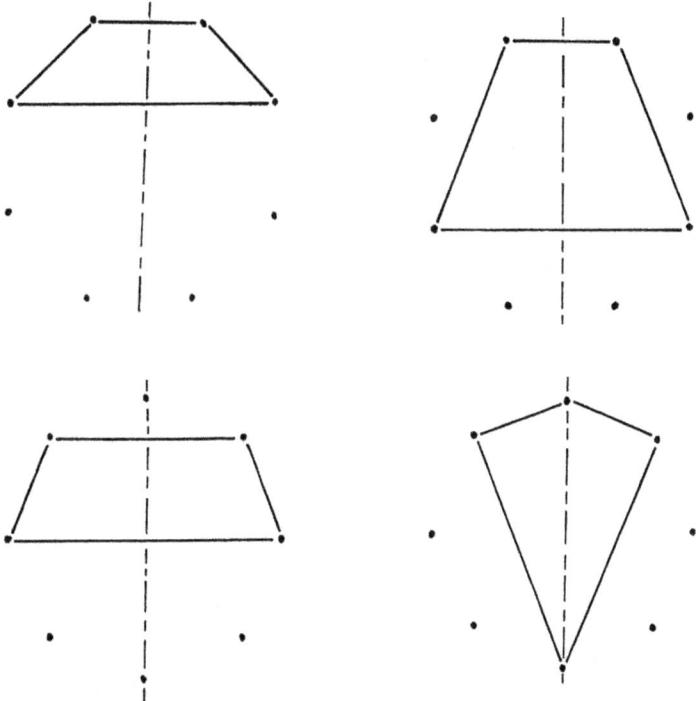

and two types of irregular quadrilateral,

each occurring 16 times.

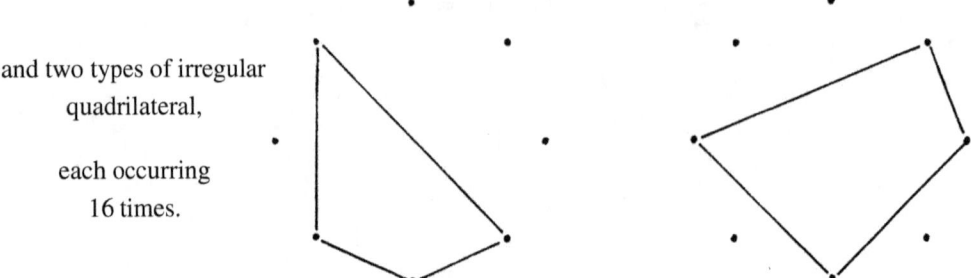

That is a total of 70 quadrilaterals.

There are in comparison fewer pentagons and fewer different pentagon forms.

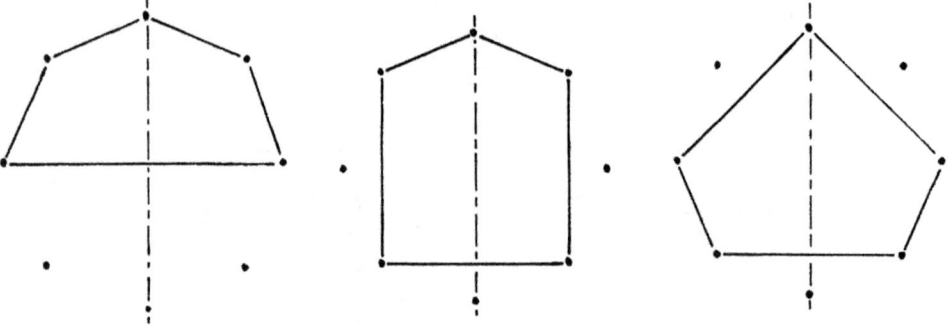

Among these there are, as with the triangles, 3 types, each with a single symmetry axis, and each type occurs 8 times.

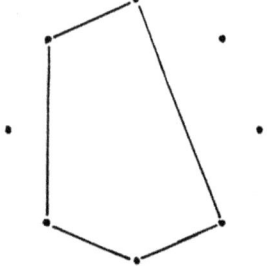
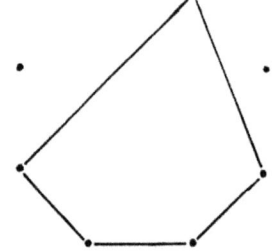

Additionally there are two types of irregular pentagon, each 16 times.

For a total of 56 pentagons.

There are even fewer hexagons,
namely 4 with two symmetry axes,

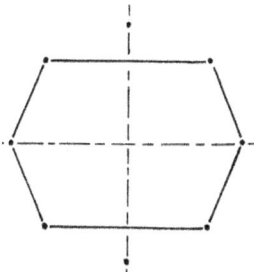

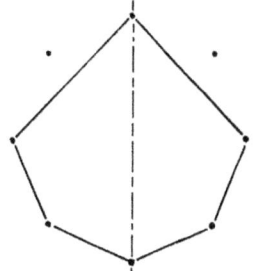 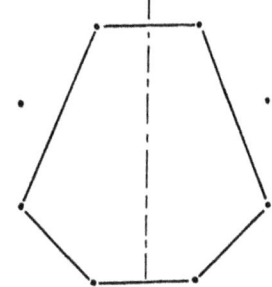 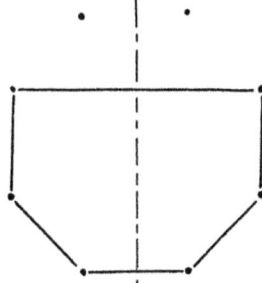

and 3 types with single symmetry axis, each occurring 8 times, for a total of 28 hexagons.

Furthermore there are 8 heptagons
and the octagon itself.

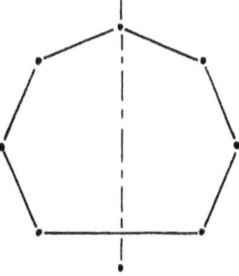

Things become much simpler when we turn to frame polygons with fewer vertices. There the portion of inscribed "legal" polygons in proportion to the "illegal" is however smaller. As a result, the number laws under investigation don't appear so clearly for small frame polygons.

In the regular **pentagon** one can only inscribe two groups of 5 triangles and 5 quadrilaterals.

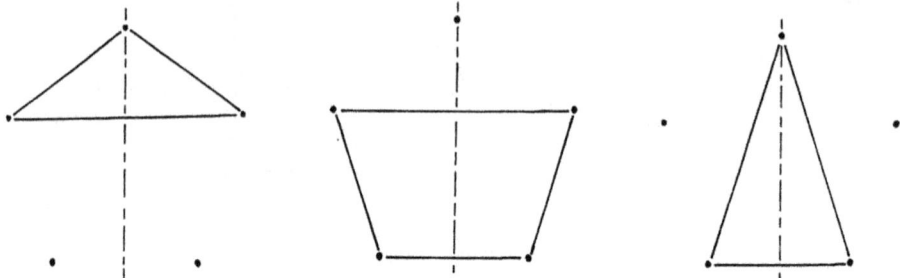

for a total of 10 triangles and 5 quadrilaterals.
Finally, there is the single pentagon itself.

In the **Square**, finally, one can inscribe only 4 triangles. And the square itself gets counted.

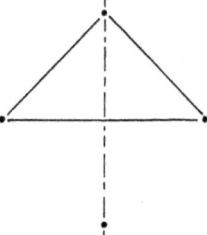

By now there should be sufficient in-depth experience accumulated, in order to realize, that it might be meaningful to integrate diagonals as 2-gons and single vertices as 1-gons in the investigation, even though they don't represent surfaces. And, finally, it's also plausible to formulate, that the decision to choose *no* point also represents *one* possible choice. But to talk about a "null configuration" or to apply the word "0-gon", doesn't belong in a ninth grade.

On the basis of these terminological problems is clear that the surfaces and their particular forms are not essential to the study undertaken here, rather the important features are the number of ways to choose so-and-so many points from an encompassing set. Nevertheless, the geometrical forms do support the organizing forces of thinking, which is the real core of combinatorics.

Also the fact that we have arranged the points in a regular way (on an invisible circle), is not essential. But it did help in handling our cluster of questions in such a way that we didn't lose the overview – not of course without application of some effort. Viewed in this way, the whole process can be seen as a gentle introduction to the art of abstraction, in the sense that the student can thereby learn to ignore what isn't essential (even when it's very concrete). Geometric forms are experienced more strongly, the more regular that they are. It's stimulating, for example, to find out how the number of the different types of triangles, quadrilaterals, etc., corresponds to their number of symmetry axes. Unsymmetric forms are the most numerous, multiple symmetry axes rather seldom.

Let's try to collect the results of our investigations together. For this, we will include as frame polygon the triangle, the "2-gon", and the "1-gon"; even that null configuration, the "0-gon" is to be included. We include them not *only* as frame polygons, but also as inscribed polygons! If one omits the 0-gon, then the Pascal triangle lacks a tip, which can be seen as an aesthetic blemish.

Number of vertices of frame polygon										Number of inscribed polygons
0					1					"0-Gon"
1				1		1				"1-Gon"
2				1	2	1				"2-Gon"
3			1	3	3	1				triangle
4			1	4	6	4	1			quadrilateral
5		1	5	10	10	5	1			pentagon
6		1	6	15	20	15	6	1		hexagon
7		1	7	21	35	35	21	7	1	heptagon
8	1	8	28	56	70	56	28	8	1	octagon

If one observes the numbers in a row of Pascals' triangle, then two things strike one.

1. The numbers are symmetric with respect to the vertical axis. This isn't hard to see, since to every inscribed polygon, there corresponds a unique complementary one, whose vertices consist of the vertices which the first one doesn't have. Hence the sum of the number of vertices of these two polygons is the number of vertices of the frame polygon. From this correspondence follows directly the truth of the formula $\binom{n}{k} = \binom{n}{n-k}$.

2. If the number of vertices of the frame polygon is prime, this prime is then a divisor of every entry of that row of Pascal's triangle, with the exception of the beginning and ending 1's. If the number of vertices is not prime, then it isn't a divisor of every entry in this way. It might seem surprising, to discover such a result by investigating geometrical forms. In the context of instruction in the 9th grade, it's not so important to give and air-tight proof of such a conjecture. But we can use our investigations of the inscribed polygons to penetrate deeper into the number laws which it reveals.

For this it's necessary to look more closely at how the numbers in the interior of the triangle come about. They are the sum of numbers, each of which corresponds to a particular form of inscribed polygon which we have studied above. Let's take as example the heptagon and octagon as frame polygons.

The heptagon

That one can inscribe 7 single "1-gons" and hexagons is immediately clear. Let's look now at the 21 2-gons, resp., pentagons, in both cases we have 3 times 7. And that's because, every possible 2-gon, resp., pentagon, has one symmetry axis. Hence the total 21 has to be a multiple of 7.

Among the triangles and quadrilaterals, that are to begin with 3 times 7 of each that have one symmetry axis, hence once again 21, a multiple of 7. There are additionally the irregular triangles and quadrilaterals. A first group of seven arises in that one lets one exemplar "'run around the circle'" and take all 7 possible positions one after the other. Then repeat this with the mirror symmetric irregular exemplar. In this way arise twice 7 of the triangles, resp., quadrilaterals, without any symmetry axis. This means that the total number of inscribed triangles, resp., quadrilaterals is composed only of multiples of 7, hence is also a multiple of 7: $35 = 7+7+7+2\cdot 7$.

The octagon

Once more its immediately clear that there are eight "1-gons", resp., heptagons that can be inscribed. Then there are 28 each of 2-gons and hexagons. 28 is not a multiple of 8. How is that? To begin with there are 3 times 8 simple axially symmetric 2-gons and hexagons, yielding $24 = 3\cdot 8$. Next come 4 exemplars with two axes of symmetry, for a total of $28 = 8+8+8+4$. The summand 4 destroys the divisibility by 8. If I take one of these inscribed polygons and let it "run around" the 8 positions of the circle, it lands on top of its previous positions half the time, meaning there are only 4 distinct exemplars instead of 8. This is only possible because these polygons have 2 different symmetry axes. Of triangles and pentagons there appear 56 of each, once more a multiple of 8. That's due to the fact, that none of these polygons have more than one symmetry axis: 3 times 8 with one symmetry axis and two times 16 with no symmetry axis, that is, once more a multiple of 8. Hence the total number $56 = 8+8+8+16+16$ is also a multiple of 8.

Finally, consider the quadrilaterals. There are two squares with 4 axes of symmetry, 4 with two symmetry axes, 4 times 8 with a single symmetry axis (trapezoid, resp., kite) and two times 16 irregular quadrilaterals, for a total of $2+4+8+8+8+8+16+16 = 70$ quadrilaterals. The divisibility of this number by 8 is disturbed by the squares and rectangles (2+4) with multiple symmetry axes.

What we've been able to observe in regard to heptagon and octagon, can be generalized.

1. If an inscribed polygon possessses no symmetry, then the total number of such polygons is twice the number of vertices of the frame polygon.

2. If the inscribed polygon has only one symmetry axis, then the total number of such polygons is equal to the number of vertices of the frame polygon.

3. If you rotate a polygon around the circle (rotating each vertex to the next vertex of the frame polygon with each step), it can happen that you arrive back at the beginning position (*qua* polygon, ignoring the labeling of the vertices). – This can only happen if the number of vertices of the frame polygon is not prime. – Further rotation doesn't create any new polygons, but repeats the sequence already found. There may still be more distinct polygons, that are obtained by mirroring the ones found so far (or repeating the process beginning with the mirror image of the original polygon). This happens if the inscribed polygon has no axes of

mirror symmetry. Mirroring doesn't produce any new polygons, if there is at least one axis of symmetry of the original polygon.

In the following cases, then, the number of inscribed polygons is smaller than the number of vertices of the frame polygon (call this number n):

a) In rotating the polygon, fewer than $\frac{n}{2}$ new polygons arise before the polygon coincides with its original position.

b) In rotating the polygon, $\frac{n}{2}$ new polygons arise before the polygon coincides with its original position, and the polygon has an axis of symmetry.

It's the contribution from such polygons that is responsible, when n doesn't divide the total number of all inscribed k-polygons.

4. When n, the number of vertices of the frame polygon, is prime, then an inscribed polygon has at most one symmetry axis. In this case, according to 1. and 2., the total number of inscribed k-polygons is divisible by n.

Finally, a remark to the symmetry of 2-gons and 1-gons. A 2-gon is a line segment, and has always, considered alone, has 2 symmetry axes: the perpendicular bisector and the line of the segment itself. The 1-gon, or single point, has in this context infinitely many symmetry axes: lines passing through the poing. When one brings these configurations in connection with the frame polygon, one arrives at:

A side or a diagonal of the frame polygon, that isn't a diameter, has only one symmetry axis in common with the frame polygon, the perpendicular bisector of the segment. A diameter has a second symmetry axis, given by the line it lies on.

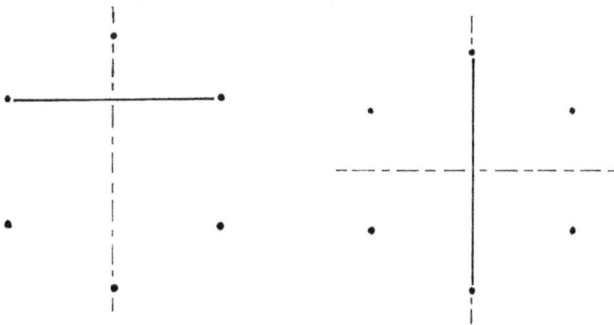

The "1-gon" has a single symmetry axis in common with the frame polygon, the diameter of the frame polygon passing through the point.

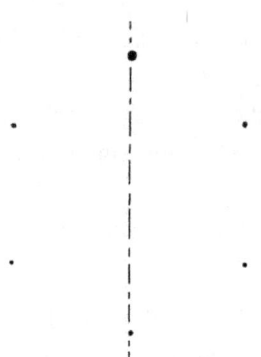

We didn't have to mention the symmetry axes of the frame polygon until now, since the symmetry axes of inscribed polygons with 3 or more vertices are also all symmetry axes of the frame polygon; only for the exceptional cases of 2-gon and 1-gon is that no longer true.

From this point of view, the symmetries of 1-gons and 2-gons fit in consistently to the chosen framework. In particular, they correspond exactly to the symmetries of the complementary polygons $((n-2)$- and $((n-1)$-gons).

Looking back at the examples presented above and the accompanying discussions, leads to the question, how one can really keep track of all the inscribed polygons when the number of vertices of the frame polygon grows. To which degree the students can show imagination, develop organization, and exhibit perseverance, will vary widely from student to student. Even the most gifted reach their limits in this process. The mathematical law of the number of ways to choose k from n elements

$$\binom{n}{k} = \frac{n!}{k! \cdot (n-k)!}$$

can hardly be discovered using the procedure outlined in the examples above. But I'm still convinced that an activity as the one described here is still a meaningful one from a pedagogical standpoint. One trains thereby a way of thinking that brings order into chaos, exactly what is needed for the ninth grade "phase of life".

When this law is finally discovered in the form of the well-known formula above (see for example the chapter by K.-Fr. Georg, especially the section "Combinations" 190 and the preparatory section "k-Permutations" 186) and one establishes that it agrees with the results which have been worked out here, it's likely that the students will experience a feeling of satisfaction. After all, it's valuable – as a kind of "life lesson" – to be able to have the experience, that it's possible to arrive by very different paths at the same goal.

I'd like to close by mentioning some points of view, that gave rise to the foregoing treatment.

The willingness of our students to learn has undergone a striking change in the past years. They tend more and more to prefer practical doing, and less and less to direct efforts to know via an intellectual process. That means that the teacher has to try harder, to stimulate the students to well-rounded practicing. The students want as much as possible to discover things for themselves.

The teacher has the never-ending task, to organize his lessons in such a way that there is a healthy alternation between more lively and more organizing phases, comparable to a healthy breathing process.

In the examples described above, the student can be active as an explorer in the domain of the variegated forms of regular and irregular polygons. Imagination and flexibility are called for. Through the associated drawing, there is also abundant opportunity for practical activity. The observation of what one has thereby created and the penetration of this with number patterns, on the other hand, has a more more organizing effect.

Last but not least, the repetition of the elementary in high school is indispensable. This repetition, however, should not take place in the same way as the corresponding exercises in the middle school, but rather in a new context; so to speak, on higher plane, thereby deepening what has been learned.

In our case we are concerned, for example, with basic geometric constructions and with various kinds of geometric symmetries, but also with elementary arithmetic, with prime numbers and divisibility of composite numbers. All of this, however, is to be handled in the context of combinatorics, the new material of the 9th grade.

The preceding treatment is intended to show, how one can satisfy the requirements of the contemporary pedagogical situation in light of the above-mentioned points of view. The theme "Combinatorics and Pascal's triangle" is one possibility, that could be replaced by others. What's important here, first and foremost, is *how* one works pedagogically with the mathematical content, and not the content itself. May this article provide stimulation in this direction.

Finally, **"IV. The general binomial theorem"** (as above)

Calculating probabilities and combinatorics

UWE HANSEN

Calculation of probabilities can serve as the introduction to a combinatorics main lesson. The underlying patterns can be found by the students operating "on their own steam". One can begin, for example, with the following

Example 1: To improve his economic situation, Mr. A plays the following dice game. He pays anyone who throws a "6" € 1,-, anyone who throws a "3", € 0,50, and whoever throws a "1", € 0,30. How much should he charge a player for throwing the dice three times so that, in the long run, he earns 10 % profit on what he takes in?

Throw	Pays out
"6"	€ 1,-
"3"	€ 0,50
"1"	€ 0,30 St

Students come up with the following explanation: On average, in 6 throws each number occurs once. Therefore, after 6 throws, Mr. A, on average, has to pay out

$$€ 1,- + 0{,}50 + 0{,}30 = € 1{,}80.$$

So, for just 3 throws he can expect to pay out € 0,90. If he charges € 1,-, for 3 throws, then he can expect to keep as profit 10 % of what he takes in.

If you let each student throw a die three times, the number of throws is already so large, that the results should lie not too far from the prediction.

If, on the other hand, one sets the following pay-outs from the "'bank'":

Throw	Pays out		Throw	Pays out
"6"	€ 0,60		"3"	€ 0,30
"5"	€ 0,50	and:	"2"	€ 0,20
"'4"	€ 0,40		"'1"	€ 0,10

and one charges € 1,- for 3 throws, then the bank can expect to pay out € 2,10 for 6 throws, but only take in € 2,- , so this game isn't a good one for the bank.

If one charges € 0,20 for a throw, and if the bank pays € 0,60 for a "6", € 0,40 for a "4", and € 0,10 for a "1" or "2", then the income and the pay-out are equal, so this game is not interesting for the bank.

The next step is to actually throw dice – each student throws 150 times as homework. Assuming there are 30 students, this gives a total of 4500 throws. In the ideal case, each number occurs 750 times. It is in general so, that each number really comes quite close to this ideal case, so the deviation is less than 1 %. Sometimes the deviation is a half or a quarter percent! That's an astounding outcome for everyone!

Example 2: There are 1 yellow, 1 red, 2 green, and 4 blue balls in a jar. One ball is taken out. After noting its color, it is returned again to the jar before the procedure is repeated.

Pulled out	Pays out
yellow	€ 1,-
red	€ 0,50
green	€ 0,10

After this "pulling out" is repeated eight times, the bank can expect to pay out € 1,- + 0,50 + 2·0,10 = 1,70. If one charges € 0,25 per "pull"', then the bank takes in € 2,- for these 8 pulls; hence it earns € 0,30, which is 15 % of the total.

Also for this game, one meets the expected results, if one plays often enough.

One can easily think out similar games: In a vase one has 1 white, 1 red, and 3 black balls, which are otherwise identical. What is the expected profit after 100 pulls, if one pull costs € 0,25, and the pay-out is € 0,70 for the white ball and € 0,30 for the red ball?

Example 3: From a deck of 32 cards (face cards, aces, and 7-8-9-10) a card is chosen.

Card	Pays out	Card	Pays out
King of hearts	€ 1,-	Ace of hearts	€ 1,-
Queen of hearts	€ 1,-	Clubs	€ 0,30
Jack of hearts	€ 1,-	Spades	€ 0,10

The charge to pull a card is € 0,25. After 32 pulls, one can expect that each cards appears on average once. During this time the expected pay-out will total

$$4 \cdot € 1,- + 8 \cdot € 0,30 + 8 \cdot € 0,10 = € 7,20$$

As the income during the same time is 32·0,25 = € 8,- then one can expect a profit of 10% on revenue.

Such examples can be endlessly multiplied. The cube (dice) can be replaced with an octahedron, icosahedron, or pentagon dodecahedron. Instead of a single cube, one can take several; one can take more jars or more balls – "with" or "without" replacement of pulled-out balls, or choose more cards at once. The crucial question then makes it appearance: "'Which outcomes are equally likely?'".

For example: at first, students can believe, when you throw 2 coins at once, there are three equally likely outcomes: both heads, both tails, or one heads and one tails. But since the two tosses are actually independent of each other, there are actually four equally likely outcomes:

HH TH

HT TT

Half the time, the coins show different sides; only a fourth of the time do they show the same, given side, for example two heads HH. This reveals already the general law governing independent outcomes, which is a multiplicative one. If the two outcomes E_1 and E_2 are independent, that the outcome "'E_1 and E_2'" occurs in half of a third of the outcomes, that is, $\frac{1}{2}\frac{1}{3} = \frac{1}{6}$ of the total outcomes.

The probability to throw an odd number with one die, is larger than the probability to throw a number divisible by 3, and this is larger than the probability to throw a "6". One sees: one compares the number of "successful" outcomes with the total number of outcomes. That leads to the classical definition of probability (when all outcomes are equally likely): The probability for the occurrence of an an event (e. g., "throw an even number") is the ratio of the number of successful outcomes (in this case, 3) to the total number of possible outcomes (in this case 6).

$$P(E) = \frac{\text{Number of successful outcomes}}{\text{Number of possible outcomes}}$$

Examples: A die is thrown once:

P(a "6") = $\frac{1}{6}$

P(an even number) = $\frac{1}{2}$

P(a prime number) = $\frac{1}{2}$

P(a number not divisible by 3) = $\frac{2}{3}$

P(anything but a "4") = $\frac{5}{6}$

P("7") = 0

Two dice are thrown:

P(two "3"s) = $\frac{1}{6} \cdot \frac{1}{6} = \frac{1}{36}$

P(a "1" and a "'2'") = $2 \cdot \frac{1}{6} \cdot \frac{1}{6} = \frac{1}{18}$

P(two even numbers) = $\frac{1}{2} \cdot \frac{1}{2} = \frac{1}{4}$

P(at least one "6") = $\frac{11}{36}$

P(sum is 4) = $\frac{3}{36} = \frac{1}{12}$

P(two different numbers) = $\frac{30}{36} = \frac{5}{6}$

Calculating probabilities and combinatorics — Uwe Hansen

One has 1 white, 2 red, and 3 black balls in a jar.

a) One ball is pulled out:
$P(\text{white}) = \frac{1}{6}$ $P(\text{red}) = \frac{1}{3}$ $P(\text{black}) = \frac{1}{2}$
$P(\text{white or black}) = \frac{2}{3}$ $P(\text{not white}) = \frac{5}{6}$

b) two balls are taken – without putting one back:
$P(\text{red, red}) = \frac{2}{6} \cdot \frac{1}{5} = \frac{1}{15}$ $P(\text{one red, one white}) = 2 \cdot \frac{2}{6} \cdot \frac{1}{5} = \frac{2}{15}$
$P(\text{black, black}) = \frac{3}{6} \cdot \frac{2}{5} = \frac{1}{5}$
$P(\text{two of the same color}) = \frac{2}{30} + \frac{6}{30} = \frac{4}{15}$

In the final exercise, note that by taking out one ball, the conditions are changed: one calculates the probability for the occurrence of E_2 assuming E_1 occurs.

On these examples the following relationships can be recognized:

$0 \leqslant P(E) \leqslant 1$ $\qquad$ $P(E) + P(\text{not } E) = 1$
$P(\text{certain event}) = 1$ $\qquad$ $P(\text{impossible event}) = 0$

$P(E_1 \text{ and } E_2) = P(E_1) \cdot P(E_2)$ when E_1 and E_2 are independent.
$P(E_1 \text{ or } E_2) = P(E_1) + P(E_2)$ for events that cannot simultaneously occur (mutually exclusive events).

The typical behavior of probability calculations is brought out by the following example: From each of two jars, one pulls out one ball. In the first jar there are one white and two black balls (otherwise identical) and in the second jar there are one white and three black balls (otherwise identical). Calculate:

$P(\text{white, white}) = P(\text{white}) \cdot P(\text{white}) = \frac{1}{3} \cdot \frac{1}{4} = \frac{1}{12}$
$P(\text{black, black}) = P(\text{black}) \cdot P(\text{black}) = \frac{2}{3} \cdot \frac{3}{4} = \frac{1}{2}$
$P(\text{one white, one black})$
$= P(\text{1st white, 2nd black oder 1st black, 2nd white})$
$= P(\text{1st white}) \cdot P(\text{2nd black}) + P(\text{1st black}) \cdot P(\text{2nd white})$
$= \frac{1}{3} \cdot \frac{3}{4} + \frac{2}{3} \cdot \frac{1}{4} = \frac{1}{4} + \frac{1}{6} = \frac{5}{12}$

Students are very satisfied when they obtain the following sum:

$$\frac{1}{12} + \frac{1}{2} + \frac{5}{12} = 1$$

This sum has to be 1, since all possibilities have been included. The students also experience the verification of the connection of the relation "and" and "or" with the arithmetic operations "multiplication", resp., "addition". Furthermore, he experiences how the whole is differentiated into parts, for example:

$$P(\text{any 2 balls}) = P(\text{two equal balls})$$
$$\text{of two different balls})$$
$$P(\text{2 equal balls}) = P(\text{2 white or 2 black balls})$$
$$P(\text{2 white balls}) = P(\text{first white and second white})$$

It should be emphasized, that the lawfulness of probability theory is not grounded in experience. If, for example, one would discover that when one throws a particular die very often, it shows "6" in a third of the cases, one would not consider this a basis for questioning the results obtained above, but rather search for the reason in the irregularity of this particular die: the laws derived above are produced completely out of the concepts which underly them.

These considerations support treating probability theory in the 9th grade. It is a means for the student to experience the power of his own thinking; he experiences, that the laws that he arrived at through his own thinking, are also valid in the world. This strengthens his feeling that he is at home in the world. It's therefore important, that the student also experiences the laws of his thinking, and probability theory can provide lots of stimulation in this direction.

Still further examples:
In a box there are three cards with the letters AIK. How large is the probability, that one draws out the three cards in the order KAI? Answer: $P(KAI) = \frac{1}{3} \cdot \frac{1}{2} \cdot \frac{1}{1} = \frac{1}{3!} = \frac{1}{6}$.

Similar exercises can be thought up with longer words, also allowing repeated letters. At this point you can introduce the factorial product $n!$.

A further example
Janie puts the letters of her name on cards and then into a box. Johanna does the same for her name, with second box. They then each take out three cards from their respective boxes. What is the probability that "JAN" is chosen?

a) by Janie $P(JAN) = \frac{1}{5} \cdot \frac{1}{4} \cdot \frac{1}{3} = \frac{1}{60}$

b) by Johanna $P(JAN) = \frac{1}{7} \cdot \frac{2}{6} \cdot \frac{2}{5} = \frac{2}{105}$

This exercise can be embedded in a humorous story. One can also extract the name of a boy in the class from the name of a girl, and vice-versa.

Exercise: In a classroom, there are 16 girls and 12 boys. 2 students leave the room. What is the probability, that it is a boy and a girl?

Solution: $W = 2 \cdot \frac{16}{28} \cdot \frac{12}{27} = \frac{32}{63}$

Extension: $P(\text{2 girls}) = \frac{20}{63}$ $P(\text{2 boys}) = \frac{11}{63}$

Exercise: Simplified lotto:
In a jar there are 3 white and 5 black balls. Three balls are pulled out.

P(three white balls) = $\frac{3}{8} \cdot \frac{2}{7} \cdot \frac{1}{6} = \frac{1}{56}$

P(exactly two white balls) = $\frac{3}{8} \cdot \frac{2}{7} \cdot \frac{5}{6} \cdot 3 = \frac{15}{56}$

P(exactly one white ball) = $\frac{3}{8} \cdot \frac{5}{7} \cdot \frac{4}{6} \cdot 3 = \frac{30}{56}$

P(no white ball) = $\frac{5}{8} \cdot \frac{4}{7} \cdot \frac{3}{6} = \frac{10}{56}$

Check: $\frac{1}{56} + \frac{15}{56} + \frac{30}{56} + \frac{10}{56} = 1$.

Exercise: From a deck of 32 cards (as above) one pulls out one card. P(7 or hearts) = P(7) + P(hearts) − P(7 of hearts).

For events, that can occur simultaneously, one has:

$P(E_1 \text{ or } E_2) = P(E_1) + P(E_2) - P(E_1 \text{ and } E_2)$.

This is obvious, since otherwise one would count twice the cases when both events occur.

Exercise: The situations can become quite elaborate. One can arrive at a cave, in which a valuable treasure is buried, by two different paths, each of which passes through 3 gates. At the first gate, a die is cast; at the second, one pulls a ball from a jar with one white, two red, and four blue balls; at the third, one draws a card from a deck of 32 cards.

Left path: one arrives at the cave, when one throws an even number, pulls out a white ball, and finally draws a black card.

Right path: one arrives at the cave, when one throws an uneven prime number, pulls out a red ball, and finally draws a face card (king, queen, or jack) – On which path does one have a higher probability to arrive at the cave?

Aufgabe Three sharp-shooters shoot at the same time at a target. On the average, each of the three hits the target once in three shots. What is the probability that the target is hit?

$$P(\text{target is hit}) = 1 - P(\text{target is not hit})$$
$$= 1 - P(\text{each shooter misses})$$
$$= 1 - \frac{2}{3} \cdot \frac{2}{3} \cdot \frac{2}{3} = \frac{19}{27}$$

The following problem shows the connection between combinatorics and probability theory very clearly.

Exercise: Each of 7 jars contains one white and one black ball. One takes one ball from each jar.

$$P(\text{all white}) = \frac{1}{2^7} \qquad P(\text{exactly one black}) = 7 \cdot \frac{1}{2^7}$$

then the 1 black ball can come from any of the 7 jars.

$$P(\text{exactly two blacks}) = \binom{7}{2} \cdot \frac{1}{2^7}$$

Why? There are $\binom{7}{2}$ ways to choose two jars from the 7 jars. One pulls the black balls from these two; and white from the ohers. One can see, these considerations agree completely with those that lead to the calculation of the binomial formulas for $(a+b)^7$ and $(a+b)^n$.

Also by the so-caled triangle of probabilities, this line of thought leads to the correct answer:

Exercise

A token stands on the mark "0" of a number line, that continues in both positive (to the right) and negative (to the left) directions. A coin is thrown. If head appears, one moves the token one step to the right; if tails, one step to the left. The coin is thrown n times. What is the probability, that the token stands ends up a particular value (of the number line)?

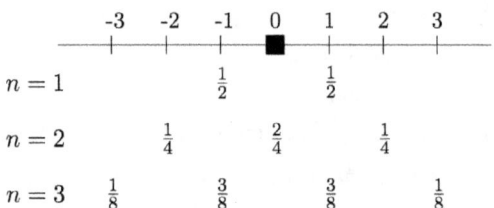

It should be clear that in the n-th row, the following numbers appear:

$$\frac{1}{2^n}\binom{n}{0}, \frac{1}{2^n}\binom{n}{1}, \frac{1}{2^n}\binom{n}{2}, \ldots, \frac{1}{2^n}\binom{n}{n}$$

The occurrence of the binomial coefficients is not mysterious: let's consider the position +3 of the number line. This position can only be arrived at if the token has moved 5 times to the right and 2 times to the left, in some order. Each such ordering can be represented as a word consisting of 5 R's and 2 L's, for example, RRRLRLR. The total number of such words is given by the number of ways to choose the position of the 2 L's from the 7 possible positions in the word. But that's exactly $\binom{7}{2}$.

Additional sources

Amos Franceschelli, "Mathematics in the Classroom: Mineshaft and Skylight", Mercury Press, Spring Valley, 1998.

Ron Jarman, "Topics in Mathematics for Waldorf High Schools" , Vol. 2, Waldorf Publications, 2017

Robert Oehlaf, "A Waldorf High School Mathematics Program", e-book, Waldorf Publications, 2015.

A. Renwick Sheen, "Geometry and the Imagination", Waldorf Publications

Herbert Swanson, "Geometry for the Waldorf High School", Waldorf Publications

Bengt Ulin, "Finding the Path: Themes and Methods for the Teaching of Mathematics in a Waldorf School", AWSNA, 1991

Jamie York, "Making Math Meaningful – A Source Book for Teaching High School Math", Jamie York Press, 2015

Index

11-check, 151
9-check, 139

algebra, 128
altitude-theorem, 59
area-transformations, 30
arithmetic, 128

binomial theorem, 193
buffon needle problem, 71

cissoid, 93
combinations, 190
combinatorics, 177, 198, 216
conchoid, 87
conic sections, 15, 18
continued fraction, 134
continued fractions, 111

division circles, 81

effective teaching habits, 78
ellipse, 18
equations, 158, 174
eucledian algorithm, 111

geometric locus, 81
geometric mean leg theorem, 57

hyperbola, 20

irrational, 103

main lesson, 25
mean proportion leg theorem, 57
mental reckoning, 25
metamorphosis of curve forms, 85
Methodology, 9

parabola, 19
pascal's triangle, 193, 211

permutations, 177
physical units, 32
plane geometry, 24
polygon, 33
probabilities, 216
product-rule, 189

shearing, 57
square roots, 118

theorem of pythagoras, 68
thread-construction, 21
transformation
    of parallelograms, 37
    of rectangles, 36

www.ingramcontent.com/pod-product-compliance
Lightning Source LLC
LaVergne TN
LVHW080312260326
834688LV00038B/1075